CONSERVATIVE JUDAISM
The New Century

CONSERVATIVE JUDAISM
The New Century

NEIL GILLMAN

 Behrman House, Inc.

About the Cover

In 1902, fifteen years after the Jewish Theological Seminary's establishment, the school's financial situation was precarious; it lived hand to mouth without any firm or consistent support. To the rescue came a group of wealthy Jews who raised enough money to put the school, and eventually the Movement, on solid ground. Thus, the Seminary and Conservative Judaism were not only saved but launched on a period of extraordinary growth through the efforts of these beneficent Jews. Appropriately, their names are carved on the pillars which surround the Seminary courtyard in New York City.

Copyright © 1993 by Neil Gillman

Project Editor: Adam Siegel
Book Design: Richard Stalzer Associates, Ltd.
Cover Design: Robert J. O'Dell
Cover Photo: Valerie Fenelon

Library of Congress Cataloging-in-Publication Data

Gillman, Neil.
    Conservative Judaism : the new century / by Neil Gillman.
        p.   cm.
    Includes bibliographical references (p.) and index.
    ISBN 0–87441–547–0
    1. Conservative Judaism—United States—History—20th century.
2. Judaism—20th century.   3. Jewish Theological Seminary of
America.   I. Title.
BM197.5.G5   1993
296.8'342'09—dc20

                                                    93–14637
                                                    CIP

Published by Behrman House, Inc.
235 Watchung Avenue
West Orange, New Jersey 07052

Manufactured in the United States of America

99 98 97 96 95   7 6 5 4 3 2

Dedication

To my students
at
The Jewish Theological Seminary
and elsewhere

CONTENTS

ACKNOWLEDGMENTS

This study was written at the invitation of Mr. Jacob Behrman, president of Behrman House Inc. What Mr. Behrman did not know was that some months before his invitation I had prepared an outline of a volume that reflected the substance of a course on Conservative Judaism that I had been teaching in The Jewish Theological Seminary's Rabbinical School.

Although both the original outline and this book pursue a roughly chronological course, it was never my intention to write a history of either the Seminary or the Movement. My purpose, rather, was to try to understand the culture of what seemed a highly enigmatic movement. The only way this could be done, I felt, was to study the contradictory impulses that led to the creation of the school and then to trace how these impulses worked themselves out in the course of time.

If I single out individuals for particular mention, I do so because I recall their contributions with particular gratitude.

I am grateful to Mr. Behrman for his patience and support throughout the process of writing and revising the manuscript. The perspective that he brought to the work, the questions that he posed, and the issues that he asked me to confront have shaped every page of the book. I cannot adequately express the respect and the gratitude I owe him.

One of the happy fruits of this assignment has been my relationship with Mr. Adam Siegel, my editor at Behrman House. No one could have been more helpful and encouraging throughout the process of bringing this book to print. Indeed, the entire Behrman House staff merit my deepest gratitude for the concern they have shown at each stage.

Earlier drafts of the manuscript were read by Mrs. Marjorie Wyler, who remains the preeminent master of Seminary lore, and by the late Rabbi Wolfe Kelman. I can think of few people who played a more central role in shaping this Movement or who understood its dynamics with more acuity than Wolfe Kelman. I was fortunate to have been able to benefit from his insight and experience in the last painful months prior to his death.

My colleague Professor Jack Wertheimer reviewed the entire manuscript and offered numerous suggestions on content and interpretation, most of which have been incorporated into the book.

I am particularly grateful to him for his unstinting generosity of time and spirit.

The bulk of the writing was completed prior to the establishment of the Joseph and Miriam Ratner Center for the Study of Conservative Judaism, which Dr. Wertheimer now directs and which is collecting archival material related to the Seminary and the Movement. The Ratner Center has begun a thoroughgoing study of the history of the Seminary, funded by the Lilly Foundation, which will culminate in the publication of a number of volumes on all of the issues covered in this book.

I am grateful to Ms. Julie Miller, the Ratner Center's Archivist, who generously shared with me the graphic material collected by the Center. Ms. Sharon Liberman-Mintz, Assistant Curator of Jewish Art at the Seminary Library, did the same with the graphics collection in the Seminary Library. They are largely responsible for supplying the photographs that grace this volume.

One of the glories of teaching at the Seminary remains the remarkable community of scholars and students with whom I come into contact every day. My colleagues have been generous in sharing their scholarship and experience with me. My students, who have been exposed to this material in class, constantly force me to sharpen my thinking and clarify my conclusions. Their imprint is on every page of this book.

I am also grateful to my former students, now colleagues in the Rabbinical Assembly, who have invited me to share my research with their congregants, even at the risk of exposing them to some painful truths about the state of the Movement and its history. Their response has reassured me that a book of this kind can serve a useful purpose in helping them understand what they stand for and in shaping the future course of Conservative Judaism.

Chancellor Ismar Schorsch's encouragement and his readiness to draw on his understanding of the dynamics of the Jewish religion in the modern age must be gratefully acknowledged.

The stage of final manuscript revision was marked by the death of the Seminary's two Chancellors Emeriti, Louis Finkelstein and Gerson D. Cohen. It was my privilege to have worked closely with both of these giants and to have spent countless hours discussing all of the issues reviewed in these pages. That they will not be present at the coming to fruition of my work is my personal loss.

On more than one occasion I felt free to draw colleague and long-time friend Rabbi Joseph Brodie away from his work to read a particular paragraph and confirm my findings. Rabbi Morton Leifman drew on his personal experience as Seminary Director of Israel Activities from 1969 to 1974 and subjected my chapter on that part of the story to a searching analysis. Rabbi Benjamin Segal helped me understand his role and the role of the Israeli Conservative rabbinate in the drafting of *Emet Ve-Emunah*. Seminary Vice Chancellor Michael Greenbaum shared with me the fruits of his research into the Finkelstein years and his understanding of the inner workings of the Seminary administration, particularly in relation to budgetary issues. Dr. Saul Shapiro, co-author of the Liebman-Shapiro report discussed in Chapter 8, helped clarify my understanding of that report and of his perspective on the emergence of the Union for Traditional Judaism.

Professors Joel Roth and Gordon Tucker, both of whom have served, and in Rabbi Roth's case, now serves again, as Dean of the Seminary's Rabbinical School, as have I, have shared with me their personal perspectives on Seminary-style rabbinic education.

At various times I turned to Rabbis David Kogen, William Lebeau, Benjamin Kreitman, Nina Cardin, Charles Simon, Leonard Levy, Simon Greenberg and to Dr. John Ruskay, Ms. Bernice Balter, Ms. Gale Labovitz, Ms. Marlee Pinsker, Ms. Amy Katz Wasser, Ms. Stephanie Coen, and Mr. Avraham Wernick for guidance and information. I am grateful to them all.

Ms. Amy Lederhendler, my research assistant during the academic year 1990–1991, worked closely with me on both substantive and stylistic issues. Even more important, she was my unfailing guide in my not overly successful efforts to master the mysteries of word processing. Mr. Ron Fish, my 1991–1992 research assistant, worked to corroborate factual details in the manuscript. Ms. Dini Lewittes Tannenbaum's assistance was indispensable in the final stages of revising and rewriting. I am particularly grateful to Ms. Ilene McGrath whose meticulous review of the entire manuscript caught many an error in content and syntax.

My daughter Debby devoted the better part of her mid-winter school break to help with the page-by-page revisions of the manuscript. Her loving and patient support and critique, together with those of her sister, Abby, and my wife, Sarah, mean more to me than I can possibly say.

In expressing my gratitude to all of these people, I am of course in no way evading responsibility for the contents of this volume.

Finally, I am grateful to God, Who has blessed me with health, energy, and a love for teaching that inspires me in all I do. May God's support and guidance remain with me as I turn now to other projects that lie ahead.

New York, N.Y.
August 1992
Erev Shabbat Nahamu
Eve of the Sabbath of Consolation 5752

INTRODUCTION

A Lover's Quarrel

I walked through the imposing wrought-iron gates of The Jewish Theological Seminary of America for the first time on a wintry day in late December 1953.

I was in my senior year at McGill University in Montreal, and I had decided to apply to the Seminary's Rabbinical School. This was to be my first meeting with Rabbi Marvin Wiener, then serving as the Rabbinical School's admissions officer. I was in fact about five hours late for that meeting because my train from Montreal was delayed by a blizzard in upstate New York. Upon arriving at Penn Station, I called the office in a state of acute anxiety, only to be reassured. My meeting had been postponed. The entire Seminary community was attending the funeral of one of the giants of its faculty, Alexander Marx, long-time Seminary Librarian and Professor of History. It was a memorable day for many reasons.

If someone had told me that day that a decade later I would be a member of that faculty, that I would eventually teach a course in Conservative Judaism and even write a book about the school and the Movement, I would have dismissed that person as a raving lunatic. I wasn't even sure then that I had much of a chance of being admitted. My early Jewish education had been next to nil. But I was admitted—to what was then the school's six-year program, a program reserved for promising newcomers to Jewish studies—and I have never left. Most of what I know about Judaism I learned here. The Seminary and the Conservative Movement constitute my primary Jewish home.

The original subtitle of this book was *A Partisan Guide to Conservative Judaism*. It is partisan in two ways. I remain, first—to use the dictionary definition of the term—a "militant advocate" of Conservative Judaism. This is not the work of a detached observer.

But I am also a partisan of my thesis, which is frequently critical of the directions both school and Movement took over the past century. I do not believe that the founders of Conservative Judaism and their successors deliberately set out to compromise what they had so lovingly created. They were simply human beings who carried their humanness with them in an unredeemed world. They were passionate Jews who did what they felt should be done in order to save Judaism in the face of new and imposing challenges. But every human decision, even the wisest one, has trade-offs. Our responsibility is to evaluate their decisions, to appreciate their wisdom, and also to discern the trade-offs. As Conservative Judaism enters its second century, the time is particularly ripe for an evaluation of this kind.

When I have taught this material at the Seminary and in various settings around the country, the two most frequently voiced criticisms remain first, "How can you be so critical of the Seminary?" and second, "How can you be so optimistic about the future of the Movement?" The fact that my thinking inspires such contradictory responses suggests to me that I am just about where I should be. I am conducting a lover's quarrel with both the school and the Movement.

Every scholar knows that the hard work of scholarship takes place in the classroom, in the thrust and parry of classroom debate. This book is no exception. It in fact began as a course in Conservative Judaism that I was asked to teach for the first time in the spring of 1984. I soon realized that the history of the course was itself a stunning statement about its subject matter and about the Seminary's relationship to the Movement, for the course had been offered for the first time just ten years earlier. In other words, it took the Seminary about 85 years to teach its future rabbis about the very movement that it had spawned and that they were about to lead!

In retrospect, it is clear to me that I learned about the Movement primarily from living it. While scholarly documentation served to jolt my memory, to suggest lines of inquiry, and to refine my conclusions, what was primary was the experience of living, working, and studying within the Movement: sitting in Seminary classrooms; living in its dormitory; studying with Abraham Heschel, Mordecai Kaplan, Shalom Spiegel, Saul Lieberman, and H. L. Ginsberg; attending faculty meetings; participating in Rabbinical Assembly debates; attending Conservative synagogues; serving as counselor to a bunk of adolescent boys at Camp Ramah in Wisconsin; listening to my colleagues' sermons; talking with Louis Finkelstein, Gerson Cohen, and Ismar Schorsch, the three chancellors under whom I have been privileged to serve; and not the least, sitting around tables in the Seminary dining hall and riding its elevators on those seemingly interminable trips up and down.

Seminary lore has it that when Solomon Schechter interviewed Louis Finkelstein upon the latter's application to the Seminary, Schechter asked, "Why do you want to come to the Seminary?" "To study," Finkelstein replied. Schechter retorted, "To study, all you need is a library. The only reason to come here is to associate with great men."

In the course of writing these chapters I have often had occasion to recall this anecdote. In the last analysis, after all of the accomplishments have been acknowledged and all the criticisms voiced, the greatness of this Movement is best measured by the sheer quality of the human beings it has attracted—their honesty, their breadth of spirit, their generosity to each other, their loyalty, their devotion, their passion, and their genuine concern for Judaism and the Jewish people, for their children's and grandchildren's Jewish education, for their synagogues, and for the lives they are trying to fashion for themselves as Jews in contemporary America.

These men and women populate the Conservative Movement. I meet them everywhere as I travel throughout the country. They have long felt that to identify themselves as "not Orthodox and not Reform" is simply not enough. They are searching for a way to be both authentically Jewish and thoroughly in tune with modernity. They are convinced that to be a believing Jew should not demand the slightest sacrifice of mind. I write to validate their questions and to suggest a way of finding some answers. My conviction—and all of my teaching and writing is grounded in this conviction—is that of all of the varied readings of Judaism on the contemporary scene, Conservative Judaism provides the most honest and the most fruitful setting for that inquiry.

THE EUROPEAN EXPERIENCE

"Adopt the mores and constitution of the country in which you find yourself, but be steadfast in upholding the religion of your fathers."

——Moses Mendelssohn

Beginnings Are Important

By almost any criterion, Conservative Judaism represents a stunning success story. Beginning in 1887 as a rabbinical school with an enrollment of eight, the Movement now includes an academic center with five distinct degree-granting schools and a range and depth of resources that are unequaled anywhere in the world outside of Israel; a rabbinic body with a membership of over 1,300; and a congregational arm composed of over 800 congregations and well over 255,000 member families in the United States and Canada, plus offshoots in Israel, Europe, and South America. In addition, the Movement has spawned a host of affiliated schools, youth programs, summer camps, men's and women's organizations, and publications—and all of this the fruit of efforts that began barely a century ago. The most recent (1990) demographic survey of American Jews indicates that Conservative Judaism has attracted more synagogue-affiliated households than either of the other two major American Jewish religious movements.

Yet despite these accomplishments, serious questions about the Movement's strength continue to be voiced, both by dispassionate students of American Judaism and by the Movement's own leadership.

First, there is a general consensus that Conservative Judaism has failed to create a significant body of committed, observant lay Jews—Jews who keep a kosher home, who attend synagogue weekly, and who participate in a serious adult education program, to use three commonly accepted criteria of Jewish commitment. There is no firm statistical basis for this claim, but most Conservative rabbis questioned by this observer have estimated the committed core of their congregations to be somewhere between 10 and 15 percent of their membership.

Second, most Conservative Jews would likely have great difficulty answering the question, "What does it mean to be a Conservative Jew?" A common answer to that question is "Well, I guess it means being not Orthodox and not Reform"—hardly a triumphant or positive answer. And this despite the availability of *Emet Ve-Emunah*, the Movement's first formally articulated Statement of Principles.

Finally, Conservative Judaism shares the fate of all center movements. It exists in a state of perpetual tension, constantly pulled both to the right and to the left on any significant issue—yesterday women's ordination, today the range of issues raised by a newly articulate Jewish gay and lesbian community, tomorrow some other issue. More than Orthodoxy on the right and Reform on the left, it is a movement that is held together by a consensus often on the edge of fragmentation.

In retrospect, both the Movement's accomplishments and its persistent dilemmas could have been anticipated over a century ago. Both are inherent in the dynamics that created the Movement in America near the turn of the century. But the emergence of Conservative Judaism as an American religious movement is actually the result of an earlier and far more fundamental impulse—the need of a religious community to respond to the challenges of modernity. In mid-nineteenth-century Germany, the Jewish community's response to that need created a specific method of reading classical Jewish texts, a particular way of interpreting Jewish history, and an innovative way of making decisions about what Jews are to believe and how Jews are to live in a world that was strikingly different from the one in which those beliefs and practices originally came into being.

The earliest formal expression of this new approach can be discerned in a watershed decision made by a German rabbi, Zechariah Frankel, on May 17, 1845. On that day, Frankel withdrew from a conference of Reform rabbis that was being held in Frankfurt, Germany. That withdrawal—the issue over which he withdrew and his defense of that decision—marks the first overt expression of what we today understand as a Conservative approach to Judaism. To understand Frankel's decision, we must first trace the broader cultural context in which Frankel lived and worked.

■ PERHAPS NOTHING more vividly symbolizes the separation of Jews from the secular world than the ghettos in which Jews were forced to live throughout Europe.

In the early Middle Ages, as an expression of their distinct identity, Jews voluntarily chose to live in a specific area of the town. But by the sixteenth century, in the wake of growing Christian intolerance, the term *ghetto* was applied to a compulsory residential quarter surrounded by a wall, forcibly shutting Jews off from the rest of the population. The ghetto gates were bolted at night, living conditions were crowded and unsanitary, and this forced isolation was accompanied by the requirement that Jews wear a badge, by restrictions on professions, and by compulsory attendance at sermons meant to convert Jews to Christianity.

With the dawn of the Enlightenment at the close of the eighteenth century, the ghetto walls began to crumble, irrevocably changing the relationship between Judaism and the secular world. Pictured here is the Frankfurt *Judengasse* (or "Jews' Lane") about 1870.

Judaism Encounters Modernity

Most historians agree that the modern age in Jewish history had its beginnings toward the middle of the eighteenth century. It was about this time that Jews encountered the two movements that transformed the character of both the Jewish people and Judaism and that have shaped the Jewish agenda to our own day. Those two movements were the Enlightenment (or *Haskalah*, from the Hebrew root *s-kh-l*, "to understand"), and its political counterpart, the Emancipation.

Enlightenment and Emancipation represent two faces of one process: the gradual integration of the Jewish community into the political, socioeconomic, cultural, and intellectual structures of European civilization. Enlightenment refers to the cultural or intellectual dimension of that process: Jews began to absorb the intellectual currents in the community at large, enter universities, read books in foreign languages, and study new disciplines; they began to think like their European contemporaries, and more important, they began to apply these new ways of understanding to Judaism. Emancipation refers to the political dimension of the process: Jews became citizens of emerging national states—France in 1789, America in 1791—with the same rights and responsibilities as all citizens of those states.

In short, the Jewish encounter with modernity led to the collapse of the walls, both intellectual and political, that separated the Jewish community from the rest of the world. In the process, everything Jewish would be radically transformed, including the beliefs and practices of Jewish religion. For it was Jewish religion above all that had created those very walls that were now on the point of collapsing.

But neither the Enlightenment nor the emancipatory movement can be understood without reference to the broader European cultural context in which Jews found themselves during the eighteenth century.

The Enlightenment

The European Enlightenment was a movement that synthesized a set of new ideas concerning the human being, nature, social and political organization, and inevitably, God and religion. This revolutionary new worldview quickly gained wide assent, decisively transforming European and world culture.

The Enlightenment was, as its name implies, the process of "letting in the light" into the presumed "darkness" of the age that preceded it. The "light" that was to be let in was primarily the light of reason. Reason, not received tradition or external authority, was to be the ultimate source of truth in all areas of human understanding. The work of scientists such as Isaac Newton and philosophers such as John Locke demonstrated that both the natural world and the human mind are accessible to human understanding. Reason was the human faculty *par excellence*, the faculty that distinguished the human being from the rest of creation. To exalt reason was to propound a new humanism, to proclaim confidence in human powers and in the human ability to understand the world and oneself, and then to apply that knowledge in the creation of better and happier lives.

■ MUCH OF what we take for granted about the world we live in today—the flowering of the natural sciences and modern technology, for example—stems directly from Enlightenment assumptions. This new delight with science, exalting confidence in the power of human beings to understand and control their world, is captured in this illustration from 1770, which was meant to provide an optical basis for our perception of the rainbow.

The German philosopher Immanuel Kant characterized enlightenment as "the human being's release from self-imposed tutelage." By "tutelage," Kant meant our tendency to accept external authority as our guide in determining what we are to believe and how we are to live. That tutelage is "self-imposed," Kant notes, when we are really free to break with the received authority but do not have the courage to do so. The Enlightenment was thus a powerful force for human liberation from all imposed ideas about human life and the world.

But if human beings using their natural powers could attain an adequate understanding of the world, who needed religion? Indeed, if there was a symbol for the "darkness" that the Enlightenment was designed to banish, it was religion, or more specifically in the European context, the Catholic Church. Voltaire's cry *"Ecrasez l'infame!"* ("Crush the infamous thing!") set the tone. The Church stood for authority over freedom; for faith over reason; for superstition, ignorance, and prejudice over understanding; for the primacy of the supernatural over the natural, the other-worldly over the this-worldly, the divine over the human. The Church, and by extension, religion as a whole, was seen as the enemy.

REASON, REVOLUTION, AND RELIGION

The extent to which the Church felt threatened by the ideas of the Enlightenment was evident as far back as the seventeenth century, when Galileo proved that the earth was not the center of the universe but rather revolved around the sun with the other planets. Such a proclamation, removing man from his exalted position and relegating him to nothing greater or less than anything else in the universe, was perceived as heresy. The Church brought Galileo to trial in 1633 and forced him to renounce his discoveries. Accounts of the trial have concluded with the legendary statement that Galileo, as he arose from his knees, uttered *sotto voce*, "*E pur si muove*" ("Nevertheless it does move").

Finally, in political theory, the Enlightenment dispensed with the notion of the state as an approximation on earth of some heavenly ideal. The belief in the divine right of kings, whereby rulers justified their authority and power by claiming they had been chosen by God, was abandoned. In its place, Thomas Hobbes propounded the doctrine of the social contract, whereby the state was founded on an agreement among human beings to devise an order that would protect natural rights and self-interest. Theories of this kind led directly to the two major political upheavals of the age, the American and the French revolutions of 1776 and 1789, respectively.

■ AMERICA CAME into being as an expression of Enlightenment ideals. The founders of the United States—among them Thomas Paine, Benjamin Franklin, and Thomas Jefferson—were prominent Enlightenment figures who had imbibed the thought of Rousseau and Voltaire, Locke and Hobbes. The American system of checks and balances, its suspicion of excessively centralized government, and the doctrine of the separation of church and state reflect the Enlightenment's emphasis on preserving the individual's freedoms and liberties. The humanism, progressivism, and optimism that are so integrally part of the American temper were central to the spirit of the Enlightenment.

Emancipation

The movement for political emancipation was very much the child of the Enlightenment. Since reason was the universal attribute of all human beings, to celebrate reason was to open the way for new and revolutionary political theories founded on the liberal and democratic values of emancipatory movements worldwide.

European medieval civilization was a structured, hierarchical society in which different groupings or communities, called estates, formed separate and distinct corporate bodies. Among these were the nobility, the clergy, the merchants or burghers, and the masses of villeins or serfs, who constituted the majority of the population. Medieval Jews formed one of these corporate bodies.

The divisions between these estates set clear boundaries around what an individual was and was not permitted to do. Before Emancipation spread throughout Europe, Jews could not own land or enter universities; they could not chose where to live, often being forced to live in ghettos, where they were locked in at night; and they were prohibited from entering many professions. Often Jews were allowed to enter only vocations that were considered undesirable or degrading, such as money lending. However, the premier Jewish historian of our century, the late Salo Baron, has reminded us that the status from which Jews were being emancipated was not totally bad. In the medieval hierarchy, the Jews enjoyed fewer rights than the clergy and the nobility but incomparably more rights than the villeins. The often-held view of the preemancipation period as a time of unrelieved oppression, bondage, and suffering is simply inaccurate.

Jewish Emancipation

The emancipation of the Jews was a complicated affair. First, it did not come about in one sudden, dramatic moment as the act of a single benevolent authority figure. Rather, it was a long and slow process marked by many reversals, particularly in Central Europe. In fact, we can claim that in regard to Russian Jewry, the process of emancipation is only beginning to reach fruition today.

Second, just as medieval life was not totally bad for the Jews, the emancipatory age was not an unmixed blessing. The very nature of the old corporate society gave Jews internal autonomy: the right to conduct their internal affairs according to their own codes of law, essentially the Bible and its interpretation in the Babylonian Talmud. It also guaranteed the ethnic integrity of the Jewish community, for the walls between the corporate bodies were not easily breached. The substitution of an egalitarian society for the corporate society gave Jews the vote and a measure of equality, but it also took away the ethnic, religious, and political separateness that for centuries had served as the main guarantor of Jewish distinctiveness.

Some sense of the pain accompanying the process of emancipation may be gleaned from the declaration adopted by the Assembly of Jewish Notables in 1806. The Assembly was convened by Napoleon to debate answers to a set of questions that were to determine whether or not French Jewry was genuinely prepared to forfeit Jewish nationhood and accept French citizenship. Napoleon's questions clearly embarrassed the members of the Assembly. How were they supposed to deal with issues such as these: In the eyes of Jews, are Frenchmen considered as brethren or as strangers? In either case, what conduct does their law prescribe toward Frenchmen not of their religion? Do the Jews born in France and treated by the law as French citizens acknowledge France as their country? Are they bound to defend it? Are they bound to obey the laws and to follow the direction of the civil code?

The Notables deliberated for close to two weeks. Some questions could be handled easily; others were avoided. Still others must have generated a good deal of anguish. To the question regarding acknowledging France as their country, the Assembly replied: "The love of the country is in the heart of Jews a sentiment so natural, so powerful, and so consonant to their religious opinions that a French Jew considers himself, in England, as among strangers, although he may be among Jews; and the case is the same with English Jews in France. To such a pitch is this sentiment carried among them that, during the last war, French Jews have been seen fighting desperately against other Jews, the subjects of countries then at war with France."

But the reality was that European Jews simply had no choice whether or not to accept the new freedoms and privileges emancipation provided them. There was no room in the emerging national states for a separate corporate group. One either became a member of the state and enjoyed all of the rights and responsibilities of citizenship, or one left. Much later in the century a Jewish nationalist

■ IN 1806 Napoleon convened the Assembly of Jewish Notables in response to the pleas of French farmers and landowners who viewed the policies of the Jewish money lenders as extortionary. In addition, others had complained to the emperor that Jews were evading military conscription. In response to these complaints, Napoleon declared a one-year moratorium on all debts owed to Jews, and he convened a meeting at which French Jews would formally accept a series of statements, carefully crafted by a committee of rabbis and laypeople, proclaiming the primary loyalty of French Jewry to France and to French law. In return for this declaration, Jews were to be given full rights and participation in French society. However ambivalent French Jewry may have felt about this declaration, Napoleon was perceived as having liberated the Jews from the anguish of medieval persecution, in return for which Jews owed France and its emperor undying gratitude and loyalty.

movement—political Zionism—advocated doing just that—namely, leaving Europe and establishing a national state in some other corner of the world. But that reaction against emancipation was long in coming. At the outset, most Jews simply felt that there was no alternative but to accept emancipation and then struggle with the implications of that decision as best they could.

One conclusion is clear: The major item on the agenda of all modern Jewish movements was to try to juggle a complex set of demands: to accommodate to modernity, to a radically new outside world, to new intellectual currents, and to new political realities while in the process trying to retain some measure of Jewish national identity and religious integrity. It was not a simple task.

THE SCIENCE OF JUDAISM

The Science of Judaism (German, *Wissenschaft des Judentums*) school was an integral part of the Emancipation-Enlightenment movement in mid-nineteenth-century Europe. As its name implies, it was a scholarly movement founded on the assumption that if Jews were to be integrated into European political life, then the scholarly study of Judaism should also be integrated into European scholarly culture. In principle, Judaism should be studied much as we would study any other human institution, using all of the resources available to modern scholarship. Jewish scholarship had to be emancipated from Jewish belief. Whatever the scholars' private commitments, their scholarly stance had to be "scientific," that is, detached, neutral, dispassionate, welcoming the "truth" whatever its source or its implications. As we shall see, the adoption of this scholarly approach to the study of Torah was to have major repercussions in the Conservative Movement.

The Paradigmatic Modern Jew: Moses Mendelssohn

In its Jewish garb, the Enlightenment was precisely the impulse for Jews to adopt European manners, mores, customs, and ways of thinking. It tried to abolish the exclusiveness and separateness that characterized traditional forms of Jewish identity. It encouraged the mastery of non-Jewish languages and secular learning. It fostered the modernization of Hebrew and the scientific study of Jewish texts and ideas. It fought superstition, primitiveness, and fanaticism. Most important, it required looking anew at all forms of Jewish belief and practice in the light of the new spirit of the age. In short, if Jews were to be emancipated, then Judaism would have to be emancipated as well—emancipated from all that was primitive, undignified, superstitious, irrational, or generally not worthy of being embraced by a modern, sophisticated European. Inevitably, the Enlightenment led to religious skepticism, atheism, and the abandonment, by many *Maskilim* (followers of *Haskalah*), of all forms of religious expression.

■ MOSES MENDELSSOHN (1729–1786) was the paradigm of the best that Jewish modernity was supposed to create. An observant Jew who was also a philosopher and an art and literary critic, fluent in both Hebrew and German, Mendelssohn was at home in both the Jewish and secular worlds. But that delicate balance proved to be too precarious to be transmitted, even to his own family. Two generations later most of Mendelssohn's fourteen grandchildren, the most prominent of whom was the composer Felix, had converted to Christianity.

The first passionate advocate of an enlightened approach to Judaism in an emancipated Europe was the German-Jewish philosopher Moses Mendelssohn. Mendelssohn may not have been the first modern Jew, but he was certainly the first articulate modern Jew. He was the first to spell out in detail the dream of a new and reinvigorated Judaism, one that would be clearly and authentically Jewish but also fully integrated into the cultural and political life of the European nations.

Mendelssohn's major work, *Jerusalem or On Religious Power and Judaism,* is a powerful tract urging Western European nations to grant Jews political equality and urging Jews to welcome this new status, which, he insisted, would not demand the slightest sacrifice of Jewish religion. Mendelssohn addresses his fellow Jews with the following words: "Adopt the mores and constitution of the country in which you find yourself, but be steadfast in upholding the religion of your fathers, too. Bear both burdens as well as you can."

Mendelssohn was very aware of the tensions and ambiguities of his position, however. The closing lines of *Jerusalem* are permeated with the dread that the package would not hold, that integration into European life and culture would lead to assimilation and conversion to Christianity: "And you, my brothers and fellowmen, who are the followers of the teachings of Jesus, how can you blame us for doing what the founder of your religion has himself done? Can you seriously believe that you cannot reciprocate our love as citizens as long as we are outwardly distinguished from you by our ceremonial law, do not eat with you, or do not marry you?" "It is beyond our power to yield on this matter," he continues. "Show us ways and provide us with means of becoming better fellow residents, and let us enjoy, together with you, the rights of humanity. . . . We cannot forsake the law in good conscience—and without a conscience, of what use would fellow citizens be to you?"

The major fallacy in Mendelssohn's prescription for Jewish survival in the modern age was his belief that Jewish religion—specifically the ritual law, along with Judaism's institutional structure, the rabbinate, the synagogue, and the service of worship—could be retained intact in a strikingly new climate. That was an impossible dream.

It was precisely this religious system that was the source of much of Judaism's separateness. It dictated what Jews could and could not do every waking moment. It had a great deal to say, as Mendelssohn acknowledged, about whom they ate with and whom they could marry. It also had Jews praising God for "having chosen us from among the nations" and praying that God "bring us in peace from the four corners of the earth and lead us upright to our land." "Our land" in this context was most certainly not Germany or France. But how could one claim to belong to these national states and at the same time pray for a return to Zion? Even more, in this new egalitarian setting everything Jews did and said would be exposed for all to see. Not only Jews, but Judaism as well, would have to earn the respect of the new world.

■ MORE THAN any other aspect of traditional Jewish observance, it is the laws governing the consumption of food that distinguish Jews from their non-Jewish friends and the Jewish home from that of its neighbors. But to "distinguish" means to "separate," and one of the purposes of the Jewish dietary laws is precisely to separate the Jewish people from other peoples. The assumption is that eating is a powerful social experience; if you cannot eat with other people, you will not join them. But once the Enlightenment began to grant Jews the right to enter the non-Jewish world, the very value or purpose of being separated was called into question and with it the value of the dietary laws. Pictured here is the engraving *Jewish Entertainment During the Feast of Tabernacles* by the eighteenth-century Dutch artist Bernard Picart.

Reform Judaism

The movement that took the lead in trying to reshape and thus retain the core of Jewish religion within the culture of the Enlightenment was the Reform Movement. It is impossible to overestimate the contribution of those early Reformers. They were deeply devoted Jews. They cared desperately about the future of Judaism. Whatever decisions they made were based on the firm conviction that this was the only way to save Judaism for the ages. They also faced challenges that were unprecedented. All the other Jewish responses to modernity—Conservative Judaism, Modern Orthodoxy, and even political Zionism—can be seen as reactions to the work of these Reformers. It's no exaggeration to say that Reform Judaism set the agenda for all modern Jewish movements.

Those early Reform Jews who worked and taught between 1810 and 1840 had neither a consistent set of principles nor a firm program of action. By and large, they improvised as they went along. Much like our own Democratic and Republican parties, they formed a shifting coalition made up of various perspectives ranging from traditional to liberal. They shared a common assumption that some aspects of Judaism had to change but that broad agreement glossed over a number of potentially divisive issues.

The disagreements within Reform focused on two main questions: What aspects of Judaism had to be changed? And how were those changes to be effectuated?

First, what was to be changed? Were these changes to be esthetic only, touching upon the more superficial aspects of Jewish life—a sermon in German instead of Yiddish or Hebrew, a more decorous synagogue service, an abbreviated liturgy, more modern choral music—or were they to affect the heart of Jewish ritual? Were the dietary laws, for example, to be dismissed because they separated Jews from their non-Jewish friends and neighbors? Was the wearing of *tefillin* to be abolished because they were viewed as magical amulets? Were prayers for the return to Zion to be eliminated from the prayerbook (for what did emancipation mean if not that Jews now viewed themselves as completely at home in their European settings)?

Second, how were these changes to be effectuated? By fiat? By the decision of individual rabbis and leaders who would simply dictate the changes to their new Reform communities? Or rather, by the congregants themselves, who would "vote with their feet," intuitively retaining certain aspects of tradition and rejecting others? Would the changes emerge by revolution, a simple overthrow of outdated practices and beliefs? Or by evolution, as the process gradually worked itself out in congregation after congregation.

Some sense of the substance and tone of the debate within Reform may be gleaned from a short excerpt of a letter by Abraham Geiger (1810–1874), responding to statements from Leopold Zunz (1794–1886), the preeminent scholar of his generation. Zunz was an early, passionate supporter of Reform, but in his later years he distanced himself from the Reformers and concentrated on his scholarly work. Geiger was the moving force behind Reform at mid-century and one of the most articulate and learned representatives of the Movement. Geiger's letter, dated March 19, 1845, begins with a gentle critique of Zunz's published views on the value of wearing *tefillin*. He then turns to the rite of circumcision, which Zunz had also insisted on retaining. Geiger writes:

> The fact remains that it is a barbaric, gory rite which fills the infant's father with fear and subjects the new mother to harmful emotional strain. . . . The sense of sacrifice . . . has long since vanished from our midst. . . . True, in the olden days a religious

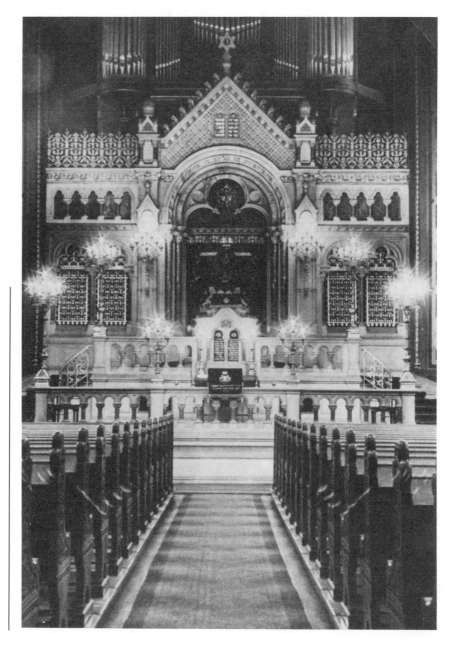

■ TO THE traditionalist Jews, the introduction of organ music into the service of worship on Sabbath and festivals, one of Reform's earliest innovations, was offensive in two ways. First, it violated the *halakhic* prohibition against the use of musical instruments on the Sabbath and festivals. Second, in some less clearly defined way, it represented a borrowing by Jews of a preeminently Christian mode of worship. Traditionalist Jews felt a powerful need to keep the boundaries between Judaism and Christianity sharp and clear. Even if the organ were to be used only on a weekday, this kind of appropriation worked to blur the differences between Judaism and Christianity and was thus to be resisted. Pictured here is the organ in the Lindenstrasse synagogue in Berlin.

sentiment may well have clung to it; at present, however, its only foundations are habit and fear, and we surely have no desire to dedicate temples to either.

Geiger then turns to the dietary laws.

It is precisely these dietary laws that are so void of rationale and . . . such a hindrance to the development of social relationships. Truly, the ideal of the deeper sense of brotherhood among men should have priority over the revival of that sense of separation. . . . Consequently, I could attach more value to almost anything rather than to this particular branch of rabbinic legal practice that has been cultivated from micrology to almost sheer madness.

Those are fighting words. They also reveal a movement ridden with debate and uncertainty.

This coalition of early Reformers had its liberal, center, and conservative wings. Despite the fundamental nature of their differences, these wings enjoyed an easy coexistence for the first decades of the century. But as the Movement grew stronger and its leaders became more confident, the calls for greater clarity and consistency on all of these issues could not be ignored. The result was a series of conferences convened by the rabbis of the Movement, designed to provide a forum for achieving consensus on the substance and pace of Reform. The second of these conferences, held in Frankfurt in May 1845, proved to be a watershed in the history of modern Judaism.

2

THE LEGACY OF FRANKEL

"True, Judaism demands religious activity, but the people is not altogether mere clay to be molded by the will of theologians and scholars. In religious activities, as in those of ordinary life, it decides for itself. This right was conceded by Judaism to the people."

——Zechariah Frankel

Zechariah Frankel and the Frankfurt Conference

■ A RESPECTED scholar and editor, Rabbi Zechariah Frankel (1801–1875) had been an ardent spokesman for the more traditionalist wing of the Reform coalition. Frankel advocated a more gradualist or evolutionary approach toward changes in religious practice, limiting those reforms to the more superficial aspects of Jewish religious life. He insisted that rabbis should not impose changes that the community was not prepared to adopt on its own.

At the time of the second Reform rabbinic conference, Rabbi Zechariah Frankel was serving as Chief Rabbi of Dresden. Frankel had declined to attend the first Reform rabbinic conference, held a year earlier in Brunswick, Germany. When he had bitterly attacked the conclusions of that conference as excessively radical, his colleagues responded that he had only himself to blame: By not participating in the deliberations he had forfeited the right to influence their outcome. This criticism must have had some impact because May 1845 found Frankel in Frankfurt for the second conference. On the third day of the conference, May 17, he resigned and returned to Dresden.

The topic under discussion that day was "Is prayer in the Hebrew tongue objectively necessary?" It may seem strange today that this was the issue that prompted the break between the traditional and the more liberal Reform Jews. Jewish law is extraordinarily lenient in permitting prayer in any language. To this day, the mourner's *Kaddish*, probably the most frequently recited piece of the traditional liturgy, is recited not in Hebrew but in Aramaic, the language spoken by most Jews in the early rabbinic period. Why then make a fuss about the possibility of reciting some prayers in German when far more substantial issues were being deliberated, such as the Jewish marriage laws?

Morgen-Gottesdienſt für den Sabbath. 7

שְׁמַע יִשְׂרָאֵל יְיָ אֱלֹהֵינוּ יְיָ אֶחָד:

Chor und Gemeinde.

שְׁמַע יִשְׂרָאֵל יְיָ אֱלֹהֵינוּ יְיָ אֶחָד:

Vorbeter.

בָּרוּךְ שֵׁם כְּבוֹד מַלְכוּתוֹ לְעוֹלָם וָעֶד:

Chor und Gemeinde.

בָּרוּךְ שֵׁם כְּבוֹד מַלְכוּתוֹ לְעוֹלָם וָעֶד:

(Die Gemeinde nimmt ihre Plätze wieder ein.)

Vorbeter.

וְאָהַבְתָּ אֵת יְיָ אֱלֹהֶיךָ בְּכָל־לְבָבְךָ וּבְכָל־נַפְשְׁךָ וּבְכָל־מְאֹדֶךָ: וְהָיוּ הַדְּבָרִים הָאֵלֶה אֲשֶׁר אָנֹכִי מְצַוְּךָ הַיּוֹם עַל־לְבָבֶךָ: וְשִׁנַּנְתָּם לְבָנֶיךָ וְדִבַּרְתָּ בָּם בְּשִׁבְתְּךָ בְּבֵיתֶךָ וּבְלֶכְתְּךָ בַדֶּרֶךְ וּבְשָׁכְבְּךָ וּבְקוּמֶךָ: וּקְשַׁרְתָּם לְאוֹת עַל־יָדֶךָ וְהָיוּ לְטֹטָפֹת בֵּין עֵינֶיךָ: וּכְתַבְתָּם עַל־מְזֻזוֹת בֵּיתֶךָ וּבִשְׁעָרֶיךָ:

_____

*) Höre Iſrael, Gott, unſer Herr, iſt der einzige Gott!
**) Geprieſen ſei ſein Name, ſein Reich und ſeine Herrlichkeit in Ewigkeit.
***) Und lieben ſollſt Du Gott, deinen Herrn, mit ganzem Herzen, ganzer Seele und ganzem Vermögen. Und es ſollen dieſe Worte, die ich dir heute befehle, in deinem Herzen ſein. Du ſollſt ſie einſchärfen deinen Kindern, und von ihnen reden, wenn du ſitzeſt in deinem Hauſe, wenn du gehſt auf dem Wege, wenn du dich niederlegſt und wenn du aufſtehſt. Trage

■ THERE IS no more complex or subtle form of religious expression than prayer. This is doubtless why the talmudic rabbis explicitly permit us to recite even the *Shema*, the core portion of the daily morning and evening service, in any language we wish (Bab. Talmud, Tractate *B'rakhot*, 13a). Why add a language barrier to all the others that so often impede the free flow of our feelings in prayer!

Despite this leniency, the Hebrew language remained the language of the synagogue and the gateway to classical Jewish texts. It also retained a powerful hold on the sentiment and loyalties of Jewish communities throughout the ages as a primary form of Jewish national expression. It was precisely this latter dimension of the issue that divided Zechariah Frankel and his colleagues at the 1845 conference of Reform rabbis in Frankfurt. Pictured here is a page from the prayerbook *Olat Tamid* (1856) composed mainly in German by the radical Reform Rabbi, David Einhorn (1809–1879) for his Har Sinai congregation in Baltimore.

Upon closer examination, however, it is clear that all of the conferees appreciated the enormous symbolic power of the Hebrew language. For the Jewish people, Hebrew represented kinship, a sense of belonging, a tie to the Jewish past and to every other Jewish community. It was a powerful symbol of Jewish nationhood. That is precisely why Frankel's pro-emancipation colleagues wanted to weaken its position in the synagogue service and why Frankel wanted to strengthen it.

The case against the exclusive primacy of Hebrew was made by Abraham Adler, a representative of the more radical wing of German Reform. Adler argued that Hebrew, as the language of the Jewish community, had in fact died, that it was not understandable even to the people who prayed regularly. Further, he claimed, no language can claim inherent sanctity; a language becomes sacred when what it conveys is sacred. "If I speak the truth in German, then that German word is sacred. If I lie in Hebrew, then that Hebrew word is unholy." Finally, if Hebrew is to survive, it will survive on its own; "It needs no crutches."

The disagreement was in fact a narrow one. No one wanted to dispense with Hebrew completely, and everyone, even Frankel, agreed that some German should be included. Why then the passion of this debate? Clearly because of its symbolic value. First was the issue itself: Hebrew represented the bond that had united Jews for over two thousand years. Second was the very fact that some form of departure from the past was being effected. What was at stake was the crucial issue facing Reform: How was this process of reform to work itself out?

The vote on the issue was hardly decisive. Fifteen conference members voted that Hebrew should not be "objectively necessary," thirteen voted that it should be, and three abstained. Frankel had spoken passionately against the majority position. Upon hearing the result, he walked out.

Two months later, on July 18, 1845, Frankel defended his action in a letter to his colleagues. That letter is a document that Conservative Jews should study with care, as one of those policy statements that have haunted Conservative Judaism to this day. Frankel was fully aware that Hebrew prayer is not mandated by Jewish law. His appeal was to history and tradition, to the wishes of the community, clearly expressed since antiquity. Hebrew, he wrote, has been "sanctified by millennia"; it is the language of Scripture, the language of prayer, the tie that binds Jews from widely different cultures. Banish Hebrew from the service and it will soon disappear from the school as well. Hebrew embodies the devotion, the religious force, the sanctity, and the "edifying powers" of Jewish prayer.

In short, Frankel disagreed with the "tendency of the decision" because "it eliminates the historical element which has weight and power in every religion." He felt it was "not the spirit of preserving but of destroying positive historical Judaism." Because of this difference of opinion, he said, he could "neither sit nor vote in [the assembly's] midst." Although he knew his action might be misinterpreted, "the honest man values his conviction above all. . . . All other considerations yield before those of religion and truth."

This appeal to history ("sanctified by millennia") and to the wishes of the community, as well as the formula "positive historical Judaism," were to become, a generation later, the calling cards of Conservative Judaism in America. At the time, however, it was the first attempt to define a new and distinctive approach to living as a religious Jew in the modern age.

What was that distinctive stance? What were the alternatives? What positions was Frankel rejecting?

First, Frankel was rejecting the approach of German Reform, which he saw as capricious, radical, and hasty. He perceived it as breaking too sharply with the wishes of the broader community, both past and current. Frankel saw Reform as divisive and undisciplined.

But Frankel was also rejecting the position that any change in the central beliefs and practices of Judaism is impossible. He did not endorse the view that Jewish religion, in all of its details, represents the explicit will of God and is therefore immune from cultural and historical influences. In Frankel's day, that position was being articulated by Rabbi Samson Raphael Hirsch, now commonly recognized as the father of Modern Orthodoxy.

Samson Raphael Hirsch

■ BY ANY criterion, Samson Raphael Hirsch (1808–1888) was one of the most influential of modern Jewish thinkers. First and foremost, he was a great rabbi. Although not a renowned scholar, he was a passionate polemicist, an articulate debater, and a shrewd and skilled political leader. He created schools, translated and wrote commentaries on the prayerbook, the *Humash,* and the Psalms and published a series of books and articles expounding his vision of Judaism in thoroughly modern terms. In 1851, after serving as rabbi in three distinguished communities, Hirsch accepted the invitation of a small group of dissident traditionalists in one of German Reform's most powerful strongholds, the city of Frankfurt. He served there until his death, and during the almost four decades of his rabbinate, he created Europe's most prestigious Modern Orthodox congregation.

It was Samson Raphael Hirsch who set the terms for the Orthodox response to Reform Judaism. One of his most powerful statements, an essay entitled "Religion Allied to Progress" (1854), puts the issue succinctly: "To them [Reform], progress is the absolute and religion is governed by it; to us, religion is the absolute. . . . That is all the difference. But this difference is abysmal." Judaism is "the gift and the word of God, an untouchable sanctuary which must not be subjected to human judgment nor subordinated to human considerations." If Judaism and modernity conflict, then it is modernity that must yield.

Hirsch's primary religious opponent was the emerging Reform Movement, but as we shall see, he was equally suspicious of Frankel. Frankel may have hoped that his vigorous opposition to Reform, coupled with the traditionalist cast of his thinking, would shield him from attacks by the religious right—but that was not to be. To Hirsch, Frankel's position was just as threatening as Reform, and its traditionalist garb perhaps made it even more dangerous.

In 1854, nine years after Frankel walked out of the Frankfurt conference, he became the head of a new rabbinical school. Two aspects of that move are worth noting. First, the "conservative" reaction to the increasing liberalization of German Reform Judaism led to the creation of such a school. Second, note the name of that school: The Jewish Theological Seminary of Breslau.

When Frankel assumed its leadership, Hirsch challenged him to answer a series of questions he published, focusing on the ideological stance of the new seminary: "What will revelation mean in the forthcoming Seminary? What will the Bible mean? What will tradition mean?" Hirsch provided his own answers. Revelation is "the divine word of the personal, one God to man." Hirsch believes in "the divine authority of the whole Bible." He knows nothing of a tradition that "had a history in the course of the ages."

Tellingly, Frankel remained silent.

Hirsch's suspicions regarding Frankel's ideological stance were amply confirmed in 1859 by the publication of Frankel's magnum opus, *Darkhei HaMishnah* (literally, *The Ways of the Mishnah*). In this work, Frankel amassed considerable scholarly support for the contention that Jewish law had always developed in response to changing historical conditions. He never outlined the theological assumptions of his position, but by acknowledging the possibility of change and development in Jewish religion and by locating the authority for that change within the community, Frankel was implying that whatever God had to do with Torah, its fate had now been rendered into the hands of a human community, which was subject to changing conditions of history. This community had always determined and would continue to determine the shape of Jewish belief and practice in every generation.

In contrast to the polar positions of Reform and Orthodoxy, Frankel was proposing a program of development that would be carefully disciplined, academically justified, and communally based. He attempted to authenticate his approach through an appeal to history and community. He was saying, in effect, that there was nothing radically new in his approach. Since the community had always sanctioned changes in Jewish beliefs and practices over time, it was in fact he, and not Hirsch, who had captured the dynamic of Judaism over the ages.

At the same time, however, Frankel was trying to delineate the parameters within which this process of development took place. Above all, he insisted, the integrity of both the Jewish past and the Jewish community as a whole had to be preserved. It was this broader concern that Frankel felt had been sacrificed by Reform.

Frankel's position was an extraordinary vote of confidence both in the internal dynamics of Jewish life and in the inherent goodwill of the Jewish religious community. He had faith that the caring core of the community, under the guidance of its rabbinic and scholarly leadership, would intuitively continue to locate the fine balance between continuity and development, between what to retain and what to change. His leap of faith was that Jews would not let Judaism die.

JUDAISM HAS HAD A HISTORY

A classic illustration of how the Jewish community changed traditional Jewish law in order to accommodate its current needs is a ruling by the first-century C.E. sage Hillel, as recorded in *Mishnah Shvi'it* 10:3. According to Deuteronomy 15:2, all debts accrued between Jews were automatically canceled by the sabbatical year. Consequently, as the sabbatical year approached, Jews simply stopped making loans, and the poor suffered. To alleviate the plight of the poor, Hillel legislated that a debt could be transferred to the court, where it would be sheltered during the sabbatical year, and at the end of the year it would revert to the creditor and could be re-claimed. The declaration whereby the debt was transferred to the court was called *Prozbul* (from the Greek for "before the assembly"). In effect, Hillel used a legal fiction to circumvent a biblical law that, because of changing economic conditions, had come to subvert the broader social vision of the Torah.

Reform in America

From about 1840 to 1885, the center of Jewish life had begun to shift from the Continent to America. But the evolution of American Reform Judaism and its conservative reaction followed the pattern of the European experience.

The first generation of American Reformers, immigrants from Germany, began changing religious practices almost improvisationally, by addressing the esthetics of the synagogue service—including a sermon in English or German, a more decorous service, and a choir singing nontraditional synagogue music. Here, too, as the Movement gained strength and confidence, it generated a more radical wing that questioned the relevance of more substantive areas—the belief in the return to Zion, Sabbath observance, and the dietary laws. This wing also advocated moving the main service of the week from Saturday morning to Sunday.

■ OF THE many reforms instituted by the early Jewish Reformers, one of the most radical was shifting the observance of the Sabbath from Saturday to Sunday. When Samuel Holdheim made that proposal at the conference of Reform rabbis in Breslau in 1846, he anticipated that it would be "rejected with indignation," and it was. Still, Sunday services were held in a number of American Reform congregations around the turn of the century, although a generation later their attraction had faded.

Not surprisingly, Holdheim believed that the change to Sunday was necessary precisely to preserve the Sabbath. Saturday observance placed the Jew in conflict with his or her economic life, Holdheim contended, and this was a conflict that Judaism could not possibly win. The shift to Sunday would free the Jew to celebrate the Sabbath not only by rest, which Holdheim understood as a passive or negative way of observing the day, but also by providing a setting for spiritual edification.

"My House shall be called a House of Prayer for All Peoples"

Temple Berith Kodesh
ROCHESTER · NEW YORK

SUNDAY SERVICE

As in Germany, a series of rabbinic conferences was convened—most notably one in Philadelphia in 1869—to give the Movement greater coherence and direction. Again, as the radical wing gained momentum, the traditionalist or "conservative" faction pleaded for the centrality of Hebrew as the language of the liturgy, for the retention of the traditional Sabbath and Saturday morning service, and for the ongoing relevance of the dietary laws.

Despite its internal strains, the American Reform coalition held together long enough to establish the institutional structure of the Movement. The year 1873 saw the founding of its congregational arm, the Union of American Hebrew Congregations, and 1875, its school, the Hebrew Union College in Cincinnati.

That the traditionalists supported these efforts is evidence of their lingering hope that they might still control the direction of the Movement. To a degree, that expectation was nourished by the man who is considered to be the founder of American Reform, Rabbi Isaac Mayer Wise.

■ ISAAC MAYER WISE (1819–1900) emerges as a seminal figure in the annals of American Reform. He was the architect of the institutional structure of Reform, the founder of the Union of American Hebrew Congregations, the first President of the College, a master fund-raiser, a wily political strategist, a man of great energy and ambition. In ideological matters, he showed an uncanny ability to straddle the issues, effectively keeping both radicals and traditionalists in league. But he was a difficult person to work with. One of his colleagues, writing in his personal diary, branded him as "envious" and of a "jealous disposition." "He cannot endure that anyone should stand near him, independent in thought and action; he must rule; the name the Jewish Pope has been well applied to him."

Wise was aware that he needed the support of the traditionalists if the Movement were to be launched on firm footing. He founded the College as a "nondenominational" school, and in its early years the school had a clear traditionalist cast, with a required curriculum of Hebrew and Aramaic, Mishnah, Gemara, Midrash, and the later codifications of Jewish law. But the split within Reform was not long in coming. It surfaced over the infamous *trefah* banquet.

■ RABBI WISE repeatedly denied any personal responsibility for the menu of the *trefah* banquet (pictured below), insisting that an "unscrupulous caterer" was to blame. But it was a *faux pas* of such major proportions that it could hardly have come about by accident. The decision seems to have been made by some of Wise's lay supporters in the movement, maybe without his knowledge. Still, Wise's behavior after the fact was unambiguous. He bitterly denounced the traditionalists for their concern over what he disparaged as "kitchen Judaism." "It is about time to stop that noise over the culinary department of Judaism. The American Hebrew's religion centers not in kitchen and stomach. . . . It has some more important matters to attend to."

The *Trefah* Banquet

A banquet was convened to celebrate the College's first graduation exercises in July 1883. The first rabbinic ordination ever held in the United States, it was the climax of a glorious day in the history of the Movement. The banquet was attended by a panoply of men and women associated with the Movement. To the shock of the traditionalists, the menu included Little Neck clams, soft-shell crabs, shrimp, frog's legs, beef, ice cream, and cheese. Appalled, they walked out of the banquet.

The *trefah* banquet effectively shattered the illusions of the traditionalists. But the final collapse of the Reform coalition in America, the American parallel to the watershed 1845 Frankfurt conference, took place two years later at a conference of Reform rabbis in Pittsburgh in November 1885. After three days of meetings under the chairmanship of Rabbi Wise, nineteen rabbis issued a landmark document that was to determine the shape of Reform Judaism for at least the next half century, the Pittsburgh Platform.

MENU.

Little Neck Clams (Half Shell).
"Amontillado"
Sherry.

POTAGES.

Consomme Royal.
"Sauternes."

POISSONS.

Fillet de Boef, aux Champignons.
Soft Shell Crabs,
a l'Amerique, Pommes Duchesse.
Salade of Shrimp.
"St. Julien."

ENTREE.

Sweet Breads, a la Monglas.
Petits Pois, a la Francaise.
"Deidesheimer."

RELEVEE.

Poulets, a la Viennoise.
Asperges Sauce, Vinaigrette Pommes
"Punch Romain." [Pate.
Grenouiles a la Creme and Cauliflower.

ROTI.

Vol au Vents de Pigeons, a la Tyrolienne.
Salade de Saitue.
"G. H. Mumm Extra Dry."

HORS-D'OEUVERS.

Bouchies de Volaille, a la Regeurs.
Olives Caviv, Sardelles de Hollande.
Brissotins au Supreme Tomatoe,
Mayonaise.

SUCRES.

Ice Cream.
Assorted and Ornamented Cakes.

ENTREMENTS.

Fromages Varies.   Fruits Varies.
"Martell Cognac."   Cafe Noir.

The Pittsburgh Platform

Rabbi Wise, the recognized institutional head of the Reform Movement, was the logical choice to chair the Pittsburgh Conference, but the man who convened it and shaped its outcome was the leader of its radical wing, Kaufmann Kohler (1843–1926). Kohler came to Pittsburgh with a position paper consisting of ten propositions. In his opening address he defined the agenda for the deliberations, and much of his material came to be embodied in the Platform.

Kohler's stance toward traditional Jewish ritual was clear from his opening address:

> We can no longer be blind to the fact that Mosaic-Rabbinical Judaism, as based upon Law and Tradition, has actually and irrevocably lost its hold upon the modern Jew. Whether they have justificatory reasons for doing so or not, the overwhelming majority of Jews within the domain of modern culture disregard altogether the Mosaic-Rabbinical laws concerning diet or dress, concerning work or the kindling of lights on Sabbath, or any other ancient rite.

Kohler was clear about the purpose of the conference. "Judaism is a historical growth. . . . We must accentuate and define what is essential and vital amidst its ever-changing forms and ever-fluctuating conditions. We must declare before the world *what Judaism is and what Reform Judaism means and aims at*" [emphasis Kohler's].

The Pittsburgh Platform unambiguously did just that, marking the triumph of American Reform's radical wing. In eight sharply worded paragraphs, it dismisses "such Mosaic and rabbinical laws as regulate diet, priestly purity and dress" as anachronisms that can only obstruct spirituality in the modern age; it accepts as binding only the moral laws of Judaism and those ceremonies that "elevate and sanctify our lives," rejecting those that are "not adapted to the views and habits of modern civilization"; it claims that Jews no longer consider themselves a nation and "therefore expect neither a return to Palestine, nor a sacrificial worship under the sons of Aaron, nor the restoration of any of the laws concerning the Jewish state"; it rejects the belief in bodily resurrection; it accepts "the providential mission" of Christianity and Islam and welcomes their aid "in the spreading of monotheism and moral truth."

The Pittsburgh Platform was indeed, as Isaac Mayer Wise dubbed it, a "Declaration of Independence." It reduced Judaism from an intricate blend of religion and peoplehood to a religion alone (much on the model of Christianity), to a matter of belief in the monotheistic God, a commitment to ethics and social justice, and to activity in furthering the Messianic age, in which all peoples will acknowledge the one God and establish an era of "truth and righteousness among men." It was also a red flag waved in the face of the traditionalists in the coalition who, not surprisingly, had absented themselves from the conference.

The traditionalists responded much as their predecessor Zechariah Frankel had 40 years earlier in Germany. On January 31, 1886, ten weeks after the Pittsburgh Conference, a group of men met in the Trustee Room of the Shearith Israel Synagogue in New York City (more commonly known today as the Spanish and Portuguese Synagogue) and announced the founding of a rabbinical seminary "in conservative Jewish principles." A year later, on January 3, 1887, eight students began their rabbinical studies at this new school, which was named—in a direct parallel to the German experience—The Jewish Theological Seminary of New York.

■ JUDAISM DIVIDES the *mitzvot* into two broad categories, those governing interpersonal relationships (e.g., giving charity, avoiding slander) and those dealing with one's relationship with God (e.g., the dietary laws, the wearing of *tallit* and *tefillin*, observance of Sabbath and festivals).

The first group make eminent sense; we could well have come up with them even without God's command. But the latter seem arbitrary. Why is tuna fish kosher and pork *treif*? Jews who believe that the Torah represents the explicit will and word of God have no trouble fulfilling these commands; we do them because God commanded us to. Once the belief that God spoke at Sinai begins to weaken, however, these rituals become questionable. Reform Jews had one other reason for dispensing with these rituals: They were inherently separatist, tending to erect barriers between the Jew and the non-Jew. Since Reform was interested in breaking down these barriers, rituals such as the laying of *tefillin*, pictured here, were left behind. Within the past few decades, however, Reform Jews have begun to realize that it is impossible to do away with ritual, that every community has its own distinctive rituals, and that they are a powerful tool for religious expression and education. It is no longer unusual to find Reform Jews who observe many of the traditional rituals of Jewish life.

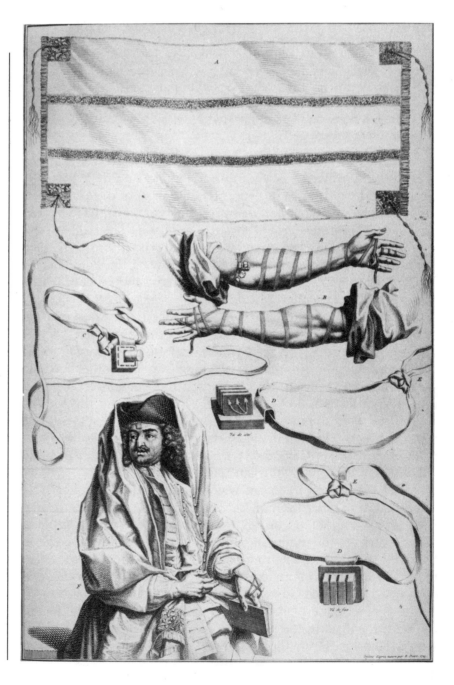

An American Frankel?
Alexander Kohut and Sabato Morais

The name of Zechariah Frankel dominates European Conservative Judaism; one has to look long and hard to find another personality of note who had any influence on the shape of the Movement in Germany. Was there a counterpart in America? Two names come to mind.

The first is Rabbi Alexander Kohut. Six months before the Pittsburgh Conference, Kohut began a series of lectures from his pulpit, sharply attacking the emerging shape of American Reform and presenting his own ideology as a more authentic alternative. Kohut's attack on Reform had an enormous impact. It impelled an equally passionate rebuttal in the form of sermons delivered by Kaufmann Kohler, the convener of the Pittsburgh Conference. The Kohut–Kohler Controversy dominated the pages of the American Jewish press throughout the summer of 1885. Kohut's attack was instrumental in forcing the hand of the Reformers. It led to the convening of the Pittsburgh Conference as a forum for declaring what American Reform stood for. And Kohler's sermons provided the basis for the draft platform he introduced at Pittsburgh.

■ ALEXANDER KOHUT (1842–1894) was ordained at the Breslau Seminary, served as a congregational rabbi in Hungary and Germany, and established his considerable scholarly reputation with a series of noteworthy publications on Jewish history and rabbinics. He came to the United States in 1885 and served in New York both as a congregational rabbi and as a member of the New York Seminary's faculty, until his untimely death in 1894. Kohut was a passionate and articulate thinker and speaker, and in those short nine years he became the ideological champion of the Conservative reaction to American Reform. Almost single-handedly, he was responsible for transmitting the Frankel-Breslau approach to Judaism from Europe to the United States.

Kohut had studied at the Breslau Seminary, and much of his thinking reflects the ideas of Zechariah Frankel. Kohut's debt to Frankel emerges clearly in this passage from an article published in June 1885, just after his arrival in America: "The sphere of Reform must be limited, and nothing must be admitted whose results and conclusions cannot be foreseen, for the law must always be firmly established and irrevocable so far as concerns the revealed Law and Religion. . . . The true idea of Liberty excludes the idea of License. Development does not mean Destruction. Recasting is a very different process from casting aside."

Who decides what is to be retained and what cast off? Clearly, echoing Frankel, the community, "that which still has a hold upon the hearts of men and women, which still retains vitality, should be preserved as sacred; attempting to destroy it is equivalent to Temple sacrilege."

If Kohut is the ideological father of Conservative Judaism in America, its institutional father is Sabato Morais.

■ SABATO MORAIS (1823–1897), Italian born and trained, came to America in 1851 and served as rabbi of Congregation Mikve Israel in Philadelphia until his death. An outspoken opponent of slavery and a passionate supporter of the Union during the Civil War, Morais was deeply involved in a wide range of social and political causes in the country at large. Though he was not in Kohut's league as a critical scholar, he had published in the field of Hebrew literature and was acknowledged to be a master teacher.

Rabbi Sabato Morais, more than any other person, championed the Conservative reaction to American Reform. Ideologically, Morais was the principal exponent of what has been called "enlightened Orthodoxy." In the decades prior to the Pittsburgh Conference he had been a voice for moderation within the coalition of Reformers. He had opposed the more radical changes in synagogue practice, but he was open to moderate changes introduced at a deliberate pace and in a way that would not offend the traditionalists. After the publication of the Pittsburgh Platform, however, Morais recognized the futility of his efforts and turned his attention to the new Seminary.

When the Seminary's founders chose someone to guide their fledgling institution, they turned not to Kohut, the newcomer to America, but rather to Morais. Morais knew American Jewry, he was a veteran of the political and ideological struggles within the Reform coalition, and he was widely respected.

The 62-year-old Morais agreed to commute weekly from his congregation in Philadelphia to New York. He took upon himself the responsibility for all aspects of the new institution—its curriculum, administration, financing, staff, and the rest. He served as President of the Seminary until his death a decade later.

The Legacy of Frankel

There are three aspects of this early history of Conservative Judaism that are especially noteworthy. They exemplify the early decisions that determined the shape of the Movement and have influenced it to this day.

First, both in Europe and in America, the Movement began with the creation of a school. Conservative Judaism's rabbinic arm, the Alumni Association of the Seminary (later to become the Rabbinical Assembly), was founded fourteen years later, in 1901. The congregational arm, the United Synagogue of America, was not established until 1913. In the Reform Movement, in contrast, it was the congregational movement that came first—The Union of American Hebrew Congregations, founded in 1873—then the school—the Hebrew Union College in Cincinnati, in 1875—and finally the Central Conference of American Rabbis, in 1889.

Because the Seminary was the founding institution of the Conservative Movement, it was able to exert a powerful influence over the other two branches. Both the religious authority and political power centered in this one institution were to have long-range consequences for the development of the Movement as a whole.

A second contrast with Reform is in ideological clarity. From the outset, the American Reform Movement published a platform that articulated its ideological position clearly and coherently. Indeed, the Pittsburgh Platform was but the first in a series of platforms to be published during the next century. In contrast, it took Conservative Judaism over 100 years to prepare its very first platform: *Emet Ve-Emunah* was not published until 1987.

Finally, when Zechariah Frankel appealed to history and to the will of the community as sources of authority, he could not possibly have appreciated the ultimate significance of this step. In retrospect, however, it emerges as the first, tentative attempt to define the subtle but distinctive approach of what was to become Conservative Judaism.

That complex and subtle message, transmitted to America by Alexander Kohut and shared by Morais and the founding faculty of the new Seminary, continues to define the distinctive stance of Conservative Judaism to this day. We shall see that this position is hardly trouble-free. It shares the ambiguity of all middle-of-the-road positions, it eludes clear definition, and it is inherently more complex than the polar positions. It also requires a substantive theological grounding, which for the better part of a century the leadership of the Movement did not provide. But it also represents a forthright attempt to confront the challenges of being an authentic religious Jew in the modern age by recognizing the claims of both the past and the present.

It is to the eternal credit of Conservative Judaism that from the very outset it attempted to confront that tension openly and candidly. That effort is the core of Frankel's legacy to Conservative Judaism.

3 From School to Movement

You must make something great out of your institution if the Torah and wisdom are to remain among us. Everything is at a standstill in Germany; England has too few Jews to excercise any real influence. What will happen to Jewish learning if America remains indifferent? //

——Solomon Schechter to Alexander Kohut

Two Movements, Not Three

For most of this century American Judaism was commonly understood to be composed of three religious movements: Reform on the left of the religious spectrum, Orthodoxy on the right, and Conservative Judaism in the center. More recently, a small but vigorous fourth movement has emerged. Reconstructionism, founded by longtime Seminary faculty member Mordecai Kaplan, has had a significant impact on the left side of the religious spectrum.

But the existence of even that earlier tripartite division is a relatively recent development. Some would argue that Orthodoxy did not become a full-fledged, broad-based movement until the 1950s. Whatever the merits of that claim, it is clear that back in 1886 the founders of the Seminary did not think in terms of three movements, and they most certainly did not see themselves as creating a middle movement.

These men over a century ago saw American Jewry as divided into two large groupings, Reform and everyone else. Their hope was that the Seminary would become the institutional center of the "everyone else" group. By 1886, Reform was well on its way to becoming a religious movement. It had a school, the Hebrew Union College in Cincinnati; a set of ideological principles, the Pittsburgh Platform; and a significantly large and wealthy lay body organized into its Union of American Hebrew Congregations. It was soon (in 1889) to have a rabbinic association, the Central Conference of American Rabbis. It had also made significant inroads into the American Jewish population, which by 1890 numbered close to 450,000. The "everyone else" group, in contrast, had the Seminary, a handful of small, European-style talmudic academies or *yeshivot*, and little else.

SAVING JUDAISM IN AMERICA

No religious leader, no matter how revolutionary the message, deliberately strives to destroy his or her community and its traditions. The very opposite is the case. Every religious radical is convinced that this particular program is the only one that will preserve the community for all time. The early Jewish Reformers were convinced that their program alone guaranteed the survival of Judaism and the Jewish people. The leaders of Conservative Judaism insisted that it was *their* program that would save Judaism. Without this conviction, the Conservative Movement would have lacked its primary source of energy and its integrity. From the Movement's beginning, its leaders believed that the success of Conservative Judaism was absolutely indispensable to the health and vitality of the American Jewish community.

The "conservative" group of men who founded the Seminary followed the lead of the early Reformers in trying to create a coalition. The unifying impulse behind this coalition was to fight Reform. To be a legitimate member of this coalition, one had to be firmly opposed to the growing radicalization of Reform as evidenced in the Pittsburgh Platform.

Such a criterion, of course, is wholly negative. It says nothing explicit about what a Jew should believe or how a Jew should live— only about what one shouldn't believe and how one shouldn't live. Much like the early Reformers, this coalition was able to survive as long as it did because it repressed a host of potentially divisive issues. The founders of the Seminary never published a platform of principles on the model of Reform's Pittsburgh Platform because they had learned their lesson well: After the Pittsburgh Conference the Reform coalition split up! Platforms are potentially divisive. If you specify clearly what you believe, you open the door to criticisms from all corners. The very enterprise of outlining a clear and consistent ideology and program might have stymied the traditionalists' efforts to combat Reform from the very beginning.

Though these men may not have articulated an explicit ideology, they certainly did share an implicit one. We will try to unearth this ideology in the next chapter, but for now we can say that they espoused an "enlightened traditionalism." They felt that much of the traditional package of Jewish beliefs and practices had to be retained. They recognized the need for some changes, but they insisted that the changes should be relatively superficial or esthetic—Morais, for example, advocated a shortened Sabbath service with a triennial rather than an annual cycle for the Torah reading—and held that these changes should be instituted slowly and deliberately under the guidance of recognized scholars.

What, then, made this traditionalism "enlightened"? Their willingness to adopt a more modern, critical, open approach to the study of Judaism and to appropriate the Science of Judaism methodology of their European predecessors. To this day in most traditional *yeshivot*, the curriculum is devoted exclusively to the study of Talmud, with its traditional interpreters, and to the codifications of Jewish law, particularly Maimonides' *Mishneh Torah* and Joseph Karo's *Shulhan Arukh* and their commentaries. In contrast, the curricula of both the Hebrew Union College and the new Seminary were modeled on the curriculum of an American university, with courses in Jewish philosophy, Jewish history, Jewish literature, Hebrew language, and of course, Talmud and Bible. Most of the founding members of the original European Reform coalition, including Abraham Geiger and Zechariah Frankel, appropriated the goals and methods of *Wissenschaft*. Their students, in turn, transmitted the approach to the new American setting, where it became the cornerstone of both the Hebrew Union College and the new Seminary.

But this package of "enlightened traditionalism" obviously represents an uneasy compromise. In fact, the very term *conservative* is ambiguous. It is a relative term. One is conservative in relation to or in comparison with a more liberal posture. Of course, that idea is precisely what the founders wanted to indicate: This new approach was to be conservative in relation to Reform. In fact, in the early literature of the Movement the terms *conservative, traditional*, and even *orthodox* are used almost synonymously, confirmation that this new grouping defined itself primarily in terms of the movement to its left. It also reveals the hope that the Seminary would serve as the academic and institutional center of the right side of the religious spectrum. We shall see that this dream proved to be unrealistic, however difficult it would be for the Movement to relinquish it.

The New School: Can the Center Hold?

■ IN THE course of its history the Seminary has had several locations in New York City. It was born in 1886 in the Trustee Room of Shearith Israel Synagogue, then at 5 West 19th Street. In October 1887 it moved to Cooper Union, some blocks away, and four years later to a brownstone at 736 Lexington Avenue. In 1902, with the reorganization of the Seminary and the arrival of Solomon Schechter, it moved uptown, to 531 West 123rd Street, in Manhattan's Morningside Heights (pictured here), where it was to remain until 1929, when it moved around the corner to its present campus which extends along Broadway from 122nd Street to 123rd Street.

The name The Jewish Theological Seminary of New York appears for the first time in a resolution passed on January 31, 1886—just ten weeks after the Pittsburgh Conference—at a meeting that took place at Shearith Israel Synagogue in New York City. That resolution, now a historic document, reads, "Resolved that it is indispensable to the welfare and progress of Judaism in this country that there should be founded a seminary for the training of teachers of the future generations in sympathy with the spirit of Conservative Judaism, to be called, 'The Jewish Theological Seminary of New York.'" Those attending the meeting also approved resolutions to recruit students, raise funds, and enlist the support of congregations that might be sympathetic to the group's opposition to the Reform Movement.

THE BIRTH OF A MOVEMENT

The preamble to the constitution of The Jewish Theological Association announces its goals to be the preservation of "the knowledge and practice of historical Judaism as ordained in the Law of Moses and expounded by the prophets and sages of Israel in Biblical and Talmudic writings. . . ." The phrase *historical Judaism*, soon to become a catchword of the new enterprise, harks back to Zechariah Frankel and his appeal to history as the source of authenticity for modern Jewish forms of expression. It was, as we shall soon see, a singularly problematic choice.

The decision to create the Seminary enraged the Reformers. Writing two months later, in March 1886, Isaac Mayer Wise brands the new school an "orthodox Rabbinical School" created by men ". . . who are themselves *poshim* [sinners] in the eyes not only of the genuines of Poland and Hungary, but also of the leaders of that class in Germany and Italy," and claims it was created solely for the purpose of opposing the Hebrew Union College.

According to Wise, the new school was fraudulent from the start. His labeling it orthodox was designed to discourage the moderate Reformers from associating with the enterprise. Wise was protecting his own coalition, and his tactic was to polarize the opposition: If you were not Reform, then you were orthodox. There was nothing in between, no legitimate "enlightened traditionalism."

But the founders of the Seminary were creating their own coalition. It was in their interest to blur the differences between their own stance and that of moderate Reform on the left and the more traditionalist Jews on the right. What was needed, Kohut wrote, was a Seminary that would be "purely and truly Jewish. We do not desire it to be destined for a sect, whether reform, conservative or orthodox, we would have it be a Jewish theological seminary, like that of Breslau, for example."

That Reform should have fought the new school is not surprising. What might be surprising, however, was the opposition from the religious right. Writing in the Yiddish press, an eminent Orthodox scholar, Rabbi J. D. Eisenstein, also brands the new school fraudulent: "In my opinion, the objective of Conservatism and the law of the Radicals lead to the same path, the only difference between them is the time," that is, the time frame during which changes would be introduced into Judaism. Reform does it quickly; the Conservatives, slowly. Eisenstein urges the Seminary founders to break completely with their Reform forebears and explicitly define themselves as Orthodox.

Notice how both Wise and Eisenstein locate the Seminary as a "centrist" school and then dismiss it for being there. In fact, all middle-of-the-road positions are inherently problematic. They are invariably compromises and, as such, are suspect in the eyes of the polar positions. To the Reformers, the Seminary was Orthodox; to the Orthodox, it was Reform. To both, it was a fraudulent enterprise.

Despite the opposition, the Seminary founders proceeded to round up support for their cause. The year 1886 was devoted to a series of meetings designed to raise funds and enlist congregations in what was called The Jewish Theological Seminary Association, a corporate body that would become the sponsor of the new school. During this year, some 25 congregations allied themselves with the Seminary Association. As the year drew to a close, the first eight students were admitted to the school. Opening ceremonies were held on January 2, 1887, and the next day classes began. The Jewish Theological Seminary was born.

■ THE ONLY one of the original eight students to be ordained by the new Jewish Theological Seminary of New York was Joseph Hertz (1872–1946). Hertz went on to become Chief Rabbi of the British Empire and to edit the version of the *Humash* that is currently used in most English-speaking Conservative and Orthodox synagogues.

Creating a Movement

As attacks from both left and right indicated, this new coalition barely suppressed serious internal tensions. The founders of the Seminary were comfortable with the mixed package of enlightened traditionalism that they had designed. But it was a far different matter to reach out beyond the school to create a congregational base and a support group of wealthy lay Jews sympathetic to the goals of this new coalition. The founders could not but envy the support that Reform's Union of American Hebrew Congregations lent to its college. Not the least significant aspect of that support was financial. A school needs funding, and the Seminary's early years were marked by continuous precariousness because of the lack of assured financial support.

But money was only part of the story. The Seminary was not simply an academic institution. It was committed to a distinctive approach to living as a religious Jew in a new historical and cultural setting. Its ultimate goal was to create a community of religious Jews, so it needed congregations for its rabbis and a constituency that would attend to its message.

As the century drew to a close, the Jewish population in America numbered over 1 million. Roughly one-quarter of that number were the descendants of the Sephardic and German Jews who had inhabited the country since colonial times. The remaining three-quarters were newly arrived Eastern European Jews, who flooded the country in the mass immigrations of the last two decades of the century. The Seminary's initial support was drawn from the Sephardic-German community. To expand that support, it was only natural that the founders would turn to the more numerous and still rapidly growing Eastern European population.

EASTERN EUROPEAN JEWS

The new immigrant Jews from Eastern Europe were fresh out of small towns and villages. Inclined to be much more traditionalist in belief and practice than their German-Sephardic cousins, they were relatively unfamiliar with the culture of modernity. They had largely been spared the challenges that the Emancipation and Enlightenment had brought to Western European Jewry, but that very fact made them much more vulnerable to the shock of being introduced into American life.

The Eastern European Immigration

The Seminary's combination of Jewish traditionalism with an American idiom seemed tailor-made for the new Eastern European community. Those immigrant Jews who sought to retain some semblance of traditional religious life organized themselves into the small synagogues familiar to them from their Eastern European background. They were also strongly opposed to Reform. The Seminary founders were convinced that their coalition was broad enough to include this new population, and that including them would be a natural way of broadening the base of support for the new school.

What followed is a fascinating and totally unanticipated chapter in the history of American Judaism. In effect, the Seminary served as the catalyst for the eventual emergence of a strong and independent American Orthodoxy.

■ THE SHOCK of the transplanted Eastern European Jews was economic, cultural, and religious. Their poverty was pervasive; they had to learn a new language and adjust to a very different lifestyle; and for many, their religious traditions seemed to retard or even prevent their acculturation. How could a poor peddler or a small retail merchant observe the Sabbath, potentially his busiest day of the week?

The Yom Kippur Ball

The Eastern European Jews responded to America in many different ways. For some, the openness of the American setting stimulated a latent antireligious impulse. Anarchists, socialists, Yiddishists, and secular culturalists of all stripes competed for allegiance. A dramatic statement of that antireligious impulse was the Yom Kippur ball held on Kol Nidre night, where these Jews ate, drank, and danced the night away as their fellow Jews fasted and prayed in their synagogues.

Once again, the watershed was a series of conferences held under the auspices of the Seminary, in 1898, 1900, and 1902. The first of these was held at Shearith Israel. The delegates represented about fifty congregations, some old-line German-Sephardic but most of them the new Eastern European traditional congregations. The conference, conducted in English, began with an announcement of a newly created organization—note the name—the Orthodox Jewish Congregational Union of America. The principles of the new body were an almost point-by-point refutation of the Pittsburgh Platform: All Jewish ritual remains binding; Judaism is both a religion and a national collectivity; belief in the divine revelation of Torah, in a personal Messiah, and in the return to Zion is reaffirmed.

The second conference of the Union took place not at Shearith Israel but in the Eldridge Street Synagogue, on New York's Lower East Side, the bastion of the newly arrived "downtown"—that is, Eastern European—Jews. That shift portended what was to come. A major address delivered in Yiddish denounced all Jewish immigration to America: How could one retain one's Jewishness in such a secular society? Soon the Seminary itself came under attack: Its language of instruction was English; its *Wissenschaft* assumptions were modeled on those of the modern, Western university rather than on those of the traditional European *yeshivah*. A proposal to raise funds on its behalf was passed but with the proviso that half of these funds were to be allotted to one of the Lower East Side's Eastern European–style *yeshivot*, Etz Chayim. (Etz Chayim was later to merge with another traditionalist *yeshivah*, Rabbi Isaac Elhanan, to form the nucleus of what is now Yeshiva University, the academic and institutional bastion of modern American Orthodoxy.)

By the time of the third conference, in 1902, the new Union had been totally captured by the Eastern European population. The language of the conference was Yiddish, and Etz Chayim became the sole beneficiary of funds raised. The Seminary pulled out, and the Orthodox Congregational Union went its own way to become the congregational base of an independent American Orthodoxy. It was not until 1913 that the Seminary would succeed in creating its own congregational movement, the United Synagogue of America.

"Uptown" and "Downtown": A Shaky Coalition

In retrospect, the unhappy story of the Seminary's entanglement with the Orthodox Congregational Union could have been predicted a decade earlier. It was an accurate reflection of the strains inherent in this conservative coalition.

The strains were multidimensional. Part was a sociological or cultural clash between the wealthy, sophisticated, established "uptown" (i.e., German-Sephardic) Jews and the poor, uneducated, newly arrived "downtown" masses from Eastern Europe. Part was a matter of language: English as opposed to Yiddish. Part was a conflict of intellectual backgrounds. The old-line Jews had appropriated the values of the Enlightenment: Many had a secular education and had read extensively in non-Jewish literature, science and philosophy. The new Jews were largely uneducated, apart from whatever Jewish education they had garnered in the European *yeshivot* or their American replicas. One group was sympathetic to some measure of reform; the other was staunchly traditionalist.

■ THE WEALTHY German Jews, shown here at a Purim ball in New York in 1877, had little in common socially, economically, or intellectually with the recently arrived Eastern European immigrants. As a result, the Seminary, which was supported primarily by German Jews, encountered great difficulty when it tried to incorporate this new population into the fledgling Conservative Movement.

The Seminary itself served as a barrier between these two groups. It was the creation of the old-line community. Its leaders were German and Sephardic. The school could not but reflect their values. The language of instruction had to be English; a secular undergraduate education was a prerequisite. The curriculum was radically different from that of the traditional *yeshivah*, where students concentrated exclusively on Talmud and the later codifications of Jewish law. Seminary students studied Bible, Hebrew language and grammar, Jewish history, modern Hebrew literature, and Jewish philosophy, not to mention pedagogy, homiletics, and subjects relating to the professional work of the rabbi. The Seminary was, in fact, closer to a modern, Western graduate school than to the traditional *yeshivah*.

Another source of strain was the fact that, at least until 1885, the Seminary founders had been more or less comfortable members of the Reform coalition. They brought much of the Reform culture with them to the new enterprise, particularly the Western-style, scholarly assumptions of the *Wissenschaft* school. That was the "enlightened" piece of the "enlightened traditionalism" they represented. It was on matters of ideology that the Seminary founders broke with Reform—the return to Zion, the resurrection of the dead, the divine revelation of Torah, and the personal Messiah—and on matters of practice—including observance of the Sabbath, festivals, and the dietary laws. That was the "traditionalism" piece of the package. The founders appeal to the downtown Jews rested on their hope that this traditionalism would outweigh the enlightened intellectualism. In this case—because of the powerful cultural factors that were at work—it simply didn't.

That rejection, then, could have been predicted. It was amply clear, close to six decades earlier, that even Zechariah Frankel's version of enlightened traditionalism was profoundly suspect to the traditionalists in mid-nineteenth-century Germany. The focus of that opposition, as noted in the preceding chapter, was Rabbi Samson Raphael Hirsch, who can be credited with launching what came to be called the "modern Orthodox" reading of Judaism. (We will discuss the emergence of American Orthodoxy at greater length later.) Since the Seminary was the American embodiment of *Wissenschaft*, it inevitably inherited all of its ideological complexities. The full impact of that tension in this new American setting may have been delayed, but its germ was present from the outset.

Crisis at the Seminary

The failure of these early attempts to create a congregational movement could not have come at a worse time for the Seminary. By the turn of the century its two most prominent spokesmen had died—Kohut in 1894 and Morais in 1897. Its student body remained small;

by 1902, fifteen years after its establishment, it had ordained the grand number of seventeen rabbis. Its financial position was precarious; it lived from hand to mouth, raising its roughly $20,000 annual budget through a constant stream of "emergency" appeals to its constituency. It had no firm and consistent support.

The turning point in the Seminary's fortunes was as unanticipated as its role in promoting American Orthodoxy. In effect, the Seminary and Conservative Judaism were not only saved but was launched on a period of extraordinary growth through the efforts of a small group of wealthy, largely Reform Jews, members of Temple Emanu-El, New York's most prestigious Reform congregation.

The roster of names who participated in this effort—Jacob Schiff, Isidor Straus, Mayer Sulzberger, Louis Marshall, Leonard Lewisohn, Samuel and Daniel Guggenheim—reads like a *Who's Who* of American Jewish lay leadership at the turn of the century, all old-line Jews, all Reform, all wealthy. Appropriately, their names are carved in stone on the pillars that surround the present Seminary courtyard. Their catalyst was the premier institution builder of American Jewry, Cyrus Adler.

Adler had been drawn into the affairs of the Seminary from the outset through Sabato Morais, who had been his private tutor. Adler became a member of the Seminary's Board of Directors and was actively involved in soliciting funds for the school. He himself was not wealthy, but he was an intimate of America's wealthiest Jews, and he used his network of relationships in support of all the causes in which he was involved.

How did this group of wealthy Reform Jews come to rescue an institution that was specifically created to oppose the growth of Reform? Their motives were quite clear. They understood that the new wave of Eastern European Jewish immigration would never join Reform congregations. Nevertheless, they had a vested interest in helping the new immigrants to become Americanized, learn English, give their children a secular education, and yet find forms of Jewish religious expression that would preserve their traditional Jewish lifestyle. The Seminary may have failed to co-opt this population in its attempts to form its own union of congregations, but it was also clear that Etz Chayim and the other transplanted *yeshivot* could never produce a rabbinic leadership that would further the process of acculturation in America. This Seminary could. Its rabbis and teachers could serve as role models and educators for this new type of American Jew.

What impelled this group of Reform Jews, then, was a sense of communal responsibility. Their efforts proved to be decisive. In late 1901, after a series of meetings at which a sum of $500,000 was raised, Professor Solomon Schechter, then Reader in Rabbinics at Cambridge University in England, was invited to come to New York and assume the presidency of the school. Schechter arrived in March 1902. The rest is history.

Solomon Schechter

Prominently displayed in the lobby of the Seminary's new Library Building is a portrait of Solomon Schechter, robed in the scarlet gown of the Cambridge professor, white-bearded, crowned with an unruly shock of gray hair, peering imperiously at the observer. This writer finds it impossible to pass this portrait without pausing to look at it again and again. The man exudes power, majesty, and authority.

Schechter was the architect of Conservative Judaism. Born in Romania, educated first in Eastern European *yeshivot* and later in the schools of Western learning in Vienna and Berlin, Schechter had been serving as Reader in Rabbinics at Cambridge when in 1896 he achieved international renown as the scholar who unearthed the Cairo Genizah.

From the Seminary's very first years, Schechter had been wooed by representatives of the school. As early as 1890 Morais had written to invite him to join its faculty, but Schechter was unhappy with the remuneration proposed and was not yet convinced that the new school was financially secure enough to ensure its future. In

1895 Schechter visited the United States, lectured in Philadelphia and Baltimore, and held extensive conversations with Adler and his colleagues. Again negotiations came to nought. Upon Morais' death in 1897 another offer was made, with a higher remuneration. Again Schechter questioned the adequacy of the school's financial resources.

Finally, in late 1901, following Adler's fund-raising efforts, the agreement was in place. The Seminary Association was merged into a new entity called The Jewish Theological Seminary of America, the Seminary Board was reorganized with Adler as its President, an endowment fund was established, and Schechter agreed to move to New York.

Schechter's presidency was to last only thirteen years, but in this brief period he launched both school and movement on a period of unparalleled growth. He assembled the faculty of scholarly giants who established the Seminary's reputation as the foremost center for advanced Jewish studies in the world. In a series of letters and papers he articulated an ideology for the new Movement. And in 1913 he presided over the creation of the Movement's long-desired congregational arm, the United Synagogue of America. (The name was carefully chosen to reflect the coalition-building goals of the new school, but in 1991, when the Movement's agenda had changed, the name was also changed to the United Synagogue of Conservative Judaism.) He served as the United Synagogue's first President and then as its Honorary President until his death.

■ SINCE ANTIQUITY, Jews have been reluctant to dispose of anything written in Hebrew. Hebrew is the language of revelation, the language of Torah; it should never be profaned by being relegated to the garbage heap. Instead, this material was usually hidden away in some storage place (the Hebrew word *genizah* literally means "hiding place") until it could be buried in the grave of a rabbi or other pious man.

Toward the end of the nineteenth century, isolated manuscripts, legal contracts, letters, and other documents from the early Middle Ages were pilfered from one of these archives and filtered into the hands of European scholars. One of these manuscripts—a piece of the original Hebrew version of the apocryphal book of Ecclesiasticus, whose existence had been suspected but never confirmed—was shown to Schechter, and he was able to trace its provenance to Cairo.

In 1896 Schechter traveled to Egypt, established contact with the leaders of Egyptian Jewry, and was led to the long-unused garret of an old synagogue, a room without windows or doors and accessible only if one climbed a ladder and entered through a hole in the wall. There Schechter discovered material of such richness and in such quantity that to this very day scholars in schools and museums around the world are still busy trying to decipher its contents. It is no exaggeration to claim that the contents of the Cairo Genizah have enabled us, for the first time, to write an accurate history of the Jewish Middle Ages. Schechter is pictured here at Cambridge University examining fragments from the Cairo Genizah.

Schechter's Synthesis

Schechter represented in his very person the kind of integration that was at the heart of everything the Seminary stood for. He spoke both Yiddish and English (as well as German and Hebrew); he had studied both in the Romanian *yeshivot* and in the Science of Judaism schools in Vienna (and Berlin and London); he had written on the mystics of Safed and on Abraham Lincoln (one of his heroes from early childhood); he was at home with the "downtown" Jews and the "uptown" Jews; he was open-minded intellectually and traditionalist in practice.

Schechter's inaugural address, delivered on November 20, 1902, is a perfect illustration of the ideological integration central to Conservative Judaism. The address is liberally sprinkled with references to Western learning, to the writings of Thackeray, Whitman, Goethe, Lincoln, Montaigne, George Eliot, and Renan, along with biblical, talmudic, and liturgical passages. It is unapologetic about its commitment to modernity. It protests against that attitude of mind that:

> cognizant of the fact that there were such things as the eighteenth and nineteenth century, with their various movements and revolutions in all departments of human thought, somehow manages to reduce them to a blank, as if they had not been. My friends, they have been! There has been such a thing as rationalism. . . . There has been such a thing as a critical school. . . . There has been such a thing as a historical school. . . . All these movements are solemn facts, and they can as little be argued away by mere silence as pain and suffering can be removed from the world by the methods of Christian Science.

As to the school's religious tendency, Schechter is unequivocal:

> The religion in which the Jewish ministry should be trained must be specifically and purely Jewish, without any alloy or adulteration. Judaism must stand or fall by that which distinguishes it from other religions. . . . Judaism is *not* [emphasis Schechter's] a religion which does not oppose itself to anything in particular. Judaism is opposed to any number of things. . . . It permeates the whole of your life. It demands control over all your actions, and interferes even with your menu. It sanctifies the seasons, and regulates your history, both in the past and in the future. Above all, it teaches that disobedience is the strength of sin.

How are these two impulses—intellectual openness and traditional observance—to be balanced? Schechter is clearly aware of the ambiguities of his position:

> I would consider my work . . . a complete failure if this institution would not in the future produce such extremes as on the one side a raving mystic who would denounce me as a sober Philistine; on the other side, an advanced critic, who would rail at me as a narrow-minded fanatic, while a third devotee of

strict orthodoxy would raise protest against any critical views I may entertain.

There is nothing new in this state of affairs: "The Torah gave spiritual accommodation for thousands of years to all sorts and conditions of men, sages, philosophers, scholars, mystics, casuists, school men and skeptics; and it should also prove broad enough to harbor the different minds of the present century."

Still, the center of gravity must remain within Torah: "The teaching in the Seminary will be . . . confined to the exposition and elucidation of historical Judaism in its various manifestations. There is no other Jewish religion but that taught by the Torah and confirmed by history and tradition, and sunk into the conscience of Catholic Israel."

From Frankel to Schechter

We will look at Schechter's ideology much more closely, but even in this preliminary discussion the continuity between Frankel's vision of Judaism in the modern age and the vision of Schechter's can be seen.

Like Frankel, Schechter was delicately balancing two opposing impulses. On one hand, modernity was here to stay. His espousal of the critical and historical approach to Judaism decisively distances him from Hirsch and his Modern Orthodox descendants. He had too much intellectual integrity to compartmentalize his mind, to use a modern mental set to study secular culture and a traditionalist one to study Torah. On the other hand, the central religious thrust of classical Judaism remains binding. Reform's reckless abandonment of classical forms of Jewish religious expression, he felt, was perilous to the Jewish future. Neither of these impulses can be denied.

But how are these contrary impulses to be accommodated? How does one balance the claims of both authenticity and modernity? Not surprisingly, by an appeal to historical Judaism and community, to what Schechter dubbed—and we will return to this puzzling term—Catholic Israel. Like Frankel, Schechter avoided dealing with the theological assumptions that underlay this accommodation. He was aware that the position was subtle, that it would expose him to criticism from all sides, but he was convinced that it represented the authentic tradition and that it was the only way to deal with the challenges of modernity.

This attempt to capture a reading of Judaism that would be both authentic and in tune with the temper of modernity was Schechter's implicit acknowledgment of Frankel's vote of confidence in the Jewish community and in the intuitive dynamics of Jewish tradition. Through Schechter, that position became the cornerstone of both the school and the Movement that it spawned.

THE FOUNDING IDEOLOGY

Unless we succeed in effecting an organization which, while loyal to the Torah, to the teachings of our sages, to the traditions of our fathers, to the usages and customs of Israel, shall at the same time introduce the English sermon, and adopt scientific methods in our seminaries, in our training of rabbis and schoolmasters, for our synagogues and Talmud Torahs, and bring order and decorum in our synagogues . . . , traditional Judaism will not survive another generation in this country.

——Solomon Schechter

Good Reasons and the Real Reason

There are three reasons why the founders of Conservative Judaism did not publish their own statement of principles. Two of these can be called good reasons; the third is the real reason.

This distinction between good reasons and real reasons assumes that the motivations that impel human decision making are complex. Some of these motivations may be perfectly adequate without being decisive. These were the good reasons for not publishing a platform, those that were publicly articulated and openly discussed. What was decisive was the real reason, one that has to be inferred from the dynamics of institution building at work in Conservative Judaism's early history.

The first good reason was alluded to in the preceding chapter. Ideological platforms are inherently divisive. As long as Reform's ideology remained vague and implicit, its founding coalition held together. When it became explicit, the movement split in two. The new movement was not going to repeat Reform's mistake.

Second, the leaders of the Seminary did not feel that they had a responsibility to articulate a platform. Reform did because it initiated the break with the established tradition. When the United States declared its independence from England, its leaders, too, had to justify their break. They wrote a Declaration of Independence. England didn't have to say a word. The Seminary, then, was England. It stood for classical Judaism, the Torah, the Talmud, and the liturgy of the prayerbook. That was its statement of principles. What else was there to say? So much for the good reasons. The real reason lay elsewhere.

In retrospect, the real reason the Seminary founders never wrote a statement of principles was that any such statement would have seemed ridden with tensions and internal contradictions, particularly in comparison with the Pittsburgh Platform. Better to leave it vague, open, and undefined. That way it could not be criticized. Their judgment proved accurate. For the first six decades of the twentieth century the Movement flowered. Undoubtedly, one of the reasons for this growth was its ideological openness.

The Founding Ideology

There is an ideology buried within the extensive writings of the Movement's founders, but it has to be dug out. Here is one attempt to do just that, using primarily the writings of Solomon Schechter, the most articulate, thoughtful, and influential of the founders of Conservative Judaism. It consists of nine building blocks.

1. America is different.

Somewhat surprisingly for a generation of immigrants, in all the writings of the Seminary founders there is not an ounce of nostalgia for their European home. On the contrary, there is an excitement about being in America, a conviction that Judaism will flower in this new land. This attitude did not derive simply from the fact that as the twentieth century began, European Jewry seemed to be more and more in a state of disarray, although this was certainly a factor. Much more, their positive stance stemmed from an intuitive conviction that America would be different—because it was a democracy, because it was founded on biblical principles, and because the American Constitution protects the religious freedom of its citizens. "In this great, glorious and free country," Schechter wrote, "we Jews need not sacrifice a single iota of our Torah; and in the enjoyment of absolute equality with our fellow citizens we can live to carry out those ideals for which our ancestors so often had to die." The future of Judaism in America is bright.

■ THE PRELIMINARY design for the U.S. Seal depicted the miraculous splitting of the Sea of Reeds and the Children of Israel escaping the pursuing Egyptian army, as recounted in Exodus 14. Note the Israelites on the shore across the sea, the Egyptians drowning as the waters return to cover the sea, and in between the two the pillars of cloud and fire, which symbolize God's protective presence over Israel. Throughout history, the biblical account of the Exodus has inspired and shaped revolutionary movements for the liberation of oppressed peoples. This preliminary version of the seal was America's acknowledgment of its debt to biblical Israel.

2. Judaism can deal with modernity.

There is a hardheaded realism in this belief, but there is also much more: an unshakable confidence that Judaism has the resources to deal with modernity and that it will emerge from that encounter strengthened and enriched. That optimism infused the culture of the school. From the very outset, every Seminary-trained rabbi had to complete a secular undergraduate education; at the turn of the century, that was a controversial move. To this day, in some Orthodox circles secular studies are absolutely forbidden.

3. If we are to deal with modernity, we must study Judaism in a modern way.

Doing that meant appropriating the methods of the Enlightenment's scientific temper for the study of Judaism. As we have noted, the Science of Judaism school, which originated in Germany at the dawn of the Emancipation, believed that if Jews were to be accepted into European culture, it was essential that Judaism be studied in the same way as any other civilization. The Jewish scholar had to adopt a totally objective stance toward this discipline and use any and every tool in the search for the truth, whatever that truth might be. The success of this enterprise would be marked by the introduction of Judaic studies into the curricula of European universities.

In practical terms, that undertaking meant adapting the methods of modern criticism to the study of the Bible and Talmud, comparing Jewish religious forms with those of other religions and cultures, and accepting the fact that at every stage of its development Judaism was influenced by the sociological, economic, and cultural conditions that existed outside the Jewish world, in the general community at large. Every page of the Bible reveals the influence of Ancient Near Eastern literature; Roman and Hellenistic law helped shape talmudic law; Arabic poetics influenced medieval Hebrew poetry. If these facts were what scholarship disclosed, so be it, whatever the impact on Jewish religion. In effect, these men were saying that for Judaism to be emancipated, Jewish scholarship had to be emancipated as well—emancipated from its ties to a system of beliefs that accorded particular sanctity to the text.

The ultimate implication of this approach, rarely articulated explicitly, was that Torah, in its broadest sense as the entire body of traditional Jewish teaching, lost its distinctive status as sacred literature. This represented a radical break from the traditional methods of studying Torah. To this day in schools run according to Orthodox teachings, Torah is studied as the explicit word of God. It is seen as a unique document, totally consistent and coherent throughout the generations and completely immune from outside influences. The Torah's teachings—primarily Jewish law, or *halakhah*—are eternally binding. The early emancipators simply dismissed this approach as "artificial ignorance." Schechter wrote, "We must insist that the teaching in the Seminary be conducted along scientific lines. . . . This is the only way to save Judaism in this country and elsewhere. We cannot and will not perpetuate 'Sluzch' or 'Bialistock' here." (Sluzch and Bialistock were two of the foremost bastions of traditional Jewish learning in Eastern Europe.)

The Seminary soon became the most influential outpost of scientific Jewish scholarship in the world, and its graduates populated departments of Jewish studies in universities throughout the country. What it did not foresee, however, was the impact of this approach on Judaism as a living religious tradition. We will return to this issue shortly.

■ ON THE opposite page is a photo of a *heder* in Poland. The Conservative Movement showed no great nostalgia for the past, no longing to return to the Middle Ages, or to the civilization of Eastern European Jewry. Judaism did not need to run scared from the encounter with modernity. Schechter was critical of the person who though "cognizant of the fact that there were such things as the eighteenth century and nineteenth century, with all their various movements and revolutions in all departments of human thought, somehow manages to reduce them to a blank, as if they had not been. My friends, they have been!"

■ HAMMURABI (ca. 1728–1686 B.C.E.), King of Babylon, is best remembered for his law code, which is inscribed on the stele, or upright stone, the top of which is pictured here. It is a document of major importance for the light it sheds on law and social and political organization in antiquity and for its numerous parallels to the laws of the Torah. An example is the case of *lex talionis*. The Bible on three separate occasions—Exodus 21: 22–25, Leviticus 24: 17–22, and Deuteronomy 19: 16–21—instructs that physical injury is to be punished with equivalent retaliation: eye for eye, tooth for tooth, hand for hand, and so forth. (In the talmudic tradition this provision is understood to mean monetary compensation, not actual physical retaliation.) Similarly, Hammurabi's code reads, "If a seignor has destroyed the eye of a member of aristocracy, they shall destroy his eye. . . . If a seignor has knocked out the tooth of a seignor of his own rank, they shall knock out his tooth."

Hammurabi's code predates the Israelite Exodus from Egypt (usually dated in the thirteenth century B.C.E.) by about 400 years. The precise relationship between these two codes is a matter of scholarly dispute, but it is clear that at the very least the two codes share many common concerns.

4. Judaism has had a history.

This was the primary discovery of the scientific study of Judaism. The early Science of Judaism scholars were all historians. They delighted in structuring Jewish history in specific periods, showing how each period differed from its predecessor and what factors in both the Jewish and the non-Jewish worlds led to the changes. If Judaism in every generation is influenced by the broader conditions under which Jews lived, and if those conditions changed from generation to generation, then Judaism has changed as well. In short, Judaism as a religion has had a history of its own.

In the early nineteenth century this idea constituted a radical break from the traditional understanding of Judaism. For the traditionalists, of course, nothing Jewish ever changed, particularly God's revealed law. How could God's explicit word be affected by changing historical conditions?

The early Reformers used this pattern of ongoing change to justify the changes they introduced into Jewish religious life. If Judaism has always changed, they said, then we today can change it again, consciously and deliberately.

But the Conservative Movement was in a bind. In *Darkhei HaMishnah*, Frankel argued that Jewish law had always changed, and he and his American successors were perfectly ready to accept some changes under specific conditions. But when Frankel pleaded for retaining Hebrew as the language of the liturgy, he also appealed to history, though now with a very different goal. Here, he argued that history teaches us not only what has constantly changed but also what has remained unchanged. One of the continuities in Jewish life was fidelity to Hebrew.

This appeal to history was the Pandora's box that Frankel opened for Conservative Judaism. It was a double-edged sword. Reform used it to justify abandoning traditional practices; Frankel and his successors used it to justify retaining some forms and dropping others. Once we appeal to history, however, it's not always possible to control how it will be used.

■ HOWEVER DIFFICULT it may be for us to imagine, our ancestors quite certainly did worship God in the Temple according to the rites prescribed in Leviticus, chapters 1–7, and in the Mishnah of the order of *Kodashim,* with animal sacrifices on weekdays, Sabbaths, and festivals. But after the destruction of the Temple in 70 C.E., Judaism was totally transformed: The synagogue replaced the Temple, the liturgy replaced sacrifices, the rabbi emerged as the leader of the community, and in effect, every Jew became a high priest, capable of approaching God on his or her own behalf at any moment and at any place on earth. The magnitude of this self-transformation was overwhelming. That Judaism not only survived this transformation but even flourished under these new conditions is testimony to its inner vitality and creative spirit and is reflective of the religion's adaptability to new historical settings.

Here we might pause and look at the first four of the nine building blocks. What is immediately striking is that on each of these issues the leaders of Reform and Conservative Judaism spoke as one. The leaders of Reform also welcomed America and were confident that Judaism could handle modernity. They, too, were committed to the scientific study of Judaism and appealed to history as a source of authority even when breaking with Jewish tradition. In fact, it can be claimed that the Seminary leadership took these four points with them when they broke with Reform. They were part of the pre–Pittsburgh Platform ideology of the Reform coalition, to which the Seminary founders belonged. True, the Reformers understood the last three of these in different ways than did the traditionalists, but these differences were in interpretation, not in policy and certainly not in ideology.

The sharp break with Reform emerges in the next five building blocks.

5. The community becomes the authority.

If in principle every Jewish practice can change, who then decides what is to be preserved and what changed? The answer can be found only through the consensus of caring, committed Jews. It was to this consensus that Frankel appealed in his argument to retain Hebrew.

But, Schechter insisted, so it was in Judaism from the beginning. The Bible itself never served as authority in matters of belief and practice. What did serve in that function was the Bible *as it was interpreted by Jews through the ages,* what Schechter called the Bible's secondary meaning, his term for the Talmud or, more generally, for the later rabbinic understanding of the Bible. And since this interpretation "is mainly a product of changing historical influences, it follows that the center of authority is . . . placed in some living body, which . . . is best able to interpret the nature of its [the Bible's] Secondary Meaning. This living body, however, is not represented by . . . any corporate priesthood or Rabbihood, but by the collective conscience of Catholic Israel."

Catholic Israel! What a strange term, and how often it has been misunderstood. It is quite clear what Schechter did not mean. He clearly did not mean that if we want to know what Judaism stands for, we should simply look at how most Jews act and what they believe. By that criterion, Judaism would have been declared long dead. Nor did he feel that rabbis and scholars should have no influence on the community's understanding of Judaism. He was far too much an intellectual elitist to believe that.

The adjective *catholic*—with a lower-case *c*—simply means "universal," "broad," or "comprehensive," the opposite of narrow, denominational, sectarian, or partial. Schechter seems to be saying that throughout the centuries and across the length and breadth of the Jewish community there has remained a core of serious Jews who want to live their Judaism fully. In a totally natural and intuitive way, these Jews retain certain patterns of belief and behavior, drop others, create new ones—all in the name of keeping Jewish religion alive. We must trust the instincts of this core group of Jews.

The term *Catholic Israel* is a powerful vote of confidence in the Jewish people's will to live. It is also a clear voice for the democratization of Jewish authority. Of course, the rabbis and scholars of every age influence the lives of Jews, but they in turn are themselves influenced by what the community wants. In fact, the community chooses its leaders. There is a sharing of power and authority between leaders and followers in Jewish life. Schechter wanted to make sure that that balance would be preserved.

This democratization of the Jewish authority structure clearly causes tension in the authoritarian structure of traditional Orthodoxy. In that world the rabbi is the authority, and his interpretation of Jewish law is binding on the community. Whether or not the rabbi in fact allowed himself to be influenced by the wishes of his community, the rhetoric of Orthodoxy, at least, affirms that the rabbi's ruling represents the will of God for the community.

But Schechter's appeal to Catholic Israel also places him in conflict with one of the basic principles of classical Reform: its insistence on personal autonomy in determining what a Jew is to believe and how a Jew is to practice Judaism in the modern age. The autonomy of the person was a centerpiece of Enlightenment thinking.

■ DESPITE ITS apparent simplicity, Hanukkah is an extremely puzzling festival. It is our only post-biblical festival, and despite the fact that we praise God for having commanded us to light the Hanukkah candles, there is no such explicit divine command. What the lighting of the Hanukkah candles does reflect is our ancestors' creativity in adopting new forms of worship and celebration. It demonstrates that the community has instituted and will continue to institute new practices and traditions of its own accord, with or without a biblical foundation.

From the outset, Reform thinkers had affirmed that the ultimate authority in belief and practice was the individual Jew, who was to legislate for him or herself according to the dictates of conscience. To this day, the individual Reform rabbi or lay Jew has the absolute right to determine what to believe and how to practice Judaism.

The concept of Catholic Israel breaks with that individualistic impulse. It insists that the community must set broad parameters, particularly in areas of observance, and that these are binding on its members. The insistence on the primacy of community over the individual remains a benchmark between Reform and Conservative Judaism to this day. We shall see how that difference is manifested in practice.

Just like the appeal to history, however, the community is often an ambiguous entity, speaking in multiple voices. The Reformers knew this well. When Frankel perceived the community as intuitively working to preserve Hebrew, the Reformers urged him to look at their communities. They saw precious little evidence of preservation there. Who then constitutes the community? Who forms the consensus? And what happens when its voice is not clear? Reform's answer to these questions led to the affirmation of personal autonomy. Schechter disagreed. We will return to these questions.

6. Hebrew must remain the language of the Jewish people.

The Seminary founders understood well that English would become the language of American Jewry; sermons would be delivered in English, and classes in the schools of Conservative congregations would be taught in English. But the language of the synagogue, of the prayerbook, and of the Torah reading would have to remain Hebrew, and every Jewish child would have to be taught to read and understand Hebrew. According to Schechter,

> [Hebrew] . . . is the sacred language, it is the language of the Bible, it is the language of the Prayer Book and the depository of all the sublimest thoughts and noblest sentiments that Israel taught and felt for more than three thousand years. It is the tie that unites us with millions of worshippers in the same sacred language, who are our brothers and brethren. . . . It is the natural language of the Jew when he is in communion with his God. . . . Translations are a poor makeshift at best, and more often a miserable caricature. . . . We must thus insist on Hebrew.

DICKDOOK LESHON GNEBREET.

A

GRAMMAR
OF THE
Hebrew Tongue,

BEING

An ESSAY

To bring the Hebrew Grammar into English,
to Facilitate the

INSTRUCTION

Of all those who are desirous of acquiring a clear Idea of this

Primitive Tongue

by their own Studies ;

In order to their more distinct Acquaintance with the SACRED ORACLES of
the Old Testament, according to the Original. And
Published more especially for the Use of the STUDENTS of *HARVARD-COLLEGE*
at *Cambridge*, in NEW-ENGLAND.

Composed and accurately Corrected,

By JUDAH MONIS, *M. A.*

BOSTON, N. *England*
Printed by JONAS GREEN, and are to be Sold by the AUTHOR
at his House in *Cambridge*. MDCCXXXV.

■ NO MATTER what other language Jews spoke in the course of their wanderings through history, Hebrew remained the language of Torah and of worship. Since the Torah was understood to be divinely revealed, the Hebrew language itself was sacred; it was, in effect, the divine tongue. To this day, a Jew who has not mastered Hebrew is shut out from the classical texts of our tradition. In America, the importance of learning Hebrew was reaffirmed, as is seen by this early *Grammar of the Hebrew Tongue*, published in 1735 by Harvard's Hebrew instructor Judah Monis.

7. Zionism is a positive force in Jewish history, and it should be encouraged.

For the better part of its first century Reform vigorously opposed Zionism because it challenged Reform's conviction that the Jewish people had to surrender its sense of nationhood if it were to achieve emancipation. Among the first prayers to be eliminated from early Reform prayerbooks were those that spoke of the eventual return to Zion.

The leaders of the Seminary could not go that far; such a stand was simply too radical a break with the tradition. Yet the very attempt to create a school that would serve diaspora Jews assumed the ongoing legitimacy and even vitality of Jewish life outside the Holy Land. How then could the Seminary honestly encourage the efforts of the Zionist movement?

They could if they defined carefully what Zionism did and did not mean to them. For Schechter, it was not a movement that urged a mass emigration of all Jews to the Holy Land and the creation of a modern, secular, national state. Rather, it was "a bulwark against assimilation."

But Schechter was very much aware that he was speaking only for himself and not for the school he headed, which "has never committed itself to the [Zionist] Movement, leaving this for the individual inclination of the students and faculty, composed of Zionists, anti-Zionists, and indifferentists." It could not be otherwise because the Movement's leaders had committed themselves to living as Jews in America and to serving American Jewry. To a significant degree, much of their ambivalence continues to this day.

■ ZIONISM, IN its modern political garb, was an alternative response to the challenges of emancipation. Zionists taught that instead of joining the emerging European nation states, Jews should create their own national home. By and large, European religious Jewry opposed Zionism—Reform, because Zionism marked a resurgence of Jewish nationalism they had rejected, and Orthodoxy, because only God could bring about the return to Zion.

While early Seminary spokesmen never espoused a vigorous anti-Zionism, Schechter, who viewed Zionism as religiously significant, was a lonely, courageous, and—as he himself noted—quite controversial voice. Pictured here are early Zionists cultivating the land of Israel.

8. Halakhah remains the preeminent form of Jewish religious expression.

On this issue, the break with Reform is complete. But it is also on this issue that the Conservative Movement's founding ideology reveals its deepest internal tensions.

For centuries traditional Judaism was tied to its *halakhah*, traditional Jewish law. The word itself comes from the Hebrew root *halokh,* which means "to go" or "to walk." *Halakhah*, then, is the traditional way or the path of Jewish living. The authentic Jew was the observant Jew. The ultimate authority for *halakhah* was God, whose will was revealed to the Jewish people at Sinai; consequently, the entire body of Jewish law is binding on every Jew.

Reform rejected that system of belief, certainly as it applied to the rituals pertaining to diet, marriage, divorce, conversion, the laws of the Sabbath and festivals, and the wearing of *tefillin*. Reform argued that these observances may have had value in the early stages of Jewish history, but today, in America, they are out-of-date, spiritually meaningless, and a barrier to Jewish emancipation.

If any single issue impelled the Seminary founders to break with Reform, it was the debate over the binding nature of all Jewish law. Schechter described his Seminary addresses as "a plea for traditional Judaism." They "advocate a deeper devotion to the laws distinctly characteristic of the Jewish conception of holiness, leading to a more strict observance of the precepts of the Torah." He characterized Reform's abrogation of the laws of the Torah as contradicting "the teachings of the Bible, the teachings of the Talmud, and all Jewish opinion that has come down to us from antiquity, from the Middle Ages, and even from modern times as late as the middle of the last century. . . . In brief, it is non-Jewish and un-Jewish."

On this issue, Schechter's successors, Cyrus Adler and Louis Finkelstein, were equally adamant. Finkelstein put it this way: "Because on the one hand we regard the laws of the Torah as prophetically inspired, and because on the other, we regard the legalism of the rabbis as the finest and highest expression of human ethics, we accept both the written and oral law as binding and authoritative on ourselves and on our children after us."

In its later development, however, the Conservative Movement did redefine a good deal of traditional Jewish law. Today it permits men and women to sit together in the synagogue and worshipers to drive to the synagogue on the Sabbath. More recently, it permitted women to assume a totally equal role in synagogue rituals and to become rabbis and cantors. What would Schechter have made of these developments? Part of the answer lies in the final building block of the founding ideology.

■ THE WORD *halakhah* signifies the distinctive pattern of Jewish behavior outlined in the Bible, elaborated in infinite detail in the writings of the talmudic rabbis, and codified in anthologies of Jewish law. *Halakhah* addresses almost every aspect of life, from agriculture to business, from prayer to charity, from how to get up in the morning to how to go to sleep at night. It instructs the Jew what may or may not be eaten, what clothing may or may not be worn, whom he or she may or may not marry; it creates the rites of passage and teaches Jews how to celebrate the Sabbath and the festivals of the year—such as the searching for leaven before Passover, pictured here by the eighteenth-century Dutch artist Bernard Picart.

9. Halakhah does change and develop to meet new situations, but this process is gradual, evolutionary, limited to the more superficial areas of Jewish life, and always under the guidance of recognized authorities in Jewish law.

This is an extension of point 4, the appeal to history, and it reflects the same ambivalence.

This ambivalence can be seen in Frankel's article entitled "On Changes in Judaism," which he published in 1845, the very year in which he broke with Reform. On one hand, Frankel was convinced that Reform's eagerness to abolish the laws was a tragic mistake. On the other, he was sufficiently grounded in the modern age to realize that the Judaism of antiquity could not be retained untouched. He tries desperately to find some middle ground between these two poles.

> [True,] . . . the word which issued from the mouth of God is rooted in eternity. But time has a force and might which must be taken account of. . . . Judaism must be saved for all time. It affirms both the divine value and historical basis of Judaism and, therefore, believes that by introducing some changes it may achieve some agreement with the concepts and conditions of the time.

AN EYE FOR AN EYE

Zechariah Frankel's *Darkhei HaMishnah* is a major book on the development of Jewish law. Frankel's thesis is that Jewish law has had a history, that it manifests a pattern of constant change in response to the conditions in which Jews lived at each stage of their history. In Frankel's "On Changes in Judaism," published in 1845, he singles out one of the most noted of these changes in Jewish law. Exodus 21:23–25 is the biblical source of what came to called *lex talionis* or "retributive law": "But if other damage ensues, the penalty shall be life for life, eye for eye, tooth for tooth, hand for hand, foot for foot, burn for burn, wound for wound, bruise for bruise." However, the Pharisaic rabbis ruled that this text was not to be interpreted literally but, rather, as requiring a corresponding monetary compensation for these damages. (Bab. Tal., Tractate *Baba Kamma*, 83b). This interpretation led Frankel to the conclusion that "the letter of the law is not decisive, but rather that the spirit must animate the law."

Who decides what to change? The community, what Schechter later called "Catholic Israel." "When the people allows certain practices to fall into disuse," wrote Frankel, "then the practices cease to exist. There is in such cases no danger for faith." But what Frankel gave with the right hand, he withdrew with the left. "The whole community is a heavy unharmonious body and its will is difficult to recognize. . . . We must find a way to carry on such changes in the proper manner, and this can be done by the help of the scholars." The role of the teachers, as he saw it, was to guard the community's "sense of piety" and bring the "truths of faith" nearer to the people. "If the people then cease to practice some unimportant customs and forms of observances it will not be a matter of great concern."

Years later Finkelstein would share Frankel's ambivalence on the way in which changes in Jewish tradition should be implemented: "If the shifting of values and the introduction of new devices will actually bring Jews back to God, to the Torah and to the synagogue, they will then doubtless be accepted. . . . But pending such proof of the value of these changes, and pending their acceptance by all Israel, some of us prefer to stand aside and watch."

Tensions and Contradictions

The statements of both Frankel and Finkelstein are riddled with inner tensions: Torah is the eternally binding word of God, but it is also responsive to changing times; the people decide what to change, but the scholars have to inspire the people so that they may know what to change and what to retain. And if any change can be validated only by its ultimate effects years later, how do we know at the outset what to change and what to preserve?

But as we have already seen, the founding ideology as a whole is studded with tensions and contradictions. We saw that the appeal to history as legitimatizing a contemporary program is a double-edged sword, for history teaches both change and continuity. Which message do we want to read? The same applies to the appeal to Catholic Israel as the authority for determining what we keep and what we change. Which of the community's many voices do we attend to? The Movement's Zionist impulse, too, is clearly ambivalent.

Even more significant, however, is the tension between the scholarly approach to Judaism and the Movement's commitment to the centrality and binding quality of *halakhah*. To put it concisely, if Torah can be studied as one more cultural document, then why are its laws binding? But if the law is God's explicit revelation and is eternally binding, then Torah is hardly a cultural document, open to study by scientific methodologies.

In other words, Reform and Orthodoxy are consistent. The first denies the literal revelation of the Torah and encourages modern methods of study. The latter affirms that Torah is God's explicit words and rejects modern scholarship. Conservative Judaism wants to affirm both. This paradox was created when the Conservative Movement applied the methods of *Wissenschaft* to the study of a text considered divine in origin.

One can maintain these contradictory positions provided he or she acknowledges that since Torah is viewed as emerging from the community, then the authority for establishing parameters of authentic belief and practice has in fact been vested in that community. Therefore, the community has the right to change those parameters if it wishes to do so, but it does not have to do so if it chooses not to. It can exercise its authority to retain all or much of the tradition as binding simply because doing so places this community where it wants to be. If individual members of the community disagree with those parameters, either they will accept them in order to maintain the community intact, or they will join an alternative community.

A statement of this kind would have resolved the ideological tensions from the outset, but the founders of the Seminary did not take this tack. Instead, they deliberately avoided any explicit statement on the issue of authority or, for that matter, on any ideological issue. Despite much hand wringing about ideological vagueness, and many failed attempts to produce such a statement, Conservative Judaism successfully avoided doing so for the better part of a century. It put a positive face on this avoidance by affirming pluralism as a distinctive characteristic of the Movement. Pluralism became a Conservative code word meaning that this coalition did not demand uniformity of belief and practice from its adherents. It also served, however, to conceal the internal contradictions that pervaded its ideology.

As much as the Seminary founders shunned ideological clarity, they also avoided theology. The absence, in all of the writings of the founders, of any sustained, disciplined inquiry into the central issues of Jewish theology—the nature of God, revelation (What did happen at Sinai?), *halakhic* authority (Why is Jewish law binding?), theodicy (Why do good people suffer?), and eschatology (What will be at the end of days?)—is striking. In 1909 Schechter wrote what is still one of the best books on the theology of the talmudic rabbis, *Some Aspects of Rabbinic Theology,* but we know almost nothing at all about what he himself believed on all of these issues. A systematic study of the issue of revelation, for example, would have forced him to confront just what Torah is, how it came to be, and why it retains any authority in our lives. Such a study would have brought many of the ideological tensions to the surface. That may be why he avoided it.

Success

Yet the early founders succeeded. "Nothing succeeds like success" we are told, and the Movement flourished. It offered an attractive mix of classical, authentic Judaism—a largely traditional prayer-book, familiar synagogue melodies, Hebrew prayer, and festival rituals—together with a touch of modern Americanism—mixed seating, English sermons and readings, strikingly designed modern synagogues, and a three-day-a-week congregational school for the children. The Conservative Movement was perfectly positioned to capture the loyalty of an immigrant and first-generation American Jewish population.

In retrospect, whether or not the Movement's ideological vagueness was a conscious, deliberate choice, it proved to be eminently successful as a strategy for growth, at least in the short run. In the long run, however, many of the problems it created could not be denied.

But this is a far too negative evaluation of these early efforts. In fact, a case can be made—and will be made in detail—that this founding ideology constituted the most honest, direct, and forthright attempt to deal with the central tension in the history of any religious tradition: the tension between the claims of the past and those of the present, between authenticity and modernity. These first-generation Conservative Jews saw clearly that the new set of challenges confronting Judaism in a modern and democratic America could not be dealt with by a simple, uncritical reaffirmation of tradition or by its reckless abandonment. The alternative, middle course was subtle, complex, and tension-ridden, but it had to be pursued, and it is to their eternal credit that they undertook the struggle.

We will get to the problems in time. First, the period of growth.

5 | MATURITY

"To put the whole matter in a word, we are the only group in Israel who have a modern mind and a Jewish heart, prophetic passion and western science. . . . And it is because we are alone in combining the two elements that can make a rational religion that we may rest convinced that, given due sacrifice and willingness on our part, the Judaism of the next generation will be saved by us. Certainly it can be saved by no other group. "

——Louis Finkelstein

From 1915 to 1972

Statistics dealing with the religious affiliation of American citizens are not precise, but what is beyond question is the speed with which the Movement grew in the 57 years between the death of Solomon Schechter in 1915 and the retirement of Louis Finkelstein, the Seminary's fourth president, in 1972.

These two dates are used as landmarks in the history of the Movement because the head of the Seminary has always served as the leader and spokesperson for the Movement as a whole; a change in Seminary leadership has usually marked a change in the Movement's culture as well. Whereas Schechter's presidency put the Movement on its feet, Finkelstein's retirement, in 1972, set the stage for a significant transformation in the Movement's religious approach. The symbol of that transformation was the Seminary's 1983 decision to admit women to training for the rabbinate, a decision that would have been inconceivable under Finkelstein's presidency. Finally, by 1970 the period of rapid growth, at least for the congregational arm of the Movement, had come to an end. In the two decades since 1970 the Movement may not have lost ground, but it has stopped growing.

But within this 57-year period the Seminary grew from a rabbinical school with an enrollment of about twenty students to the Western world's preeminent academy devoted exclusively to higher

Jewish studies, with five academic departments, a student enrollment of about 500, and a faculty of about 50 full-time scholars. The United Synagogue of America (now the United Synagogue of Conservative Judaism), founded in 1913 with 22 congregations, grew to a membership of about 800 congregations. Finally, the Rabbinical Assembly, founded originally in 1901 as the Seminary's Alumni Association, became an international body of over 1,300 rabbis.

STATISTICS TELL THE TALE

The most recent demographic study of American Jews (conducted in 1990 by the Council of Jewish Federations) indicates that 37.8 percent of adult American Jews who were born Jews and report their current religion as Jewish identify their denominational preference as Conservative, in contrast to 42.4 percent Reform and 6.6 percent Orthodox. The denominational preference of households is 40.4 percent Conservative, 41.4 percent Reform, and 6.8 percent Orthodox. The total reported population in each of the above categories is 3.2 million adults in slightly less than 2 million households. Thus, slightly more than 1.2 million adult Jews who were born Jewish and report their current religion as Jewish identify themselves as Conservative, as do 806,000 households.

The Reform plurality in denominational preference does not, however, translate into synagogue affiliation. Of the 860,000 synagogue-affiliated households reporting, 43 percent (or about 370,000) are in Conservative synagogues, as opposed to 35 percent in Reform, and 16 percent in Orthodox. (This synopsis of the data does not reflect the survey information regarding other groupings within the American Jewish population, such as "Jews by choice" and "born Jews with no religion.")

Leadership:
Cyrus Adler and Louis Finkelstein

Currently university presidents are not known for the length of their tenure; ten years is considered to be the average. It is noteworthy, then, that throughout this 57-year period the Seminary and hence the Movement were led by only two men: Cyrus Adler, who became president of the school upon Schechter's death in 1915, and Louis Finkelstein, who served as president from 1940 and as chancellor from 1951 until his retirement, in 1972.

These two men were as different from one another as men can be. Adler was the model administrator, the classic Jewish civil servant. Though he had a doctorate in Semitics from Johns Hopkins University and was an observant Jew, he is not remembered as a scholar or as a religious spokesperson. His fame is as the premier institution builder of American Jewish life.

■ CYRUS ADLER (1863–1940) was the paradigm of the traditional Jew who occupied a significant position of leadership in American public life, a paradigm that is familiar to us today but was much rarer a century ago.

Born in Van Buren, Arkansas, and educated in Semitics at Johns Hopkins, this pudgy, bespectacled, somewhat stuffy-looking man became assistant secretary of the Smithsonian Institution in Washington. But much of his energy was devoted to creating the institutional structure of American Jewry. At one time or another he was associated with and frequently headed just about every major American Jewish organization, including Dropsie College and Gratz College (which he helped found), the American Jewish Committee, the Jewish Publication Society, the American Jewish Historical Society, and the Jewish Agency for Palestine. Nothing Jewish was alien to him.

Adler was the stimulus behind that small group of Reform Jews who banded together to save the Seminary from ruin in 1901. It was Adler who negotiated Solomon Schechter's acceptance of the Seminary's presidency and who served as chairman of the reconstituted Seminary Board of Directors. He also succeeded Schechter as president of the United Synagogue. Finally, upon Schechter's untimely death, though he was not nearly the scholar that Schechter had been, it was the judgment of the Seminary's Board that only Adler had the diplomatic, administrative, and fund-raising skills to guide the Seminary during the difficult years of World War I. Adler notes in his autobiography, *I Have Considered the Days*, that his initial appointment was to be for only six months. He served 25 years.

Surveying those 25 years, it is tempting to conclude that this mild-mannered, reserved, somewhat aristocratic figure, who commuted from his home in Philadelphia to New York several days a week and who was simultaneously involved in many other projects and institutions, had little to do with the flowering of either the school or the Movement, that both grew as if out of their own inner momentum. That judgment may well be accurate, at least in respect to the Movement. It is fascinating to note that *I Have Considered the Days* contains not a single index listing for Conservative Judaism, only one for United Synagogue of America, and none for Rabbinical Assembly, but Jewish Theological Seminary is very well represented throughout the volume. Adler clearly took his Seminary responsibilities very seriously. The faculty was composed of a series of great scholars, each a giant in his field, each vying for control of the Seminary's academic and religious policies. It took all of Adler's diplomatic skills to negotiate these rivalries.

Adler's leadership of the Seminary was hardly tension free, especially in the early years of his presidency. His appointment as President was not applauded by the faculty. They would have preferred a scholar on the model of Schechter or, later, Louis Finkelstein. Eli Ginzberg's *Keeper of the Law*, a biography of his father, Louis Ginzberg, reveals that Schechter had promised Ginzberg that he would succeed him, but either Schechter changed his mind, or he never acted on his promise.

Adler had a doctorate in Semitics from a respected American university, but therein was the problem. Adler had not had a traditional Jewish education as a child, he had not studied in one of the great European universities, and his field was Bible. Schechter and his colleagues had a profound antipathy for modern, critical Bible study, which they identified as a Christian enterprise marked by an implicit prejudice in favor of viewing the Hebrew Scriptures (or Old Testament, as these scholars dubbed this material) as a prelude to the Christian Scriptures (or New Testament). It is worth noting that despite their close association, Schechter never invited Adler to teach at the Seminary.

ADLER VERSUS THE FACULTY

Adler may well have enjoyed the confidence of the Seminary Board, but his relationship with the faculty remained strained. One notable flare-up occurred over Adler's appointment of Jacob Hoschander as Professor of Bible. This position had been vacant since the death, in 1920, of Israel Friedlander, one of Schechter's appointments. Adler, whose scholarly field was Bible, was determined to appoint someone congenial to him. Without consulting the faculty, he appointed Hoschander, then on the faculty of Dropsie College (which Adler also headed). Louis Ginzberg and his colleagues protested the appointment; they felt that Hoschander's scholarship was simply not up to Seminary standards. They were powerless to prevent his appointment, but we are told that Hoschander was never fully accepted by his peers.

It is clear, however, that Adler had the confidence of the Board precisely because he was an American, a capable administrator and fund-raiser, and a skilled politician. From the Board's perspective, he was a safe choice, and despite the tensions, he did preside over a period of unprecedented growth for both the school and the Movement.

■ BEYOND ADLER's administrative contributions, his skills as a fund-raiser were central in ensuring the strength and success of the Seminary. These were the years, first, of what was called the Great War—the name now seems ironically quaint—and later of the Great Depression. For all its academic standing, the Seminary was never far from financial peril. Adler's contacts with wealthy Jews throughout the community enabled the Seminary not only to remain afloat but even to grow. It was Adler who raised the funds and supervised the construction of the three buildings at the corner of Manhattan's Broadway and 122nd Street (pictured here), which remain the heart of the Seminary campus today.

Louis Finkelstein is an entirely different story. He, too, was a skilled diplomat and a talented fund-raiser. In contrast to Adler, however, Finkelstein's scholarly renown was unchallenged. He was also a charismatic figure, a fervent spokesman for religious traditionalism, and a dynamic leader who had his own clear vision regarding the singular responsibilities of both the Seminary and Conservative Judaism in twentieth-century America.

■ TALL, SLENDER, bearded, passionate, sounding much like a prophet of old, Louis Finkelstein (1895–1991) was born in Cincinnati, studied at the College of the City of New York, earned his doctorate at Columbia University, and was ordained at the Seminary in 1919. He served briefly as a congregational rabbi, but a year after his ordination he joined the Seminary faculty, teaching Talmud and later theology. He soon assumed administrative responsibilities as well. In fact, from 1934 on, although Adler was nominally President of the Seminary, it was Finkelstein who ran the school on a day-to-day basis. He was, therefore, perfectly positioned to succeed Adler.

Finkelstein represented what might be called an intellectualist model of Jewish piety, embodying the conviction that the authentic Jew is the studying Jew; he believed that what God demands most of us is the life of the mind. Maimonides would have agreed with that claim, as would most of the rabbinic authorities of the Talmud. That is why Finkelstein could see himself as the next link in that chain of tradition.

Finkelstein used to say, "When I pray, I speak to God. When I study, God speaks to me." Like Schechter before him, Finkelstein never spelled out a personal theology to help us understand what he meant by God or by God's "speaking." Yet it was clear that he was not naive, that he was a profoundly religious Jew, and that his modern, critical method of studying Torah, however different it may have been from that of his predecessors in Europe, Babylonia, and Palestine, was a genuine religious experience for him.

It was commonly said of Finkelstein's Seminary that "the only sin at the Seminary is shoddy scholarship." Shoddy scholarship may not have been the only sin, but it was certainly the cardinal sin. Finkelstein worked passionately to retain the giants of Schechter's faculty and to replace them and expand their number with recruits, first from Israel and later from among the Seminary's own graduates. He did all he could to create a setting where his colleagues could pursue their research and publish their findings. His goal was the same as that of the Science of Judaism school: to introduce the broad field of Jewish scholarship into the agenda of American academic life. And he succeeded brilliantly. A striking symbol of that success—though it predates Finkelstein's presidency—was the decision of Harvard University, on the occasion of its tercentenary in 1936, to award an honorary degree to Louis Ginzberg, Dean of Seminary Talmudists. Harvard giving an honorary degree to a scholar of Talmud? Jewish studies had indeed arrived!

FINKELSTEIN'S AGENDA

In retrospect, Finkelstein's primary goal was to ensure the continuity of the Jewish scholarly tradition in America. Finkelstein saw clearly that since antiquity the Jewish community had been led by a series of great academies: first the *yeshivot* of Palestine and Babylonia, later those of North Africa and Spain, and more recently those of Eastern and Western Europe. It was not at all clear, in 1940, that this 2,000-year tradition of scholarly leadership would survive. European Jewry was on the brink of destruction, and Israel was still only a distant dream. Where would the next generation of Jewish scholarly leaders be trained? And how could Jewry survive without a scholarly elite? Finkelstein's answer was that it would not, that they would have to be trained here in America, and that The Jewish Theological Seminary would provide the setting for that enterprise.

If the academic world was Finkelstein's primary audience, his secondary audience was the American population at large. Here his goal was to teach the world that Judaism was alive and well, not a fossil religion, not superseded by Christianity or destroyed by the Holocaust, not an affair of elderly, bearded men poring over ancient volumes and totally oblivious to the needs and challenges facing ordinary human beings in the modern age.

It was this impulse that led Finkelstein to create the prize-winning *Eternal Light* radio program (1944), which weekly brought the teachings of Judaism on a range of human and preeminently ethical issues into the homes of millions of Americans. He also founded the

Institute for Religious and Social Studies (1938), a program that pioneered interfaith dialogue between Jewish and Christian clergy, and the Conference on Science, Philosophy, and Religion (1939), an equally pioneering effort to open lines of communication among scholars in science, religion, and the humanities.

■ UNDER LOUIS FINKELSTEIN, the Seminary became a center for interreligious and intercultural dialogue, the first such center in America. Seminary students were accustomed to seeing clergy of all faiths in its hallways and its dining room. Every Tuesday during the academic year, the Institute for Religious and Social Studies conducted classes and lecture series taught by prominent scientists, theologians, authors, and politicians. These programs were central to Finkelstein's personal mission, which was to teach Judaism to American society and to open Jewish studies to the findings of other disciplines. The sight of three visiting Buddhist monks and their translator standing in front of the Seminary gate in May 1959 was not an unusual experience for Seminary students.

These programs gave the Seminary national prominence. It was no longer simply a small, parochial school for the training of rabbis, hidden away in a corner of New York City. Finkelstein had transformed the Seminary into a national treasure, recognized throughout the scholarly world as the premier school for advanced Jewish studies and as a center for transmitting the enduring message of Judaism to the world. A dramatic symbol of that transformation was the photograph of Louis Finkelstein on the cover of the October 15, 1951, issue of *Time*. American Jewry had indeed arrived!

TIME
THE WEEKLY NEWSMAGAZINE

RABBI FINKELSTEIN
The Days of Fear are over.

■ LOUIS FINKELSTEIN cultivated a friendship with Henry Luce, the founder of *Time*. The two men shared a commitment to the value of religious traditions and a concern for applying those traditions to the social and political concerns of their generation. *Time* was a bastion of the American mass media, and its cover story on Finkelstein on October 15, 1951, was a powerful symbol that his mission was being taken seriously by American society at large.

But, it is fair to ask, if Finkelstein's primary audience was American academia and his secondary audience was the American public at large, where did the Conservative Movement fit in? Only secondarily. Finkelstein believed that creating a movement was the responsibility primarily of the Seminary's rabbinic graduates. It was their task to see to the religious and spiritual well-being of the masses of Conservative congregants.

Finkelstein was the exemplar of the Seminary's founding ideology, with all its tensions and contradictions. His scholarship was remarkably open, critical, and historical, on the model of the Science of Judaism school, but he was also a confirmed traditionalist in matters of religious practice. He was a totally observant Jew. He strongly opposed any but the most peripheral deviations from Jewish law. As a professor who spent most of his entire career at an academic institution in New York City, he himself did not have to confront the real problems of how to live as a Jew in, for example, the Midwest.

Generations of Seminary rabbinical students, then, could look neither to Cyrus Adler nor to Louis Finkelstein for guidance on how to function as a religious role model in a twentieth-century American setting. But there was one man on the Seminary faculty who was only too eager to provide that kind of direction. This man quickly became the mentor for the Seminary's rabbinical students, from the time when he first joined the faculty in 1909 until his retirement in 1963, an astounding career of 54 years. The man was Mordecai Kaplan, and if Conservative Judaism as a distinctive approach to living as a Jew in modern America has a programmatic father, he remains Mordecai Kaplan.

Mordecai Kaplan's Revisionist Ideology

■ LOUIS FINKELSTEIN always spoke of Mordecai Kaplan as "my teacher." It is undeniable that on a personal level they shared a great deal of respect and even affection. At the same time, however, if Finkelstein had a serious rival for setting the religious tone of the Seminary, it was Kaplan.

Impeccably groomed, somewhat portly, and fully as passionate and eloquent as Finkelstein, Kaplan offered what was probably the most radical reinterpretation of Judaism in our century. Born in Russia in 1881, educated at the College of the City of New York, and ordained at the Seminary in 1902, Kaplan served for a few years as assistant to the rabbi of a large, Modern Orthodox synagogue in Manhattan. It is totally understandable, given what we know of the program of the Seminary's founders, that the school's early graduates would feel quite comfortable in pulpits of this kind. But Kaplan began to feel more and more uncomfortable. He sensed a growing distance between what he was coming to believe and what his congregants were prepared to hear.

Kaplan had been raised in an Orthodox environment and it took him about 30 years to break with that way of thinking. In a brief autobiographical account, Kaplan traces the process whereby his early traditionalism—his belief in a supernatural personal God, in the biblical account of the revelation of Torah at Sinai, in the authority of the system of commandments as resting in the explicit will of this God—crumbled as he studied biblical criticism, read in the social sciences and modern philosophy, and exposed his theology to hard, critical thinking.

■ MORDECAI KAPLAN (1881–1983) was ordained in 1902 on the eve of Solomon Schechter's assumption of the Seminary's presidency. In 1909, when Kaplan had decided to leave the congregational rabbinate, Schechter persuaded him to come to the Seminary to head a new school for the training of Jewish educators. Shortly thereafter, Kaplan was invited to teach as well in the Seminary's Rabbinical School, which he did until his retirement, in 1962. During this astonishing career of over five decades Kaplan decisively shaped the culture of the Seminary and of the Conservative Movement. Pictured here at a railway station in Tannersville, New York, 1910, is the young Kaplan (left) and Schechter (right).

Toward the spring of 1909 Kaplan had decided to leave the rabbinate. In June of that year, Solomon Schechter invited him to join the Seminary faculty and head the Teachers Institute, a new department designed to train teachers for Jewish schools. Kaplan was thrilled, and within a few years he was also teaching Rabbinical School courses in Midrash, philosophies of Judaism, and homiletics.

Thus began Kaplan's career of 54 stormy years, in which he shaped the thinking of Seminary-trained rabbis and teachers. Throughout this period, every single Seminary student studied with Kaplan, an experience many recall today with dread. Kaplan used his classes to expose his own personal struggle with a tradition that he believed had become out-of-date. More than any other teacher, Kaplan forced his students to acknowledge that they had to know what they themselves believed before they could go out to teach and preach to others; they had a personal responsibility to confront their belief system with ruthless honesty.

Kaplan's revisionist theology emerged as he began to ask himself some hard questions. If we accept the fact that the Pentateuch is not one internally coherent text but, rather, a composite of separate documents with multiple internal contradictions, overlappings, and borrowings from the sacred literature of other peoples, edited some seven centuries after Moses, then in what sense is it the direct word of God? But if it is not the direct word of God, then wherein lies its authority? Why should we take any of it seriously as a guide to living and thinking as Jews? Further, what does the phrase "the word of God" mean? In fact, what is God? Do we really believe in some "being" "out there" somewhere who speaks and listens, rewards and punishes, and intervenes in history?

Finally, from his readings in the social sciences, Kaplan learned that scholars had begun to investigate the phenomenon of religion itself as one of many forms of natural human activity. He read William James on the psychology of religion, Emil Durkheim on the sociology of religion, and John Dewey on the philosophy of religion, and he applied this material to his understanding of Judaism.

It became clear to the young Kaplan that first, there are many religions and most of them exhibit similar traits. What, then, what makes one religion "true" and another "false"? Can Judaism, for example, be true and Christianity false? In fact, can we speak of objective truth and falsity when we talk of religions? Are not all of these religions simply the predictable product of the intuitive nature of different communities? And if so, why be Jewish?

■ MORDECAI KAPLAN's religious and theological naturalism taught that religion is an intuitive product of a healthy community. Its origin lies not "from the outside" through the intervention of a supernatural God into history but, rather, "from the inside" through the natural expression of human needs. From this perspective, no one religion is absolutely, objectively "true." Rather, every religion is equally "true"—that is, true for the community that has produced it. Thus, religious truth becomes relative. This conclusion generated a great deal of controversy for Kaplan, not only in the Jewish religious world but within the Seminary community as well. Pictured here is a religious service at the Eiheiji Temple in Japan.

Traditional Jewish thinking begins with the supernatural God, who creates a world, intervenes in history, chooses a people, redeems them from slavery, and reveals the Torah to that community in explicit words and letters at Sinai.

Kaplan stood that entire package on its head. First, according to Kaplan, comes the community: a family, an extended family, and eventually a people. When that people enjoys a certain security and integrity, it will eventually begin to reflect on itself: where it came from, how it came to be what it is, what makes it different from other peoples. The community will also begin to grapple with the basic problems of individual and communal living: illness and death, guilt, sexuality and intimacy, moral and ethical values by which to live, its dream of what Kaplan called "salvation"—what the world would look like as perfected, complete, and totally harmonious—and how to achieve that state.

The answers to this ensemble of questions as evolved by the Jewish people over several centuries is what we call Torah. Torah—and by extension, Judaism—is very much the creation of the Jewish people. In what sense, then, is it revealed? And what does God have to do with it?

The answer to that depends on what one means by God. This issue was the final step in Kaplan's reworking of Jewish belief, his own personal leap of faith. Kaplan refused to believe that a human community could evolve salvational visions and implement them in the course of its life experience without there being some power or impulse within the human community and within the world at large that guarantees the fulfillment of those visions.

Thus, the Kaplanian God is not a being, not a personal being, certainly not supernatural, and not "beyond" nature, for there is no beyond to nature; nature is simply all there is. Rather, God is a power, a process, a force, an impulse that pervades all things and impels us to evolve and to implement visions of an ever-more-perfect social order. God is "the power that makes for salvation."

Does this God reveal? Certainly, says Kaplan, but not from a mountaintop, not in words and letters, not only from the outside in but also from the inside out, from within ourselves, through the workings of the human conscience and human creativity. God reveals through our urge to acquire knowledge in order to tame the forces of chaos in ourselves, in nature, and in history, thus bringing about the vision of the world as perfected. In fact, we can say that according to Kaplan, it is not God who reveals the Torah but, rather, the Torah that reveals the presence of God, in ourselves and in nature at large.

The above is an all-too-brief summary of a complex body of thought, but it does serve to indicate how revolutionary Kaplan's reworking of Judaism was. Most revolutionary was what we call Kaplan's naturalism—his view of God as an impulse within nature, of religion as emerging naturally out of the ordinary, intuitive functions of human communities—and his theory of revelation as the natural process by which human beings discover visions of an ever-more-perfect world order and strive to implement them. This naturalism represented a radically new way of understanding what it means to be a religious Jew in the modern age.

■ KAPLAN REPLACED the supernatural God of classical Jewish religion with the "transnatural" God of modern, naturalist religion. God is to be understood not as a separate, independent Being existing in some world beyond nature but, rather, as an impulse, power, or force totally within the natural order. There is no place beyond nature. Kaplan's God is "transnatural" because that impulse which is God can be found throughout nature, within human beings, and within human societies, for after all, human beings form part of this natural order. Pictured here is the Grand Canyon.

KAPLAN'S NOTION of Jewish civilization led to the creation of two institutions. The first is the Jewish Community Center (or JCC, as it is popularly known), which is widespread in American Jewish communities. The Center is the institutional embodiment of the civilization in the sense that within its walls Jews can participate in a wide range of activities—sports, arts, study, worship—all within a Jewish communal framework. The other institution is the University of Judaism in Los Angeles, a school that trains professional and lay Jewish leaders in the totality of Jewish life and thought. Kaplan was instrumental in creating this institution, which until recently was identified as the West Coast school of the Seminary.

Kaplan's thought culminated in the notion that became the title of his first and most important book, *Judaism as a Civilization.* Judaism, Kaplan contended, is not simply a religion, not simply a way of behaving or believing, and not simply a matter of peoplehood. It was all of this and more. A civilization, Kaplan contended, is a dynamic complex of language, history, institutions, beliefs, practices, arts, and ties to a land. One "belongs" to or participates in a civilization by identifying with any or all of these dimensions.

A unique dimension of the Jewish civilization is the role assumed by religion. Religion gives an organic quality to the rest of Judaism and lends purpose to Jewish life. Finally, Judaism is an "evolving" religious civilization because this civilization, like all others, changes as it passes through history.

What is revolutionary in this definition is the notion that Judaism, like every other civilization, is a function of the Jewish people. Peoples create civilizations in a totally intuitive way. It is the Jewish people that serves as the core of the civilization, the one constant element in a pattern of ongoing change. The implication is that Judaism is whatever the Jewish people claim it is.

To many rabbinical students, Kaplan's thought was extraordinarily liberating. In effect, Kaplan had taken the Seminary's founding ideology and resolved all of its inner tensions and contradictions. Torah was not revealed from Sinai in words and letters. Judaism was in fact the creation of the Jewish people, very much a cultural document. Therefore, it could be studied critically, historically, and scientifically. The authority for what we do and believe as Jews lies not in the explicit will of a supernatural God but, rather, in the community that remains the instrument through which God reveals. Finally, since Judaism is whatever the Jewish people at its best would like it to be, we are completely free to redefine the content of Jewish religious belief and practice in the light of our own ongoing experience of God's revelation, and in doing so we ensure the survival of Judaism and the Jewish people. (For example, in 1922 Kaplan's daughter, Judith, was the first Jewish woman to have a *bat mitzvah*.) We are doing consciously what Jews in every generation have done.

In short, Kaplan brought the implicit theology, ideology, and program of the Movement into line.

KAPLAN EXCOMMUNICATED

In 1945 Kaplan published his Reconstructionist Prayerbook, which adapted the traditional liturgy to his new theology, eliminating references to traditional doctrines, such as that of the chosen people, the resurrection of the dead, and the personal Messiah. In response, a group of Orthodox rabbis met in formal session, burned his prayerbook, and excommunicated him.

It is to Louis Finkelstein's credit that the excommunication had little effect on Kaplan's standing at the Seminary, even though three traditionalist members of the faculty—Louis Ginzberg, Dean of Seminary Talmudists; Alexander Marx, the historian and librarian; and Saul Lieberman, a younger talmudist later to succeed Ginzberg—publicly condemned Kaplan's efforts. However much Finkelstein may have disagreed with Kaplan, he insisted on Kaplan's right to teach and to publish his thought—further testimony to Finkelstein's commitment to American-style academic freedom.

Two Conservative Judaisms

From the middle of the twentieth century through 1972, Conservative Judaism presented two faces. One was the Seminary's—highly intellectual and academic, extraordinarily open to the most critical and scientific scholarly research, yet traditionalist in practice, barely tolerating changes in ritual observance, and largely unaware of the issues faced by the masses of Jews in Conservative congregations throughout the country.

This was the Conservative Judaism of the Seminary founders, of the group that broke with Reform over the Pittsburgh Platform, of Solomon Schechter and Louis Finkelstein, and of most of their colleagues on the faculty. It is worth noting, for example, that in the Seminary's own synagogue men and women sat separately until

1984, following the Seminary's decision to ordain women. (In 1984 a second, more egalitarian service was instituted, but the traditional *minyan* continues to meet today.)

The second version of Conservative Judaism was Kaplan's. To him, Judaism is the religion of the Jewish people. What the people originally created it can continue to create and recreate in line with each new generation's intuitive perception of what is demanded for Jews to achieve a sense of fulfillment. Thus, the entire body of belief and practice can be reshaped as the community, at its best, determines. And, Kaplan insisted, this enterprise is not at all an abandonment of Judaism but, in fact, is the guarantor of its survival. It is also the work of God—not the supernatural God of the Bible, but God as a process within nature and within human beings.

Kaplan was one of the handful of Seminary faculty members who functioned as a congregational rabbi while teaching, and he brought his practical experience into the classroom. What his students learned from him—apart from the passion and integrity with which they had to confront their responsibilities—was that they were not locked into the past, that they were free to change the prayerbook, the Passover Haggadah, the observance of the Sabbath and festivals and the other rituals of Jewish religious life in order to make the body of tradition more acceptable to their congregants.

Kaplan's revisionist theology did not require his followers to go as far as Reform. In fact, Kaplan was as critical of Reform as he was of Orthodoxy. He disapproved of Reform's abandoning Jewish nationhood as a dimension of Jewish identity, its abandoning Zionism and the Hebrew language, and its reducing Judaism to a religion alone on the model of Christianity.

Students' exposure to the Seminary's version of Conservative Judaism also had a decided impact on their thinking, but they did want to go further than the Seminary in introducing changes. How much of Kaplan's theory was accepted by Seminary-trained students is open to question. In effect, they made their own synthesis of Kaplan and Finkelstein, a rough-and-ready program that enabled them to preach and teach a modified traditionalism that was at the same time a modified Kaplanism.

Kaplan's approach to the liturgy can be summed up as follows: If you don't believe it, don't say it. He therefore eliminated all references to the resurrection of the dead, the chosen people, and the personal Messiah. He dropped the middle paragraph of the *Shema* (Deut. 11:13–21) because he no longer believed that a person's behavior influences rain or drought. He dropped the entire *Musaf* (the "additional" service on Sabbath and festivals) because we no longer want to pray for a return of the Temple cult with its sacrificial system.

The leadership of the Rabbinical Assembly and the United Synagogue rejected most of these proposals. They adopted a very different approach to liturgical change, and as a result, the Rabbinical Assembly–United Synagogue *Sabbath and Festival Prayer Book* (published in 1945) was far less radical than Kaplan's, yet it was also significantly different from the traditional prayerbook. Wherever possible, the traditional Hebrew text was retained. In some instances doing so was clearly impossible. For example, instead of dropping the *Musaf* service completely, this prayerbook transposed the Hebrew of the offending prayer for the restoration of sacrifices to a historical recollection of the service in antiquity. Also, the blessing that praises God "for not having made me a woman" was replaced by one, recited by both women and men, that praises God for having made me "in Thine image."

More frequently, the strategy for handling problematic liturgical texts was to retain the traditional Hebrew and shade the translation in a way that would sidestep the problem. Thus, the *Sabbath and Festival* translation of the blessing praising God for resurrecting the dead is phrased, "who callest the dead to life everlasting."

Forty years later, *Siddur Sim Shalom*, the first comprehensive prayerbook published by the Movement (i.e., for daily, Sabbath, and festival use in the home and in the synagogue) would introduce even more radical changes.

Not surprisingly, the *Sabbath and Festival Prayer Book* was not used in the Seminary synagogue until 1984, when it was introduced for the parallel egalitarian service which came into being after the decision to admit women for ordination. In 1985 the prayerbook for that parallel service became *Siddur Sim Shalom*.

These rabbis may not have followed Kaplan all the way, then, but they did accept the principle that we can change the liturgy to bring it into line with our own belief system. And even these minimal changes offended the traditionalists, both within the Movement (e.g., Finkelstein and some of his faculty) and, of course, in the Orthodox world.

■ IN 1920 Mordecai Kaplan published an article entitled "A Program for the Reconstruction of Judaism." The year 1935 saw the first appearance of a periodical called *The Reconstructionist*. The name was new but not the periodical. In its previous guise, from 1923, it had been called *S.A.J. Review* after the Society for the Advancement of Judaism, the Reconstructionist Movement's mother congregation on Manhattan's Upper West Side that Kaplan founded in 1922. By the mid 1930s the movement that embodied Kaplan's ideological and programmatic thrust came to be known as Reconstructionism.

Kaplan undoubtedly hoped that his reading of Judaism would become the ideology and program of Conservative Judaism. But after World War II and the Holocaust, American Jewry became more traditionalist, and Kaplan felt himself increasingly isolated from the Seminary community. He turned to developing Reconstructionism as a movement by creating the Reconstructionist Rabbinical College in Philadelphia in 1968. Kaplan raised the funds for the new school, created its curriculum, and then retired to Israel. This school, which competes with the Seminary for students, symbolized Kaplan's final break with the Conservative Movement. Kaplan is shown here affixing the *mezzuzah* at the dedication of the Reconstructionist Rabbinical College in October, 1968.

Kaplan himself remained at the Seminary as long as he did probably because of his expectation that he could succeed in swinging the Movement as a whole behind him. His heyday was in the years prior to World War II, when generations of rabbinical students, most of them dropouts from Orthodoxy, came to the Seminary precisely because he was teaching there. But from the 1950s on, American Jews turned more traditionalist, and the mood of the students swung against Kaplan and he felt more and more isolated. For some years his close associates had been urging him to devote his energies to the development of Reconstructionism as a separate movement. Finally, in 1963, at the age of 82, Kaplan heeded their advice. He resigned from the Seminary, created the Reconstructionist Rabbinical College in Philadelphia, and devoted all of his efforts to the development of the Reconstructionist Movement.

He later moved to Israel, took ill there, and returned to New York, where he drifted into a coma. He died on November 9, 1983, at the age of 102, just a few weeks after the Seminary faculty voted to admit women to rabbinical training. To some, this coincidence was an act of God. Kaplan himself would have scoffed.

Abraham Joshua Heschel

■ ABRAHAM JOSHUA HESCHEL (1907–1972) came to the Seminary in 1946 from the Hebrew Union College in Cincinnatti. Born in Warsaw to a family that traced its ancestry back to the circle around the Baal Shem, the founder of Hasidism, he was educated in the best of the Eastern European *yeshivah* tradition and at the University of Berlin. Heschel left Poland shortly before World War II to accept a teaching position in Cincinnatti, but he was obviously out of place in that bastion of Reform Judaism, and six years later he moved to New York to become Professor of Ethics and Mysticism at the Seminary, where he taught until his death. His personal theology was articulated in a series of books, including *The Sabbath* (1951), *Man Is Not Alone* (1952), *Man's Quest for God* (1954), and *God in Search of Man* (1956). Heschel is pictured here teaching a class at the Jewish Theological Seminary.

For decades, Kaplan's presence at the Seminary attracted students for whom Kaplan provided an ideology and a program that enabled them to function as Jewish religious role models in the modern age without sacrifice of intellectual integrity. After World War II, however, as Kaplan's star began to fade, another figure joined the Seminary faculty and began to expound a very different reading of Judaism to a new generation of students, whose agenda was quite different from that of their predecessors. Soon the reason students came to the Seminary was to study with Abraham Joshua Heschel.

In many ways, Heschel was the polar opposite of Kaplan. Kaplan's temperament was rational and scientific; Heschel's, mystical and Hasidic. Kaplan was meticulously groomed; Heschel had the rumpled look of a romantic poet, his face deeply lined (at least in his later years), bearded, and crowned with an unruly shock of hair. Kaplan's spoken English was dry and unaccented; Heschel's, lilting and touched with a Yiddish accent. Kaplan wrote straightforward expository prose; Heschel wrote poetically and impressionistically. Kaplan's thought was radical and revolutionary; Heschel's, a restatement of classical biblical and rabbinic Judaism, albeit with a strong mystical strain and in a fully modern idiom. Kaplan advocated a reconsideration of religious practice; Heschel pleaded for a return to traditional forms.

But just as Kaplan was a product of his times, so was Heschel. Kaplan's challenge was to reread Judaism so that it could survive the challenge of the modern West. Heschel's was to speak to a generation whose faith in the modern West had been irreparably shattered by the Holocaust.

The irony is that just as Kaplan was never completely at home at the Seminary, neither was Heschel, but for different reasons. Kaplan's isolation stemmed from the content of his thought and his program. Heschel was isolated because he was basically a Hasid in a faculty that looked askance at his style of being Jewish, a generalist in a faculty of specialists, a philosopher and theologian in a school that shunned the hard work of modern philosophy and theology. Ultimately Heschel was not at home at the Seminary because he became deeply involved in American and Jewish social and political issues instead of pursuing the more closeted academic career of his colleagues.

This activity brought Heschel international renown, but it also, inevitably, diluted his impact on the Seminary community and on Conservative Judaism. Where Heschel did have a decisive impact was on the education of a small group of Seminary students, many of them now occupying major academic and rabbinic positions in the community, and his influence on their lives was far from merely academic. He injected a creative spiritual dimension into what was otherwise perceived as an arid academic environment. And as the 1960s drew to a close and the American university world exploded into political radicalism, Heschel's activism served as an inspiration to his students.

■ HESCHEL INSISTED that his turn to political activism was prompted by his experience of living in Europe in the decades before World War II. He had been a personal witness to political oppression and was painfully aware that many otherwise good people stood on the sidelines and did not intervene. He was not going to repeat that pattern in America. He became the major Jewish spokesman on the liberal side of a wide range of social and political issues. He plunged into this country's racial conflict and marched from Selma to Montgomery alongside Martin Luther King, Jr. The last decade of his life was consumed by his passionate opposition to the Vietnam War.

There is no denying, however, that in contrast to Kaplan's priorities, the fate of the school and the Movement was not Heschel's primary concern. As a result, Kaplan had the greater impact on the emerging shape of Conservative Judaism. Heschel's untimely death at the relatively young age of 65 robbed the school and the Jewish world of one of its most creative thinkers and engaging personalities.

A Faculty of Giants

This writer recalls vividly his first day at the Seminary. It was on an October morning in 1954, at the *Shaharit* service that ritually marked the opening day of classes for the academic year. I walked into the Seminary synagogue that morning, and there arrayed in the front rows of the sanctuary was a group of men—in those days, they were only men—donning *tallit* and *tefillin*. It struck me at that moment that never before in Jewish history had one room contained just about every major figure in the field of Jewish scholarship. Louis Ginzberg and his intimate friend Alexander Marx had died the previous year, but Finkelstein was there, as well as Saul Lieberman, Ginzberg's successor and the foremost talmudist of his generation. Mordecai Kaplan sat next to H. L. Ginsberg, the master of Bible and Near Eastern Literature. Next to them sat the Hebrew poet Hillel Bavli and Shalom Spiegel, unparalleled as an inspiring teacher, whose field was medieval Hebrew literature but whose course on Jeremiah was an institution among Seminary rabbinical students.

Abraham Halkin, master of Arabic, Islamic studies, and medieval Jewish history sat next to Robert Gordis, one of the few men who combined both an academic career (in Bible) and the congregational rabbinate and who was later to chair the commission that wrote the Movement's first Statement of Principles in 1986. Abraham Joshua Heschel, rapidly supplanting Kaplan as the Seminary's theologian, had joined the faculty in 1946. I also recall Moshe Zucker, master pedagogue, whose most intimate friend, we used to say, was the tenth-century giant Saadia Gaon and who could teach Bible, Talmud, post-talmudic literature, and medieval philosophy with equal brilliance.

The group also included Max Arzt and Simon Greenberg, two Seminary graduates who had illustrious careers in the pulpit and whom Finkelstein had wooed to the Seminary to serve as rabbinic models for the students and to help raise funds for the school. Another Seminary graduate, historian of American Jewry Moshe Davis, was there. Davis was serving as Provost of the school and was later to publish the authoritative account of the beginnings of Conservative Judaism in America and to play a crucial role in the founding of Camp Ramah. A recent graduate, Bernard Mandelbaum, was instrumental in Seminary fund-raising efforts, in its Israel program, and in developing the school's radio and television program.

A host of younger men were in the room as well, some of them visiting from Israel. Others, such as the brilliant young historian Gerson Cohen, were destined to play a major role in the history of both school and movement in the post-Finkelstein years. I also recall Seymour Siegel, beloved teacher of theology and Talmud, who exerted a significant religious influence on generations of students until his untimely death in 1988.

Most of this group of men are no longer among the living. But collectively their impact on both the school and Movement and on Jewish culture as a whole was simply unduplicated. They created the field of Jewish scholarship in America. They also made study at the Seminary an exhilarating experience.

Living as a Conservative Jew

*"*If we are to abide by the principles informing the Conservative Movement, we must work harder to develop interest in, and commitment to, Jewish law in our communities. We cannot be effective interpreters of the law unless there is a partnership with the people trying to observe it. It is a difficult task that has been undertaken— to renew and to retain, to conserve and to progress. *"*

—Seymour Siegel

A Conservative Jewish Life: 1960

At our century's midpoint, Conservative Judaism presented two faces: the Seminary leadership's version of what the Movement stood for and the version in the field, among the rabbis who shaped the Movement. But what about the congregants who joined Conservative congregations in such large numbers? How did they understand what it meant to be a Conservative Jew?

Imagine you are a typical Conservative Jew living in the suburbs of a large Midwestern city during the 1960s. What does your Jewish lifestyle look like?

The heart of your communal life as a Jew is your synagogue. It was designed by a prominent American architect and completed within the past decade. Your family is one of its 750 member families. (Your other options are an equally large Reform temple a mile down the road—which doesn't "feel Jewish" enough to you—and a number of smaller Orthodox synagogues, which attract a much older population and insist on separating men and women.) You live about two miles from the synagogue and attend late (8:00 P.M.) Friday night services from time to time, Saturday and festival morning services much less regularly (usually for a *bar* or *bat mitzvah*), and you are always present on Rosh Hashanah and Yom Kippur.

You drive to the synagogue and back. In the sanctuary, your family sits together in a long pew facing an elevated *bimah*, from which the rabbi and cantor, garbed in black robes, conduct the service. All the males and married women cover their heads. If you are male, you wear a *tallit* when appropriate. The synagogue choir is hidden in a room above the *bimah*, and the service is accompanied by an organ.

The prayerbook you use is the familiar black-covered *Sabbath and Festival Prayer Book,* which you find in every other Conservative synagogue you attend. It contains the complete traditional liturgy with a facing English translation that is modern and poetic. The Hebrew text is familiar to you from your Orthodox childhood, although if you look carefully you may note a few changes. You do not, if you are male, praise God "for not having made me a woman," or if you are a woman, "Who has made me according to His will"; instead, everyone praises God "Who hast made me in Thine image." You may also notice a small but significant change in the tense of a verb in the *Musaf* (or additional) service on Sabbath and festival mornings. Instead of praying that God bring us back to

■ AFTER WORLD WAR II American Jews began abandoning the inner city and moving out to the suburbs, and their congregations moved with them. Their urban synagogues were left behind; the new suburban synagogue was designed to fit into the suburban landscape. Space was plentiful, so the synagogue was built out rather than up. The notion of a neighborhood community within walking distance was no longer feasible in suburbia, so a spacious parking lot became mandatory. The auditorium became an extension of the sanctuary instead of occupying the basement of the building. Attention was given to the surrounding grounds. Most important, the exterior of the building was designed to be completely in tune with suburban architecture. It served as a statement that the Jewish community "belonged," that it was completely at home in suburban America. Pictured here is Congregation B'nai Israel, Woonsocket, Rhode Island.

our land where "we will once again bring the offerings [sacrifices]" ordained for this day, you pray that God bring us back to our land where "our forefathers prepared the daily offerings."

Otherwise, the liturgy is completely traditional, and the melodies the cantor and choir sing are familiar. Most of the service is in Hebrew, which you can recite although you can't understand it without the help of the translation. Some of the prayers are recited in English, and from time to time the rabbi leads an English responsive reading from the back of the book. Pages are announced, and you are instructed when to sit and when to stand, what to read in English and what in Hebrew, what to yourself and what in unison or responsively.

The rabbi delivers a twenty-minute sermon on Friday night, usually on some issue of topical interest in Jewish life. On Saturday morning he delivers a sermon on the Torah reading of the week. Your congregation has just begun to call women to the reading of the Torah at the morning service. Some of the old-timers grumble about this departure from the tradition, but it is clearly here to stay, and you and your family are pleased.

You may also go to the synagogue during the week for a lecture or a fund-raising event for the local Federation or United Jewish Appeal (UJA). If you are a woman and not working outside of your home, you attend the occasional luncheon meeting of the congregational Sisterhood. Your pre-*bar/bat mitzvah* children attend religious school two afternoons a week and on Sunday mornings, and your high school age children are members of United Synagogue Youth (U.S.Y.). There is a Solomon Schechter Day School in your community, with a student population of about 100, but your neighborhood public school is excellent, and you are committed to public school education. Some of your children's friends attend Camp Ramah in Wisconsin, but you prefer to take your children on family vacations.

Your home is not kosher. (About 10 to 15 percent of those in your congregation are.) Although you don't bring pork products or shellfish into your kitchen, you will eat them when you eat out. On Friday nights candles are lit, not necessarily at sunset, but before you enjoy a more formal dinner. You use electricity (television, the radio, the telephone) on the Sabbath. On Saturday, whether or not you go to the synagogue in the morning, you conduct yourself much as you might on a Sunday—shopping; visiting friends, family, or a museum; working around the house; playing tennis; or paying your bills. You fast on Yom Kippur, light Hanukkah candles, conduct an abbreviated Passover seder (serving matzah and other traditional Passover dishes, eliminating bread, but not changing your dishes), and serve a festive meal on Rosh Hashanah (with apples dipped in honey). Family rites of passage, such as your children's *bar* or *bat mitzvah* and weddings, are celebrated in the synagogue.

You visited Israel once on a two-week congregational trip led by your rabbi, and your children will spend a summer in Israel on the U.S.Y. pilgrimage. You contribute annually to your local

UJA/Federation, have bought the occasional Israel Bond, and pay your annual synagogue membership and school dues. Your total annual outlay for Jewish causes comes to about $1,000.

If someone asked you why you identified with Conservative Judaism, you would probably begin by explaining why you could not be Reform or Orthodox. If pressed, you would say that you like the synagogue's school and youth program, you respect the rabbi, you find the worship services enjoyable, and your closest friends belong there, too. If pressed on issues of ideology, you would probably back down. In fact, you have never given much thought to the ideology of the Movement, nor for that matter, have you heard these issues discussed in classes, lectures, or sermons. You may have given some passing thought to questions about God, about what will happen after you die, about why Jews have to observe anything—life seems to bring these issues to the fore from time to time—but you have never been challenged to refine your thinking or to clarify what you can or cannot believe.

■ THE FIRST day school under the auspices of a Conservative synagogue was launched in 1951 in Rockaway Park, New York, by Rabbi Robert Gordis. The first day school under the Solomon Schechter rubric was launched in 1957 in Queens, New York. As of this writing, some 65 schools are affiliated with the Solomon Schechter Day School movement, almost all elementary schools. The schools attract families who want a more intensive Jewish education than can be provided by the afternoon or supplementary school, who seek a greater integration of their children's Jewish and secular learning, and who support a more typically Conservative or Seminary-style approach to the study of Jewish texts. Pictured here are morning prayers at a Solomon Schechter Day School in Boston.

Finally, if someone were to ask you, "What, in all of the above picture, do you feel unhappy about? What would you like to change?" your answer would probably be "Nothing at all. I have the option to be much more Jewish or much less, but this pattern feels to me to be just about right. I would be happy if my children ended up just about where I am."

This portrait of a typical Conservative Jewish lifestyle in the 1960s is in some ways too generous; many Conservative Jews attended synagogue only on the well-known "three days a year" (Rosh Hashanah and Yom Kippur). In other ways it is not generous enough; Ramah camps came to be filled to capacity each summer (today they serve roughly 3,500 campers, and the staff of about 1,100 is also exposed to a significant Jewish educational experience), and the number of Solomon Schechter schools did increase from year to year. If we look at the pattern overall, however, this description is reasonably accurate. It should also be added that in the past three decades the pattern has changed in significant ways; we will return to these changes shortly.

RAMAH: CREATING A JEWISH IDENTITY

At its best, Jewish education should be more than simply transmitting data (e.g., Jewish history) and teaching skills (e.g., reading prayerbook Hebrew). Neither of these presents a great challenge. What is a major educational challenge is molding a religious personality—specifically, a religious Jew, someone who feels as a Jew and conducts his or her life as a Jew. That cannot be done simply in the classroom. It demands an educational focus on the entire life experience of the student. It was with this goal in mind that Camp Ramah was created.

Founded in 1946 under sponsorship of the Seminary, Camp Ramah is a network of Hebrew-speaking educational sleep-away and day camps, six in the United States and Canada and similar ones in South America, Israel, and Europe. As a setting where Judaism can be lived 24 hours a day with a community of like-minded Jews, Camp Ramah is believed by many to be the Movement's most influential contribution to Jewish education. The founders of the Ramah movement understood that a sleep-away camp created a totally controlled environment in which every facet of the camper's life experience—what happens at the table, on the basketball court, on the lake, in the bunk, when getting up in the morning and going to sleep at night—could potentially have an educational dimension. Ramah provided a setting for experiential, as opposed to conceptual, Jewish education, and the strategies developed in Ramah have been adapted for use throughout the Jewish educational establishment.

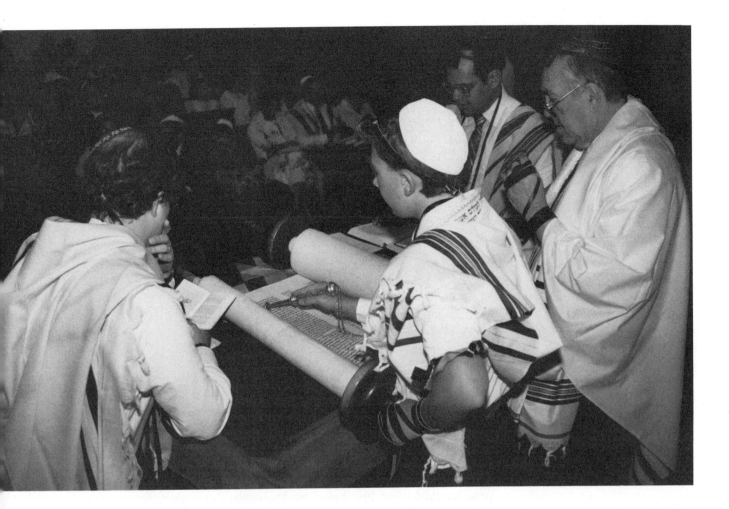

If we look at the pattern as a whole, a few conclusions emerge. First, it supports the frequently repeated definition of Conservative Judaism as not Orthodox and not Reform. The Orthodox Jew in that same suburb was more likely to have a kosher home, walk to the synagogue every Shabbat, and pray daily. The Reform Jew would have observed none of the dietary laws and would not have covered the head, worn a *tallit,* or used the traditional Hebrew prayerbook in the synagogue. Our pattern strikes a distinctive middle ground, what I called in the previous chapter "a rough-and-ready program [of] modified traditionalism [and] modified Kaplanism," or an attractive mix of Americanism and classical Judaism. Whatever it was that impelled the Movement to grow, it was certainly not its distinctive ideology but, rather, issues of style, esthetics, sociology, and a clear distaste for the alternatives.

Finally, and most important, the Conservative Jews described above did not feel any great tension about the extent of their Jewish lifestyle. Their sense was that their rabbi would have been thrilled if they observed more—if their home were kosher, for example. But he was apparently resigned to the fact that their level of observance would not change. His own lifestyle was much more traditional: His home was certainly kosher, he probably did not drive to the synagogue on the Sabbath (though some of his colleagues did), and he

■ DURING THE first half of the twentieth century a Conservative Jewish lifestyle was confined largely to the synagogue and, for the children, to the synagogue school. Little Jewish religious expression penetrated the home. The Jewishness of a typical Conservative Jew was relegated mainly to Friday nights, the High Holidays, and the rites of passage: birth (the circumcision ceremony), puberty (the *bar/bat mitzvah*), marriage, and mourning—all of which were observed mainly in the synagogue. Apart from these ritually observed moments, the rest of this lifestyle was pretty much that of the Reform Jewish family down the street. Pictured above is a *bar mitzvah* at Temple Beth Am in Los Angeles.

certainly did not shop, mow the lawn, or play golf on the Sabbath, and his congregants would have been very much upset if he did any of these. Yet he rarely made these demands on his congregants, at least not explicitly.

Was it that he felt he didn't have a chance of getting them to agree to these demands? Possibly. Perhaps he decided that by demanding too much he would distance them completely and they would reject the whole package. His strategy might have been to expect less in the hope that he would eventually get most of what he expected. Either way, the accommodation seemed to be mutually acceptable.

Process and Procedures

This typical Conservative Jewish lifestyle was the product of an extended process of evolution, sometimes informally through trial and error and sometimes after serious and extended deliberation.

For example, the practice of having men and women sit together in the synagogue was simply instituted by rabbis and their congregations. There was no debate or formal vote by any national body, almost as if the question were not even a serious one. This practice had been instituted by the early Reformers, it was very American, and it soon became commonplace in Conservative synagogues as well. (One of the last holdouts was the Seminary's own synagogue, but when the first group of women entered the Seminary's Rabbinical School in 1984, a parallel mixed-seating and egalitarian service was established.)

On the other hand, the *Sabbath and Festival Prayer Book* (1946) was the result of two years of work by a Joint Prayer Book Commission, chaired by Rabbi Robert Gordis, an eminent Conservative rabbi who also taught Bible at the Seminary. The two changes in the traditional liturgy noted earlier—removing the passage that praised God "for not having made me a woman" and changing the tense of the verb relating to sacrifices—may seem trivial in retrospect, but they represent significant symbolic departures from the traditional liturgy, coming, as they do, in passages that are talmudic in origin. A change in liturgy constituted a major departure from the prevailing style of the Movement. The changes were hotly debated, for the earlier (1927) *Festival Prayer Book* had retained the traditional text (although a limited second edition with the verb tense changed was printed and introduced into a few congregations). By the mid-1940s, however, very few Conservative rabbis felt comfortable praising God for not having made them women, and they could no longer pray for the reinstitution of sacrifices. In 1946 both of these changes became part of the Conservative prayerbook, bringing that part of the liturgy once again in line with the beliefs of most Conservative rabbis.

Similarly, issues relating to Sabbath observance, such as driving to the synagogue and using electricity, were subject to intensive study and debate by the Movement's Committee on Jewish Law and Standards.

A SYNAGOGUE GOES TO TRIAL

The practice of mixed seating in Conservative synagogues may not have generated formal discussion, but it proved bitterly divisive in many congregations. One instance, the case of Adath Israel Congregation in Cincinnati, Ohio, drew national attention. The constitution of this congregation, founded in 1853 and incorporated in 1908, stipulated that its forms of worship be in accord with "the forms and traditions of Orthodox Israelites." In 1953 the Board of Trustees voted 17–9 in favor of "Optional Family Seating"—that is, mixed seating would be permitted in the sanctuary, but a portion of the sanctuary would be reserved for those men and women who wished to sit separately. In March 1954 that policy was approved by a 289–100 vote of the congregation at large. The decision was challenged by the minority, who claimed that it was in violation of the constitution, and the issue was submitted to a "private court" consisting of three arbitrators.

The panel heard testimony from prominent American Jewish religious figures representing both the Orthodox community and the Conservative Movement. The former claimed that mixed seating was absolutely forbidden by *halakhah*. The latter claimed, first, that Jewish law is not at all clear on the issue; second, that *halakhah* has always evolved in line with cultural changes; third, that the phrase "the forms and traditions of Orthodox Israelites" did not refer to seating patterns but only to the liturgy in use; and finally, that in any case, the congregation had long ago abandoned these forms in moving the *bimah* to the front of the sanctuary, conducting the Torah reading facing the congregation, and permitting "separate but equal" seating (i.e., with simply an aisle, not a fence, separating the sexes). In December 1954 the panel voted 2–1 to maintain the congregational vote. However, in three other cases in which the issue was submitted to the civil courts (in Michigan, Louisiana, and Pennsylvania), the courts decided in favor of the traditionalists.

The Committee on Jewish Law
and Standards

The story of the makeup and procedures of the Committee on Jewish Law and Standards deserves a book-length study of its own. Briefly, during the early decades of the Movement, questions relating to Jewish law were decided through informal consultation with some authorities on the issue, frequently a talmudist on the Seminary faculty.

As the movement grew, however, a more formal structure began to emerge. The 1927 *Proceedings of the Assembly*—the first year for which these *Proceedings* were recorded—include a resolution that "a committee of ten be appointed representing the various tendencies in the Rabbinical Assembly to act in an advisory capacity to the members of the Assembly in matters of religious and legal procedure." The 1929 *Proceedings* record the first "Report of the Committee on the Interpretation of Jewish Law." This report lists the Committee's membership (among whom were both Louis Finkelstein and Mordecai Kaplan), its rules of procedure, and the questions it had studied in the previous year. The 1930–1932 *Proceedings* include a more extensive report along the same lines.

By 1948 this structure had become inadequate. That year's Rabbinical Assembly convention devoted an entire session to the topic "Towards a Philosophy of Conservative Judaism"—it fills 80 pages of the *Proceedings*—which featured three papers on the Movement's approach to Jewish law. The session culminated with a series of resolutions that were hotly debated and then voted upon.

The impact of that session can be seen in the 1949 *Proceedings*, which record the first "Report of Committee on Jewish Law and Standards" by its chair, Rabbi Morris Adler. The report reveals that the Committee now consisted of 23 members. More important, it notes that although the previous (i.e., from 1927 to 1948) Committees on Jewish Law "had been . . . self-limited to interpretation in accordance with traditional *halakhic* principles and procedures, the [1948] convention, after full consideration, decided to impose no formula and to limit the Committee to no particular method."

Rabbi Adler concludes by listing this new Committee's "field of activity." The Committee was to study *halakhah* and its precedents, the historical conditions out of which *halakhah* grew, the spiritual intent and purposes of the law, the needs and demands of modern life and thought, and the method by which Jewish living can best be aided and stimulated, and it was to plan activities that might make Judaism more inspiring and meaningful.

Though the size and procedures of the Committee have varied over the years—at this writing the Committee is made up of 25 voting representatives—certain principles have been consistently adhered to: Members of the Committee are appointed by each of the three major wings of the Movement (the Rabbinical Assembly, the Seminary, and the United Synagogue); they should be recognized scholars in rabbinic literature (although the United Synagogue appoints lay representatives, who participate in Committee deliberations without a vote); they should represent the various shades of religious opinion within the Movement; and—very important—the deliberations of the Committee may yield two or even more equally legitimate options, leaving the individual rabbi the right to choose among them. The rabbi remains, to use the traditional talmudic term, *Mara d'Atra,* literally, "Master of the Place," or ultimate authority in religious matters for the congregation.

"CHECK IT OUT IN KLEIN!"

The first book most Conservative rabbis consult when they need guidance on a matter of Jewish ritual law is Rabbi Isaac Klein's *A Guide to Jewish Religious Practice.* Published in 1979, this comprehensive survey of Jewish religious practice originated as a course which Rabbi Klein, then serving a congregation in Buffalo, was invited to teach in the Seminary's Rabbinical School. The course was designed to provide the rabbinical student of the 60s and 70s with a broad survey of those areas of Jewish law that he was most likely to encounter in his day-to-day work. A long-time member of the Movement's Law Committee and author of some of its most notable responsa, Klein was revered by his colleagues for the range and depth of his scholarship as well as for his piety. Though clearly located on the right wing of the Conservative spectrum, Klein was scrupulous in including references to Law Committee decisions whenever they applied. Close to 15,000 copies of the book have been sold, indicating that it has also entered many lay Conservative homes as well. It represents a singularly valuable educational resource for creating an observant laity along Conservative lines.

To this day, a Conservative rabbi who is confronted by an issue of Jewish law writes to the Committee; the Committee chair assigns the issue to individual members to research; their written opinions are circulated, discussed, and frequently rewritten; and then the issue is voted upon. Any position that acquires a significant backing (currently six votes, though this figure has varied over the years) is published as an acceptable practice.

How does the process work? Consider two issues: using electricity and driving on the Sabbath.

The Bible (Exod. 35:3) forbids the kindling of a flame on the Sabbath. The question then becomes, Is turning on an electric light or starting the engine of a car a case of kindling a flame and hence absolutely prohibited by the Torah? Or is it not quite kindling and thus a less stringent prohibition, merely a rabbinic edict designed to serve as a "fence about the Torah," to safeguard the main law regarding kindling? And if it is a less stringent prohibition, may such a prohibition be waived in order to encourage Jews to fulfill a *mitzvah*, such as attending the synagogue on the Sabbath?

Driving on the Sabbath raises another issue: the indirect combustion of gasoline to produce power. Again, although combustion is a form of burning, which is prohibited by the Torah, is the indirect kind of combustion involved in operating a car forbidden, or is it another rabbinic "fence" designed to safeguard the law? And thus can it be waived under current demographic conditions, with Jews living far from the synagogue?

These were technical, *halakhic* issues to be resolved. But legal decisions are rarely discussed in a vacuum. In fact, one of the major questions facing all legal systems is whether and how far extralegal factors can affect legal decision making. The extralegal factors here included the settlement of many Jewish families in American suburbia after the Second World War. Do we want to encourage these settlement patterns by allowing families to drive to the synagogue if such patterns inevitably lead to the breakdown of the traditional community of families living within walking distance of the synagogue? In addition, is participating in synagogue services on the Sabbath of such major educational importance that it should override rabbinically based prohibitions? Further, given the long-range goal of creating a more observant community, is it educationally and strategically wise to permit these practices? Will our community be able to understand that waiving some Sabbath prohibitions does not mean that we waive them all, that to permit driving to the synagogue should not be construed as permitting driving to a museum?

In 1950 a number of extended papers were written on both sides of the issue. The final vote showed a majority in favor of permitting both electricity and driving on the Sabbath. These became part of the pattern of Conservative practice.

Similarly, in 1958 the practice of using an organ in the synagogue on the Sabbath was also approved. Today the list of issues on the Committee's agenda ranges widely: euthanasia, genetic engineering, organ transplants, the *kashrut* of wines, games of chance in the synagogue, kashering microwave ovens for Passover use, conversion practices, the use of the same electric dishwasher for milk and meat dishes, cremation, civil marriage, artificial insemination, vasectomies, divorce procedures when the husband refuses to initiate the divorce, and most recently, the range of issues raised by a newly vocal group of Jewishly committed gays and lesbians and their supporters.

Is Rennet Kosher?

Over the years the Committee on Jewish Law and Standards has debated a wide range of issues: the laws of *kashrut* (Is cheese that is produced with rennet, a product made of the lining of the stomach of nonkosher animals, kosher? The answer is yes, because in the production, the rennet loses its quality of being a food and is transformed into an entirely new substance); the laws of burial (Is embalming permitted? No, because there is a traditional Jewish prohibition that should be maintained); medical ethics (Is abortion permitted? Yes, if the continuation of the pregnancy might imperil the life of the mother or cause her severe physical or psychological harm or if the fetus is judged to be defective).

Patrilineal Descent and the Role of Women in the Synagogue

It is fair to say that the large majority of Conservative congregants remain ignorant of the debates of the Committee on Jewish Law and Standards. Most congregants would drive to the synagogue and use electricity irrespective of the Committee's decisions. But the very existence of the Committee and its decisions represents a central piece of the Movement's culture. On some issues the Committee's decisions have had a decisive impact on the life of Conservative congregants. Two recent issues that prompted extensive and tension-filled debates are patrilineal descent and women's participation in synagogue rituals.

■ PATRILINEAL DESCENT is particularly troublesome because it threatens the unity of the Jewish community. In effect, it leads to two conflicting definitions of who is a Jew, for some people who are accepted as Jewish by one portion of the community are not accepted by another. What would happen if a patrilineally descended Jew wanted to marry a matrilineally descended Jew? In some circles, such a marriage would be viewed as an intermarriage. This engraving, *Wedding of Ashkenazi*, is by the eighteenth-century Dutch artist Bernard Picart.

Since talmudic times, Jewish descent has been determined by the mother. The child of a Jewish mother is Jewish; the child of a non-Jewish mother is not, whatever the religious identity of the father. The reasons for this ruling are not explicit, but they probably reflect the fact that it is much easier to establish the identity of a child's mother than its father. In 1983, Reform abandoned that principle and accepted the child of any intermarried couple as Jewish, provided the child has been raised and educated as a Jew.

The issue was brought before the Law Committee and after deliberation an overwhelming majority (21–2 with 2 abstentions) elected to maintain the traditional practice. Because of the size of the majority and because of the significance of the issue, the Committee sought to have this position declared a Standard of Rabbinic Practice so that its violation by a member of the Rabbinical Assembly could be punishable by expulsion from the Assembly. A Standard of Rabbinic Practice can be declared only by a 75-percent vote of the membership of the Assembly as a whole. In May 1986, at its annual convention, the Assembly so voted.

The issue of the place of women in synagogue ritual is far more complicated, for several reasons. First, it covers a multitude of practices: *aliyot* (can women be called to the reading of the Torah?), counting toward the *minyan* (the quorum of ten required for a formal Jewish service of worship), or leading the congregation in prayer—each of which poses its own distinctive legal issues. Second, the feminist revolution in America took a number of decades to work itself out, and the full impact of the process was not that clear when the issue was first raised. Finally, in contrast to patrilineal descent, the movement was sharply divided on these questions.

The issue is particularly fascinating because it reveals how a minority position has come to be largely accepted throughout the Movement. In 1955, for example, a majority of the Committee voted that women may be granted *aliyot* only on special occasions, such as a *bat mitzvah* or on recovery from an illness and only after the required number of *aliyot* (seven on the Sabbath) were completed by men. Today the large and growing majority of Conservative congregations grant women *aliyot* without restrictions. In 1974 a majority of the Committee voted that women may not be ordained as rabbis; by 1983 the Rabbinical Assembly was urging the Seminary to ordain women. In 1974 a majority of the Committee voted that women may not serve as cantors; in 1986 the Seminary accepted women for training as cantors.

In 1973 a majority of the Committee voted that women may be counted toward the *minyan*, but a 1974 majority voted that they should not serve as witnesses in formal Jewish legal proceedings. (Traditional Jewish law insists that only men may witness legal proceedings, such as divorce, conversion, or marriage, and only men may sign the documents testifying to their presence at such proceedings.) Today the number of Conservative congregations that count women toward the *minyan* is large and growing, and on the issue of witnessing the minority position was large enough to constitute a legitimate option and is accepted by many Conservative rabbis.

What is most important about the Law Committee is the very

fact of its existence. It is one of those benchmarks that separates Conservative Judaism from Reform. Classical Reform proclaimed the principle of individual autonomy; each Reform Jew, rabbi or lay person, is encouraged to make his or her own decisions on matters of Jewish practice in the light of conscience. In contrast, Conservative Judaism has insisted that the authorities of the community have the right and the responsibility to define the parameters of legitimate religious practice. Those parameters may be murky, may permit pluralistic options, and may change with time—the process is undeniably messy—but they are there in principle, and as in the case of patrilineal descent, the parameters of traditional Jewish practice can always be invoked. Zechariah Frankel's insistence on the interlocking roles of the community and its leadership has remained a hallmark of Conservative Judaism to this day. It represents the nucleus of Schechter's Catholic Israel.

Although it is tempting to focus exclusively on the *changes* in traditional Jewish observance that the Law Committee legitimatized, it is equally important to emphasize what it would never even think of abrogating. It may have permitted the eating of cheeses or swordfish, but it also affirmed that the large body of traditional Jewish dietary laws is still binding, that pork products and shellfish are forbidden, and that meat and milk must be separated. It may have permitted driving to the synagogue or using electricity on the Sabbath, but it also affirmed that the Sabbath remains a sacred day, that shopping, playing golf, mowing the lawn, and paying bills all remain prohibited. The bulk of festival practices and the rituals accompanying the rites of passage have also never been challenged.

What happened, then, to the part of the message that said Conservative Judaism reaffirms the ongoing validity of most Jewish ritual practice? It was certainly adhered to by the rabbis but rarely by any but a minority of the congregants. We have to realize that the message the Conservative rabbi was asked to transmit to congregants was subtle and complex. Both the Reform and Orthodox rabbi had a much easier task. The Reform rabbi had the right to dispense with any aspect of Jewish law, and the Orthodox rabbi insisted that it was all eternally binding as the explicit will of God. The Conservative rabbi, in contrast, had to make subtle distinctions: Sabbath observance is binding, but you can drive to the synagogue. The dietary laws are binding, but you can eat swordfish. The traditional synagogue ritual is retained, but women can participate equally. It was only natural, then, for the typical Conservative layperson to ask, If some things change, why don't other things change as well? If I can now eat swordfish, why can't I eat oysters as well? How do you come to these distinctions? The rabbi who had mastered the traditional texts and had deliberated their relevance may well have understood the process and could justify such subtle distinctions, but how was he to communicate them to his Jewishly uneducated and far less committed congregants?

And they were indeed largely uneducated and uncommitted. They were the first generation of American Jews to be fully at home in America, the first to enjoy the full range of its educational and professional opportunities. They had few nostalgic ties to the old world; their Jewish education, in the first generation of American synagogues, was sadly inadequate. They wanted to make it in America—socially, professionally, economically, and culturally. They were aware of their Jewishness—most of them were not about to intermarry or lose their Jewish identity—but becoming part of the American "melting pot" was a far higher priority than identifying Jewishly.

What is fascinating, however, is that they flocked to Conservative synagogues as much for these institutions' intrinsic attractions as out of a distaste for the alternatives. The mix of an authentic synagogue in a contemporary American setting combined with minimal expectations outside the synagogue walls was undoubtedly successful.

THE GAY AND LESBIAN ISSUE

The most recent major halakhic issue confronting the Movement is the status of the gay or lesbian Jew. Twice, in Leviticus 18:22 and 20:13, the Bible explicitly forbids male homosexual activity and brands it a *to'evah* (commonly translated as an "abhorrence" or "abomination"). But in the wake of significant changes in the cultural perception of sexual orientation, the Law Committee was asked to study this issue in a formal way.

This broad issue generated a number of more specific questions. Could an openly gay or lesbian person serve as a rabbi, cantor, or teacher in a synagogue school? Could he or she assume a position of lay leadership within a congregation? Could a Conservative rabbi perform a commitment ritual ceremony by which two men or two women formalize and consecrate their relationship?

A discussion of two position papers on the issue some years back had been inconclusive, and the issue was placed on the Committee's agenda once again in the Fall of 1991. Three consecutive meetings of the Committee were held in the 1991–1992 season, with a crowded group of Seminary students, faculty, and rabbis observing the proceedings, for the issue had generated a great deal of controversy within the school and in the Movement at large. The outcome of these three meetings can serve as a paradigm of how the Committee on Law and Standards operates at its very best.

At the outset, the Committee's deliberations focused on two papers, one by Rabbi Bradley Shavit Artson and one by the Committee's then chairperson, Rabbi Joel Roth. Rabbi Artson argued that the biblical prohibition applied only to exploitative, noncommitted homosexual relations, that the Bible (and by extension, the later halakhic tradition) did not know of loving, committed, long-term homosexual relations, and that therefore this latter form of relationship should not be considered halakhically forbidden. In contrast, Rabbi Roth argued that the Bible was aware of many forms of homosexual relations, that it considered them all—not the orientation itself, but the activities—prohibited, and that this prohibition should still be considered binding today. He added that his conclusions would in no way be affected by the conclusions of recent and ongoing studies of the etiology of homosexuality.

The first discussion of these two papers spawned a number of other papers, among them, one by Rabbi Elliot Dorff of the University of Judaism, a long-time member of the Committee. His paper urged the Committee to postpone a vote and, instead, establish a Movement-wide commission to study the stance of Conservative Judaism toward sexuality in general.

The third and final Committee discussion took place in March 1992. As the discussion drew to a close, a consensus emerged which became the Committee's statement of policy. This consensus affirmed that avowed homosexuals should not be admitted to the rabbinate or the cantorate, that Conservative rabbis should be prohibited from performing commitment ceremonies, but that rabbis and their congregations were free to determine for themselves the way in which homosexuals could function in other professional and lay leadership roles in the local congregation. The Committee also voted to establish the long-range study commission suggested by Rabbi Dorff.

In subsequent developments, the Seminary and the United Synagogue leadership declined to participate in Rabbi Dorff's study commission, but the commission has been established by the Rabbinical Assembly itself and has begun to meet. Finally, the membership of the Rabbinical Assembly at its May 1992 convention voted to allow the body's Placement Committee to serve gay and lesbian synagogues who turn to it for rabbinic leadership, thereby reversing the Committee's previous policy of declining to provide that service.

Effectively, the extended deliberations within the Committee led to a rejection of the two extreme positions on either side of the issue—Rabbi Artson's position that would remove all prohibitions against committed homosexual relations, and Rabbi Roth's original recommendation (withdrawn in a later revision of his paper) that the prohibition apply even on the local congregational level—in favor of a middle-of-the-road consensus which maintained the prohibition against gay or lesbian rabbis and cantors but permitted the congregation to determine its own stance on the local level.

Predictably, proponents of both of the extreme positions were dissatisfied with this conclusion, but it probably reflects the sentiments of the majority of the Movement as a whole as of this writing. It would also not be surprising if the issue were to find its way onto the agenda of the Law Committee once again—before too long.

■ JEWISH RITUAL life is to a large extent centered in the home, not in the synagogue. However, as Conservative Jews abandoned rituals such as *kashrut* and Sabbath and festival observances and as their lives as Jews came to be centered in the synagogue, they and their children lost contact with the poetry and drama that ritual can uniquely convey. The practice of building a family *sukkah* outside the home was abandoned, and those few Jews who cared used the synagogue *sukkah* in its place. In recent years, as Conservative rabbis and their congregants have begun to appreciate the educational and religious value available through Jewish home rituals, this trend has been reversed.

Imagine now that you are a typical Conservative Jew in the same congregation in 1990. Has anything changed?

A great deal. Your congregation has almost doubled in size, the building has been expanded, additional classroom space has been added, the ballroom has been redecorated, dues have tripled, and an assistant rabbi has been added to the staff.

The late Friday night service is clearly dying, to no one's regret. It has been cut to one service a month during the winter, and it continues to attract some of the old-timers, for whom it serves a valuable social function, but the younger families don't attend. Some families with very young children come to a short 5:00 P.M. family service, which also meets once a month but is geared specifically to the children (singing, storytelling, and snacks), and then they spend the rest of Shabbat evening at home. The traditional *Kabbalat Shabbat* ("Welcoming the Sabbath") service at sunset, recently instituted by the rabbi, is sparsely attended.

What has grown remarkably is the Shabbat morning service (although it has not recouped the number of congregants that used to attend on Friday night). It attracts the younger families with their children, who now participate actively in the service as Torah readers. There are other transformations in the mood and style of the synagogue service. The rabbis no longer wear gowns; the service is much more participatory, with congregants frequently leading the service; the sermon has been replaced by a study session in which the rabbi steps down from the pulpit and, standing in the aisle, engages the congregation in a discussion of the Torah reading; the entire service is now comfortably egalitarian.

Your rabbis are more traditional than their predecessors. They wear a *kippah* at all times, even at a ball game. They are also much more forceful, in their teaching and preaching, in pushing Shabbat and *kashrut* observance. Their expectations are much clearer and stronger than their predecessor's.

More interesting, you and some other members of the congregation belong to one of a number of *havurot*, informal groupings of ten to fifteen families within the congregation; each *havurah* worships together twice a month in a separate room in the synagogue and meets to study and celebrate Shabbat and festival meals in a congregant's home. This service is totally participatory, with chairs arranged in a circle, children moving in and out, and a member of the group leading the service and the study session each week—all in the interest of a greater sense of intimacy. The rabbis and leadership of the congregation are totally supportive of this development.

■ THE *HAVURAH* movement was an outgrowth of the anti-establishment mood among young Jews in the late Sixties and early Seventies. It emerged as a challenge to the institutional structure of American Jewry, including the familiar suburban synagogue service, which was perceived as impersonal, arid, and hierarchical. The attempt to infuse religious structures with a measure of spirituality took these communities outside the synagogue and into private homes. There worshipers created new liturgical and ritual forms. An important dimension of their programs was the communal "retreat" into the countryside, where Shabbat and festivals could be celebrated in nature, as in this photo of a Shavuot celebration in Nyack, New York. The influence of early Hasidism and of the Camp Ramah experience on this new religious form is notable.

The congregational prayerbook is now *Siddur Sim Shalom.* You find it somewhat bulky in comparison with the old *Sabbath and Festival Prayer Book,* and you miss some of the familiar English readings, but you are getting used to it. It has retained the liturgical changes of the old prayerbook and has added many new ones. Following the Torah reading, for example, you no longer invoke God's blessing on "this holy congregation . . . , them, their wives, their sons and daughters." Women are now recognized to be members of "this holy congregation."

In the Shabbat *Musaf* service, the older practice of simply changing the tense of the verb pertaining to sacrifices seems now to have been excessively cautious. You now must choose from among five alternative versions of the liturgy (three in English, two in Hebrew and English), all quite different from the traditional passage.

■ IT WAS the Rabbinical Assembly (in some instances along with the United Synagogue) that undertook the task of publishing prayerbooks that tried to adapt the traditional Jewish liturgy to the spiritual needs of twentieth-century Jews. Its *Sabbath and Festival Prayer Book* (1946), *Weekday Prayer Book* (1961), *Mahzor for Rosh Hashanah and Yom Kippur* (1972), and most recently, *Siddur Sim Shalom: A Prayerbook for Shabbat, Festivals, and Weekdays* (1985) are omnipresent in Conservative congregations and serve as a singular source of unity in an otherwise highly diversified set of congregational styles.

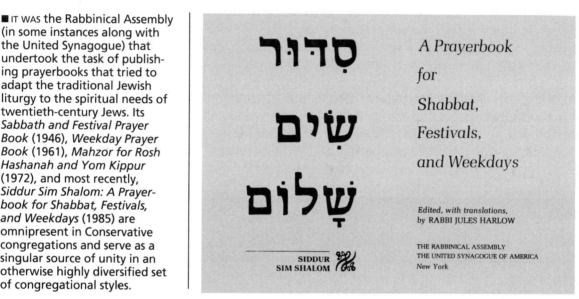

סִדּוּר שִׂים שָׁלוֹם

SIDDUR SIM SHALOM

A Prayerbook for Shabbat, Festivals, and Weekdays

Edited, with translations, by RABBI JULES HARLOW

THE RABBINICAL ASSEMBLY
THE UNITED SYNAGOGUE OF AMERICA
New York

Your home is still not kosher (the number of kosher homes in the congregation at large remains about 15 percent), although you are now somewhat defensive about that fact, especially since some of the members of your *havurah* are kosher, and you have to make provisions for their eating in your home. Your Shabbat observance is more traditional, however, because you are in the synagogue most Saturday mornings, and you frequently meet with your *havurah* for Shabbat lunch.

Friday night is a major family occasion, with time for extended conversation, a formal meal with candle lighting (before dinner), *Kiddush* said over the wine, the *Motzi* blessing over bread, and a brief *Birkat HaMazon* after the meal. Your youngest child, who is enrolled in the Solomon Schechter Day School, introduced these practices into your home. She is also expressing interest in accompanying her classmates to Camp Ramah, and although the combination of day school and Ramah tuition comes to about $10,000 a year, you don't see how you can refuse her. Altogether, your annual financial outlay for Jewish causes has increased tenfold (although a good portion of this amount is the Solomon Schechter tuition). You have been to Israel on two family visits, and your older children have visited on a U.S.Y. pilgrimage.

RELIGIOUS AND FINANCIAL OBLIGATIONS

Within the past few years, Jewish organizations have begun to express concern about the rising cost of Jewish affiliation. An informal study of the financial outlay for a family belonging to a typical Conservative congregation today would show the following: synagogue membership: $700–$1,300; religious school per child: $400–$500; nursery school per child: $2,500–$3,500; day school per child: $4,500–$7,500; Ramah per child: $3,000; Hebrew high school per child: $500–$1,000. This list does not include mandatory contributions to a building fund, charitable contributions (to synagogue, UJA/Federation, Israel Bonds, etc.), cemetery plots, JCC membership, a trip to Israel, books and publications, and the extra cost of keeping a kosher home. Many congregations use a sliding scale for dues, depending on the financial status of the family. Many congregations also have a dues structure for a single person and for the elderly.

Your older children in college are a source of anxiety. They are not that involved with Jewish life on campus and rarely attend Shabbat services in their college communities. They have taken one college course in Jewish studies (an option that was not available to you), and they come home for Rosh Hashanah and Passover, but they interdate—all the while reassuring you that dating and marriage are different. You're not quite convinced, especially since you know that the rate of Jewish intermarriage has grown precipitously over the past five years (to over 50 percent of all marriages involving a Jew). All in all, you feel more secure with the Jewishness of your younger children than with that of your older children, particularly because your own level of Jewish interest is higher now than it has ever been.

If someone were to ask you why you identify with Conservative Judaism, you might answer that you have heard about *Emet Ve-Emunah*, the Movement's first Statement of Principles, in a series of sermons delivered by your rabbi, although you haven't read the document. You welcome what seems to be its pluralism of ideological and *halakhic* options, and what you've heard of its ideology seems to fit your thinking about the world and the human experience. You appreciate your rabbi's scholarly competence and intellectual openness. In general, you are serious about intellectual issues and about the policies of the State of Israel and its place in international diplomacy, and you are prepared to devote time and energy to figuring out where you stand on these issues. The disorder of the

Movement, so threatening a generation ago, seems now to be a challenge, even though you would like a little more stability than the position is willing to grant.

Finally, if you were asked how satisfied you are with this pattern, you would probably hesitate before answering. You feel that you're in a period of transition, becoming more involved, taking more of a leadership role, exposing your children to a more intensive educational experience, expecting more from them. You are also much clearer on what this business of Conservative Judaism is all about, even though it has created some tension in your life. At the same time, the other options are even more unacceptable. You feel that Orthodoxy has gone "off the wall" on the who-is-a-Jew issue in Israel, even though you are impressed with American Orthodoxy's ability to attract young American Jews. Reform has clearly become more traditional, but its acceptance of patrilineal descent seems to you to be divisive and unwise. You are reasonably content with where you are; you sense that ten years from now you may be even more committed.

Again, this sketch is in some respects too generous—the population of Solomon Schechter schools still includes only a small minority of Conservative congregants—and in some respects not generous enough—members of *havurot* tend to have kosher homes.

But note that the balance between the synagogue and the home as the focus of Jewish life has begun to be realigned. This generation is more likely to realize that the synagogue and the synagogue school alone cannot carry the burden of transmitting Jewish identity to the next generation of American Jews.

KIPPOT: A MODERN PHENOMENON

The notion that Jewish males are obligated to cover their heads at all times is a modern phenomenon. As late as the seventeenth century, rabbinic authorities were debating whether or not Jewish law required men to cover their heads even when at prayer or study; some believed that it was simply a mark of extra piety, not a *halakhic* requirement. Gradually the use of a *kippah* during prayer and study came to be perceived as mandatory. Still later wearing it all the time became a symbol of traditionalist Jewish behavior. American Reform quickly abandoned the practice. Someone attending a Reform service some years ago might have been ordered to remove his head covering. (In most Reform synagogues covering the head is now optional.) Some members of the Seminary faculty of the Fifties routinely donned the kippah to say the blessing over bread at the beginning of the meal, removed it for the meal itself, and donned it again for the Grace after Meals!

Finally, the main difference between you and your predecessor is that the latter felt no tension about the nature and extent of his or her Jewish commitment. You do. You are Jewishly better informed. You have more free time in which to reflect on and express your Jewish identity. Even more, the "public face" of Judaism as transmitted by your new rabbis, your *havurah* experience, and your children's Ramah and Solomon Schechter experience is much more attractive.

What changed between 1960 and 1990? First, America changed. The "melting pot" is out; ethnicity is in. If black can be beautiful, so can being Jewish. Wearing a *kippah* to a ball game is a public expression of one's distinctive Jewish identity. Wear it with pride! This new generation takes its American identity for granted. It is now free to explore and solidify its Jewish roots.

Second, American Jews have become even more sharply individualistic. They reserve the right to set parameters for what they do and don't do as Jews. They are much more comfortable with the Movement's intellectualism and pluralism. Large numbers of Conservative congregation members are professionals or academicians. Many have advanced university degrees, and they want their Jewishness to be as intellectually challenging as are their other interests. They may not have any great fund of Jewish knowledge, but if presented with the information, they can think, and they want to be encouraged to think as Jews. The Conservative synagogue and its rabbi are perceived as responding to this need.

But these same developments were far from an unmixed blessing for Conservative Judaism, because the competition had also changed. Riding on the winds of the new ethnicity, the two other movements were exhibiting a totally unanticipated vitality. Reform had tossed its Pittsburgh Platform out the window and embraced Zionism, the Hebrew language, and many traditional rituals. Orthodoxy, for its part, began to attract young American Jews. A new generation of American-born, university-educated men and women were buying into the package of traditional Jewish observance. American Orthodoxy had finally become a full-fledged, independent, and vigorous movement of its own. The Seminary's founders would have been stunned!

More significantly, Conservative Judaism had begun to experience an internal crisis all its own. That crisis, to which we now turn, was the result of a growing awareness of the tensions and contradictions within the Movement—in its founding ideology, in the relationship between the Seminary and the other two wings of the Movement, and even in the Movement's distinctive congregational style. For about seven decades, as the Movement flourished, these tensions could be overlooked. Now they had to be confronted.

As the Sixties drew to a close, then, a new set of challenges had begun to emerge, both from within and from without. The result was a sense that Conservative Judaism was in crisis and that much of what it had taught and advocated would have to be rethought.

7 | THE EMERGING CRISIS

"The morale of the Conservative movement is on the decline. The present day Conservative elite . . . is no longer confident that its formula will be attractive to the younger generation . . . the Conservative crisis . . . represents a questioning of whether the Jewish people and its 'chain of tradition' can long endure on the American continent."

——Marshall Sklare (1972)

1972: A Watershed Year

By the 1970s it was abundantly clear that the vision of the Seminary's founders—the creation of a broad, traditionalist coalition of American Jews that would counter the growth of Reform—was simply unachievable. First, Reform was flourishing. Second, the religious right had become a vigorously independent American Orthodox movement, openly critical of everything Conservative Judaism stood for and competing with it for funds and affiliation. Finally, the internal tensions within the Seminary's own extended family were threatening to split the Movement apart.

The watershed year for this sense of a movement in crisis was 1972. Dates of this kind are invariably arbitrary. In life, change is gradual, and we are rarely aware of the process until it is well under way. In this case, the change in the Movement's fortunes was almost a decade old before its full effect was felt by its leadership. But in retrospect, 1972 is as good a date as any, if only because it marks the retirement of Louis Finkelstein after 32 years as President and Chancellor of the Seminary, and the election of Gerson Cohen to that position. Since the head of the Seminary has always served as the spokesperson for the Movement, any change in that position inevitably affects the culture of the Movement as well. This change was of monumental importance.

But a new Chancellor with a fresh religious vision was only part of a much more complex story. In fact, Finkelstein's retirement and Cohen's election were in part impelled by the coming together of those developments within the Movement, and in the community at large that led to what we have dubbed Conservative Judaism's "emerging crisis," a sense that if the Movement were to enjoy continued vigor and influence, its basic commitments would have to be looked at anew. What were those determining factors?

External Factor I: Modern Orthodoxy

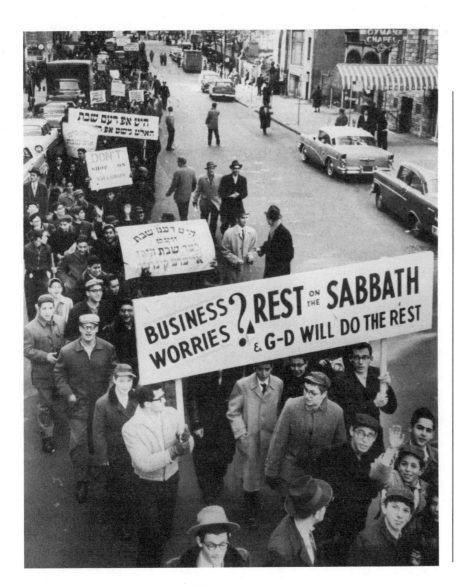

■ THE EMERGENCE of an Orthodox Movement with its own network of institutions is essentially a post-Holocaust phenomenon. True, there were many Orthodox synagogues scattered around the country, some dating from after the Civil War, and they later attracted immigrants from Eastern Europe, but there was little sense of a nationwide enterprise that set broad goals for American Jewry as a whole. All that changed in the 1950s.

To the astonishment of Reform and Conservative Jews, second- and third-generation American Jews in significant numbers began to opt for Orthodoxy over the more "modern" or "American" movements; Jewish bookstores were flooded with books, magazines, pamphlets, and prayerbooks reflecting an Orthodox ideology; and national Orthodox bodies began to argue vigorously, not only for the legitimacy of an Orthodox reading of Judaism but even for Orthodoxy as a more satisfying resource for handling the challenges of Jewish life in the modern age. Pictured here is a March for the Sabbath in New York's Lower East Side during the Fifties.

So far this book has had a great deal to say about Conservative Judaism's relationship with the Movement to its left, Reform Judaism, but it has been relatively silent about the relationship with the Movement on its right, Orthodox Judaism. There are two principle reasons for this silence. First, the founders of Conservative Judaism did not foresee, or possibly did not want to foresee, the existence of an Orthodox Movement apart from the very one they represented. They used the terms *conservative* (or *Conservative*), *traditional*, *orthodox* (or *Orthodox*), and *historical* as synonyms. These founders represented classical Judaism. They were creating a broad coalition of traditionalist Jews for the purpose of opposing Reform. They could not imagine that America would ever produce a significant body of Jews who were even more traditional than they and who would challenge their legitimacy.

Second, until the middle of the twentieth century there simply was no Orthodox Movement in American Judaism in the same sense that Reform (and later Conservative Judaism) constituted a movement—with a central academic institution, a unified congregational arm, and a rabbinic association, all with national offices, periodicals, and youth and adult programs. There were, of course, Orthodox congregations scattered throughout the country, most of them small, inner-city synagogues, most in the larger centers of population. But this activity hardly posed the kind of unified, right-wing challenge that Conservative Judaism would have to face later in the century.

We do know that as early as 1886, months before the Seminary's first entering class began its studies, there was good reason to suspect that the founders' dream of co-opting the right wing of American Jewry would be at best problematic. That was when Rabbi J. D. Eisenstein branded the new school as simply a mask for Reform. Then in 1902 the Seminary was rejected by the group of congregations it had itself assembled in its first attempt to create a supportive congregational union. That body of congregations went its own way as the Orthodox Jewish Congregational Union of America (later to be known as the Union of Orthodox Jewish Congregations, today American Orthodoxy's congregational movement.)

The representatives of the Orthodox Union rejected the Seminary's leadership because they viewed this school as far too ready to make peace with the modern age. But that very same criticism had been launched a full fifty years earlier, against the European father of Conservative Judaism, Zechariah Frankel, by the man commonly recognized as the founder of Modern Orthodoxy, Rabbi Samson Raphael Hirsch.

Frankel's modified traditionalism formed the heart of the founding ideology of the new seminary in America. Is it any wonder that the Orthodox Union felt uncomfortable with the school's leadership? The Seminary was Breslau in America. Its entire faculty was devoted to propounding Frankel's views. In fact, one of the preeminent members of the Seminary faculty, Mordecai Kaplan, was to

teach a theology that was even more heretical than anything Frankel ever conceived of, and he was untouched! Further, the Seminary's graduates soon began to translate these religious views into a program for American Jewry that had men and women sitting together in the synagogue, that permitted driving and the use of electricity on the Sabbath, and that changed the traditional liturgy.

There was, then, very little basis for hope that the Seminary and Conservative Judaism would ever be fully acceptable to the right wing of American traditionalists. During the first half of this century, however, American Orthodoxy could only stand aside and denounce; it wasn't strong enough to compete.

Then came the Holocaust, the creation of the State of Israel, the new American ethnicity, the emergence of a wave of religious fundamentalism throughout the world (the religious right in America and the Islamic brotherhood in the Middle East), and finally, the sociological conditions among third-generation American Jews that favored a return to stronger Jewish rootedness: primarily this generation's successful acculturation within American life and the subsequent death of "the melting pot" as a sociological ideal for American ethnics.

By the middle of the century, Orthodoxy had come of age. It was attracting young American professionals and academicians—many of them children of Conservative Jews—who found the syna-

■ THE HOLOCAUST was one of the two major transformative events in twentieth-century Jewish history, the other being the creation of the State of Israel. These events were transformative because in their wake nothing Jewish remained the same; everything had to be rethought. If one of the end products of modernity was the Nazi Holocaust, then for many Jews the only appropriate response to that experience was a return to Jewish traditionalism, separateness, and the belief system that our ancestors embraced before the dawn of the Enlightenment. The Holocaust was thus one of the factors that impelled the emergence of a vigorous Orthodox reading of Judaism in America over the past three decades. Pictured here is the Holocaust service We Will Never Die, held at Madison Square Garden on March 9, 1943.

gogues and education of their youth pale and wishy-washy in contrast to the vitality, security, and richness of an Orthodox Jewish lifestyle. It created new congregations and day schools (*yeshivot*), founded summer camps, and published periodicals, books, prayerbooks, and commentaries on the Bible. It became a vigorous, independent, and imperialistic third movement in American Jewish religious life.

It's important to note that Hirsch and his later American followers were far from benighted medievalists. Their motto was *Torah im Derekh Eretz*, "Torah combined with the ways of the world." They encouraged secular studies, insisted on decorous worship services, favored a full integration of Judaism with the modern world—but all with one powerful caveat: Nothing in this accommodation could lead to the abrogation of a single one of the beliefs and practices of classical Judaism. With the dawn of the second half of the century, Hirsch's vision, transplanted to America, began to flourish.

Tension Within Orthodoxy

American Orthodoxy is hardly trouble-free. It, too, has emerged as a coalition, this one designed to oppose Reform and Conservative Judaism. But the very dynamics that created this coalition have threatened the integrity of the Movement itself.

The Achilles' heel of all right-wing reactions, religious or political, is that once the move to the right has begun, it is almost impossible to stop it. One can always be more right-wing than one's neighbor; the possibilities are infinite. And particularly when we are dealing with a system as detailed and all-encompassing as Jewish law, it will not be difficult to find someone who is prepared to outflank you on your right, observe that much more than you do, and then brand you as a heretic, a covert Reform or Conservative Jew. Your impulse, in turn, will be to match his or her position, thereby drawing the entire movement one step further to the right and accentuating its polarization from the rest of the community.

The story of American Orthodoxy in the past two decades can serve as a paradigm for this process. Orthodoxy's more accommodating and more open representatives, the Modern Orthodox who now, significantly, refer to themselves as centrist—men such as Norman Lamm, the current President of Yeshiva University—are assailed by their former colleagues as covert Conservative-Reform Jews. Orthodox rabbis who officiate in mixed-seating congregations have been subject to witch-hunts and ideological-*halakhic* star-chamber proceedings as a test of their authenticity. The impulse to limit the Israeli Law of Return so that converts to Judaism would be granted automatic Israeli citizenship only if they were converted by Orthodox rabbis has met with overwhelming opposition from much of world Jewry, even in Orthodox circles. The delegitimization of non-Orthodox rabbis in Israel has alienated the majority of American Jews, including a number of Orthodox rabbis. Tactics such as denying non-Orthodox rabbis the use of an Orthodox-sponsored *mikveh* (the ritual bath used for ritual conversion and by women who observe the laws of family purity) have been viewed as petty harassment.

■ ORTHODOX THEOLOGY assumes that the Torah is divine in its origin, that it represents God's explicit will, communicated in God's words to Moses at Sinai as described in Exodus 19 and 20 and transmitted to later generations. As a result, Orthodox theology views Torah exclusively as the word of God and hence eternally and completely binding; no human community has made any substantive contribution to its original contents, nor can any later community modify or abolish its teachings.

The Orthodox believe that the only effective strategy for creating a religiously committed community is to present Torah as an uncompromising absolute that demands unquestioned loyalty. They are aware that though some Jews may well fall short of these expectations, they should understand that they have fallen short. The ideal should never be attenuated. In time, the community will come around. Pictured here is the classic Gustave Doré steel engraving of Moses descending Mount Sinai with the Ten Commandments.

More important for the long run, American Orthodoxy seems to be benefiting, as Conservative Judaism did for decades, from sociological currents among American Jews. But then Orthodoxy should learn from the experience of Conservative Judaism that a movement that lives on sociological currents alone will eventually discover that these currents are fickle. What will happen when the pendulum moves in a different direction?

These, then, are long-range questions facing American Orthodoxy: Is it more than a fad? More than a transient, sociological phenomenon? Can it survive its own internal tensions? Can it be transmitted to a fourth generation of American Jews, who will be, if anything, more sophisticated and culturally and intellectually more integrated into the broad outside world? Will the next generation of Orthodox women attorneys, doctors, stockbrokers, and executives continue to accept their traditional role in the Orthodox synagogue without protest? Evidence of unrest among these women can be seen in the many informal women's prayer groups that have sprung up in Orthodox circles around the country, in the face of vigorous opposition from the more traditionalist Orthodox rabbis.

But whatever the long-range prospects of American Orthodoxy, by 1972 Conservative Judaism found itself outflanked on its right by a movement that was wealthy, powerful, imperialistic, and growing. Most Conservative rabbis had long ago given up the dream of pleasing the religious right. The last holdout was Louis Finkelstein and his closest associates at the Seminary. His retirement marked the final shattering of that dream. It also marked the open recognition that Conservative Judaism, now clearly the middle movement in American Jewry, was free to pursue its own distinctive course without trying to accommodate American Jewish traditionalists. But what was that course to be?

■ ALL ORTHODOXIES are intrinsically isolationist; they thrive on keeping themselves apart, sociologically and intellectually, from the rest of the community. Take one example: Should a young traditionalist Jewish male attend a secular college while continuing his religious studies? The issue is hotly disputed in traditionalist circles. Yeshiva University (pictured here), the institutional heart of centrist Orthodoxy, says yes. In fact, it sponsors its own undergraduate and graduate schools, a medical school, a law school, programs in social work, clinical psychology, and other areas of study. Its opponents on the right disagree. Some permit only night school; some, only certain "safe" subjects, such as mathematics, computer programming, or engineering; some will expel from their institutions any student who goes to college. Can this style be maintained? Only time will tell.

External Factor II:
The Transformation of American
Reform Judaism

The Movement's internal struggle with self-definition was affected no less by remarkable developments within Reform Judaism. Here the changes are much easier to trace, largely because American Reform, uniquely among the three movements, has continued to issue public statements on the model of the 1885 Pittsburgh Platform. These documents, specifically the Columbus Platform of 1937 and the Centenary Perspective of 1976, define Reform's ideological positions in a formal, official manner.

The statements of 1937 and 1976 represent a stunning reversal of much of the ideology contained in the 1885 Pittsburgh Platform. In 1885 Judaism was a religion alone; in 1937 it was "the soul of which Israel is the body"; in 1976 "an uncommon union of faith and peoplehood . . . bound together . . . by language [Hebrew, no less!], land, history, culture and institutions." In 1885 only the moral laws of "Mosaic legislation" were binding, while those "ceremonies" that were not adapted to modernity were rejected; in 1937 Reform called for the "preservation of the Sabbath, festivals and Holy Days . . . and development of such customs, symbols and ceremonies as possess inspirational value"; in 1976 Judaism's claims "may begin with our ethical obligations but they extend to many other aspects of Jewish living, including: creating a Jewish home centered on family devotion; life-long study; private prayer and public worship; daily religious observance; keeping the Sabbath and the holy days. . . ."

Finally, whereas the 1885 Platform rejected the hope for a return to a Jewish national homeland, the 1937 document obliged "all Jewry to aid in [Palestine's] upbuilding . . . by endeavoring to make it . . . a center of Jewish culture and spiritual life." By 1976 the rhetoric became positively rhapsodic: "We are privileged to live in an extraordinary time. . . . We are bound to that land and to the newly reborn State of Israel. . . . We have both a stake and a responsibility in building the State of Israel. . . . We encourage *aliyah*."

Platforms of this kind are, of course, more wish lists than photographs of reality. Reform has indeed embraced Zionism; it has begun to emphasize Hebrew in its educational programs and liturgical texts; it has encouraged greater religious observance. But to what extent this posture has trickled down to the typical Reform congregant is another story. By any criterion, however, Reform's ideological and programmatic turnabout is remarkable.

In fact, Reform today might be viewed as remarkably similar to a more liberal version of congregational-style Conservative Judaism—for example, the influence of Mordecai Kaplan's thought is everywhere in the 1976 document—were it not for four other hallmarks of American Reform: its persistent commitment to individual autonomy, its tolerance of intermarriage, its espousal of patrilineal descent, and most recently, its decision to ordain gay and lesbian Jews as rabbis. Conservative Judaism, for its part, insists on the authority of its Commission on Jewish Law and Standards to legislate for the Movement as a whole. It has never sanctioned intermarriage. It vigorously repudiated patrilineal descent. Finally, in 1992 the Law Committee ruled against accepting gay and lesbian Jews into the Conservative rabbinate.

■ THE RETURN of Reform Jews to Jewish ritual life within the past decade has been motivated by many factors.

First, the Reform agenda had changed. It had become less important to combat the separatist effect of rituals such as the dietary laws than to combat the wave of assimilation and intermarriage that threatened the integrity of the Jewish community.

Second, the place of ritual as a form of human expression and culture had become a significant topic of scholarly investigation in the social sciences. It had become clear that in fact there is no escaping ritual, that the issue is never ritual versus no ritual but, rather, *which* ritual, because individuals and communities inevitably ritualize significant aspects of their lives.

Finally, there was the recognition of the inescapable power of ritual as an educational medium for conveying some of the emotional force of Jewish life. It is not uncommon now to find Reform rabbis who observe the dietary laws, who cover their head and wear *tallit* in the synagogue, and who recite the *Havdalah* service at the end of the Sabbath. Pictured here are rabbinical students at the Hebrew Union College.

There are other, less perceptible differences as well: The liturgy of the Conservative synagogue retains much more Hebrew and is much closer to the traditional text than is that of Reform; and few Reform synagogues have regularly scheduled Saturday morning services with a formal Torah-reading service, even on the triennial cycle. Only a handful of small Conservative synagogues, in contrast, do not feature a regular Shabbat morning service with a Torah reading. It is clear that the two movements are closer today than they were a century ago, but the differences between them are significant.

As of this writing, the rhetoric of American Reform Judaism has become decidedly more traditionalist. The flaunting of personal autonomy is muted, and we are hearing much more about the need for objective, communally based parameters for authentic Reform Jewish practice. The lay and rabbinic leadership of Reform Judaism has clearly been touched by these issues, but the extent to which these new emphases will persist remains an open question.

After the midpoint of our century, Reform, like Orthodoxy, began to manifest uncommon vitality, a sense that things were happening. What was happening in Conservative Judaism?

Internal Issues

The external developments—the emergence of a vigorous, independent American Orthodoxy and Reform's turn to the right—combined to exacerbate a number of long-denied but persistent dilemmas that had haunted Conservative Judaism from its inception: the vagueness and tensions of its ideological stance, its failure to articulate a clear and coherent religious program that could be aligned with its intellectual stance and create a committed laity, and the gap between the versions of Conservative Judaism espoused by the Seminary, its rabbis, and its lay community.

Ideological Vagueness
We have examined why the Movement's founders were reluctant to propound an explicit ideological platform. At that time, this posture seemed strategically sound; for the first half of the century it helped account for the rapid growth of the Movement.

But by 1972, Conservative Judaism was competing for allegiance with two other Jewish religious movements that had become explicitly and imperialistically ideological. Now the Movement's ideological vagueness had come to be counterproductive. The implicit founding ideology that we traced was just not taught, not even to its rabbis, let alone to its congregants. It was not until 1975 that a formal course in Conservative Judaism was introduced into the Seminary's Rabbinical School curriculum. To claim, as Conservative Jews had been saying for years, that "we are not Orthodox and not Reform" was simply no longer adequate. The Movement was perceived as standing for nothing, and the calls for ideological clarity, from rabbis and congregants alike, began to grow.

Ideological Tensions

If the Movement were going to clarify its distinctive ideological stance, it could no longer avoid tackling the tensions within its implicit ideology. Did history justify religious change, or did it justify continuity? In fact, it does both, but then what changes and what doesn't, and why? Does Catholic Israel as the ultimate authority want to change its religious forms, or does it want to preserve them? Again, it seems to want to do both, depending on the situation, but here again, which forms change and which do not, and why? And what is the relationship between the community and its rabbinic and scholarly authorities in determining the scope, pace, and process of change?

THE CENTRAL TENSION

The tension that illuminates all others in the Conservative Movement is this: If Torah can be studied scientifically like any other human document, why does the Movement insist on the binding character of its laws? Were Conservative rabbis justifying at least the possibility of abrogating much of traditional Jewish observance, as Hirsch and his followers insisted the Movement did? What, then, is the difference between Conservative Judaism and Reform? Is it simply a matter of style, of priorities, of strategies? Is it simply, as Reform leaders have charged, that Conservative Judaism eventually adopts all of Reform's changes but just takes longer and indulges in much more hand wringing before making them? If that tension were to be addressed, the Movement would have to deal openly with a range of theological issues: with the nature of God, with revelation, with the authority of Torah, with the nature of *mitzvah* and of sin, and with the doctrine of the end of days. The theology, ideology, and program of the Movement would have to be brought into line throughout the Movement, if not on Kaplanian terms then on others.

No Committed Laity

It is not surprising that the Movement had failed to create a genuinely committed religious lay movement. How was its subtle and complex position to be communicated to the Jewishly uneducated layperson? It simply wasn't. If we measure the size of the Movement by the number of congregations it succeeded in affiliating, we can say the Movement grew rapidly. But by 1972 even that figure had stabilized. In any case, were the laypeople who affiliated with these congregations really different from those in the Reform congregations down the road, at least in terms of the Jewishness of their lives outside the synagogue? Not really.

Three Conservative Judaisms

We have referred to the two versions of Conservative Judaism that circulated for the better part of the century—the Seminary's version and that of the rabbinic movement. In fact, there were three versions: first, the layperson's version, which was largely indistinguishable from that of his or her Reform neighbor; second, that of the Conservative rabbinate and synagogue, what we called a mix of "modified traditionalism" combined with "modified Kaplanism"; and finally, the Seminary's own distinctive mix of scholarly openness and *halakhic* traditionalism. The cynical comment that Conservative Judaism consisted of "an Orthodox faculty teaching Conservative rabbis to minister to Reform Jews" seemed sadly accurate.

What changed around 1972 was not so much the existence of these three versions but rather the growing awareness of the Movement's internal fragmentation and the recognition that in this new era the Movement could no longer tolerate this divisiveness without doing itself serious harm. Of course, divisiveness was not a new phenomenon in Jewish life. In fact, the two competing movements were also facing internal rifts. Orthodoxy was suffering from the growing polarization of its own extreme right wing, which bitterly opposed its more modern or centrist representatives; and in Reform, tension existed between those who supported and those who rejected intermarriage and patrilineal descent. But in contrast with the other two, the divisions in Conservative Judaism were structural; they separated laity from rabbis and rabbis from their teachers. The Movement as a whole seemed to lack integrity.

Finally, each of the three arms of the Movement was undergoing changes that affected not only the internal structures of each but also the total network of interrelationships.

The United Synagogue, long relegated to a passive role in the Movement's decision-making process, had begun to show a new assertiveness. It was now being led by lay Jews who were the beneficiaries of higher education, who were successful in America, and who were unwilling to stand aside and let rabbis and scholars dictate the shape of their Jewish commitment. They now wanted to participate equally in Movement-wide policy deliberations. They wanted to be heard.

The Rabbinical Assembly, for its part, had also begun to demonstrate a new assertiveness. It had published prayerbooks and it was legislating *halakhah* for the Movement as a whole—often to the displeasure of the Seminary leadership. But it had also become aware that the Conservative rabbi was a singularly lonely person. Both the Reform and the Orthodox colleagues of the Conservative rabbi enjoyed a kinship of religious vision and practice with their lay communities. In contrast, the Conservative rabbi inhabited a different world from that of the lay community. A common complaint of these rabbis was that their own children could play in precious few of their congregants' homes without seeing violations of both the Sabbath and the dietary laws. The lay community's new assertiveness compounded this unease, for not only the religious authority but even the professional security of this rabbi depended on the goodwill of the congregants.

The Seminary had claimed to be both the fountainhead of an American religious movement and a great academy for advanced Jewish studies, but for a good deal of its history it had concentrated only on the latter task, leaving the former to its rabbis. It was now confronted with the fruit of that policy. It was perceived as being remote from its constituency. "What has the Seminary done for us?" its laypeople asked more and more frequently.

In fact, the Seminary had done a great deal. It had directly provided the congregation with its rabbi, its cantor, its school principal and some of its teachers, a professor of Jewish studies and a Hillel director for its college-age children, and a culture of Jewish learning in America at large. It had decisively shaped Christian America's perception of Judaism. It had also given birth to the rest of the Movement. Yet despite these accomplishments, the fact that its constituency could still ask, "What have you done for us?" was testimony to how far removed the school seemed to be from the day-to-day life experience of Conservative Jews. Still, the school very much needed the Movement, not only for financial support but also as a constituency for its teachers and graduates. Without followers, there are no leaders.

The Conservative rabbis, for their part, were becoming poignantly aware of the deficiencies in their rabbinic education. The Seminary's curriculum might well have ensured their scholarly competence, but it had done little to prepare them for the day-to-day responsibilities of a pulpit rabbi, for counseling congregants whose child had died, whose marriage was dissolving, whose children had become alienated or were intermarrying. Courses in these professional skills were relegated to the periphery of the curriculum and the final year of training; there was no required internship. They perceived the Seminary as simply out of touch with the realities of their professional life as congregational rabbis.

The Conservative rabbi felt deprived not only professionally but religiously as well, for the school's commitment to the Science of Judaism approach to Jewish studies had succeeded only too well. *Wissenschaft* was intrinsically a secularizing impulse. It leveled the sanctity of Torah by insisting that it be studied just like any other great human document. The proponents of this method viewed it as Judaism's ticket of admission to Western modernity, and it undoubtedly served that purpose, but as the dominating impulse in a rabbinical school curriculum, it proved to be totally subversive. Whatever else the rabbis were, they were preeminently religious role models. But what did it mean to be a religious role model if your training robbed Torah of its religious significance? With the significant exception of Mordecai Kaplan and an isolated few of his colleagues, everyone at the Seminary studiously avoided that crucial issue.

To take but one example, generations of Seminary rabbinical students had studied the Bible through the modern, critical approach. The text was divided into its original documents; the internal history and provenance of each of these documents was traced; textual emendations were suggested; influences from other Middle Eastern sacred texts were traced. But the one question that was of ultimate concern to the congregational rabbis, the question that they had to be prepared to answer each time they stepped onto the pulpit on a Shabbat morning, was rarely addressed: Now that we know so much about how this text came to be, what meaning does it have for us or for our students and congregants today? Why should we read it, study it, attend to it? For that matter, why should we pray? What is supposed to happen to us when we come to the synagogue, when we observe the dietary laws, the Sabbath, or anything else? And if the rabbis couldn't deal with these questions, how could they expect their congregants to do so?

If these questions were to be addressed, the Seminary would have to rethink its educational mission from the ground up. It would have to distinguish between dispassionate graduate education and religiously committed rabbinic education. In the process, it would have to redefine its vision of the model Conservative rabbi and then create a curriculum for the training of that rabbi. This new model would not demand that the Seminary faculty abandon its commitment to *Wissenschaft*; that commitment was a matter of intellectual integrity and was not negotiable. It would, however, demand that this scientific-critical perspective be integrated with an approach that looked at the traditional texts of Judaism as a source of religious meaning and that taught the student how to extract and communicate that meaning to a congregation of modern American Jews.

Even in the task that it did take seriously, that of serving as a great academic center in the Western mold, the Seminary was hurting, paradoxically because of its very success. Its graduates had come to populate the new and multiplying departments of Jewish studies in universities across the world, even in Israel. The Seminary no longer held a monopoly on Jewish scholarship. In fact, it began to see its own faculty being wooed away by the prestige and affluence of secular American universities and by the commitment of some of its teachers to *aliyah*. It still housed the only rabbinical school that trained rabbis directly for Conservative congregations, and it had established its own graduate school, which offers advanced degrees in Judaica, but students who wanted to pursue doctoral work in Judaica could now go elsewhere if they wished. What, then, was to become of the Seminary's role as the most prestigious center for Jewish scholarship outside of Israel?

As if to confirm this sense of impending crisis, the year 1972 saw the publication of a new, augmented edition of the first book-length study of Conservative Judaism, Marshall Sklare's *Conservative Judaism: An American Religious Movement*. The original 1954 edition of this volume was a revised version of the author's doctoral dissertation in sociology at Columbia University. Sklare had studied the full range of conditions that fostered the development of the Movement, but it also focused on many of its internal conflicts: the Movement's failure to develop a coherent ideology, its theological evasiveness, and its apparent inability to articulate a clear religious program for its laity.

■ DURING THIS writer's undergraduate career (1950–1954), there were only two American universities where one could pursue advanced Jewish studies: Columbia University and Harvard. A generation later, when my children entered their undergraduate years, there were many American schools where one could study Judaica. Many prestigious universities, even those that had had a quota for the number of Jewish students accepted each year, now threw open their doors to qualified Jewish applicants. Universities established departments of Jewish studies manned by American- and Israeli-trained academicians. The Seminary, as the outstanding center for the advanced study of Judaism outside of Israel, can take credit for helping to produce that first generation of university scholars in Judaica.

In the 1972 edition, Sklare added a new concluding chapter, entitled "Recent Developments in Conservative Judaism," which begins by reviewing the Movement's genuine accomplishments in the intervening two decades: its rapid demographical growth, its "triumph" over the other two movements in developing new synagogues and affiliating new members, the emergence of the synagogue center as a home for multiple forms of Jewish activity, its emerging national lay leadership, the development of the World Council of Synagogues as a way of extending Movement affiliation outside of North America, and the accomplishments of the Ramah summer camp movement. But the tone soon grows ominous: "The morale of the Conservative movement is on the decline"; judged from the perspective of promoting religious growth among the Conservative laity, "Conservativism has been an abysmal failure." "The present-day Conservative elite . . . is no longer so confident that its formula will be attractive to the younger generation." Sklare concludes on a more cosmic note: "On a deeper level the Conservative crisis—if that be the word—represents a questioning of whether the Jewish people and its 'chain of tradition' can long endure on the American continent." Whatever one might think of that broader claim, for Conservative Judaism the crisis could no longer be ignored.

8 | THE ORDINATION OF WOMEN

*//*There is no direct halakhic objection to the acts of training and ordaining women to be a rabbi, preacher, and teacher in Israel.*//*

——Final Report of the Commission for the Study of the Ordination of Women as Rabbis

Threat and Opportunity

Crisis represents both threat and opportunity. It is to the credit of Conservative Judaism that the Movement addressed the crisis it faced as both of these.

Since the 1970s, the Conservative Movement has taken decisive steps on a variety of fronts to deal with the internal problems that had led many to question whether it had a future in American Jewish life. At the risk of oversimplification, we will focus on two issues that best symbolize this new determination. One was the 1988 publication of *Emet Ve-Emunah*, the Movement's first Statement of Principles (discussed in the next chapter). But far more dramatic in terms of its inherent interest, its impact on the Movement as a whole, and its symbolic value was the Movement's confrontation with the issue of the ordination of women. No other single issue could have more effectively forced the Movement to come to terms with its own identity. It was the right issue at the right time.

The Feminist Revolution

There is no one specific statement in all of classical Jewish literature, from the earliest pages of the Bible to the responsa of twentieth-century Jewish authorities, that explicitly forbids the ordination of women as rabbis. For that matter, neither is there a specific source that permits it. It was simply a non-issue—at least until the middle of our century.

Suddenly everything changed. Feminism became the issue of the age. We became witnesses to and participants in a revolution that touched every facet of our culture as women began to demand equal access to every area of professional life. It might seem perfectly natural to someone born in our current world to see women serving as doctors, lawyers, financial analysts, Supreme Court Justices, and senators, not to mention baggage handlers at the airport, telephone repairers, and construction workers. But to anyone who had reached adulthood prior to the onset of the revolution, all of this remains somewhat jarring. Yet even those sights are rapidly becoming part of the landscape, so thoroughly and so rapidly has the revolution achieved its goals.

Religions, however, are bastions of tradition; they shudder at the prospect of radical and rapid change, preferring to hold on to familiar patterns even after they have been exposed as problematic. Still, it was inevitable that sooner or later the feminist revolution would have an impact on religious institutions as well.

FEMINISM AND THE CHURCH

The impact of the feminist revolution on American religious bodies was first felt by American Protestantism, the more liberal form of Christianity. By 1970 roughly one-third of Protestant denominations that affiliated with the World Council of Churches were ordaining women. Though some of the more left-wing of these churches had done so for centuries (e.g., some Baptists in England since the mid-seventeenth century), the larger, more influential, and more centrist church bodies acted only in response to contemporary challenges. The Presbyterian and Methodist churches, for example, made their decision in 1956, and one group of Lutherans, in 1970. In 1976, after a long and bitter debate, the American Episcopalian church, considered by many to be the closest Christian parallel to Conservative Judaism in its religious orientation, also voted to ordain women. To this day the Catholic Church remains firmly opposed to giving women any but the most peripheral role in public ritual (as, of course, does Orthodox Judaism).

Women and Judaism: A Historical Background

■ THERE IS no biblical source that stipulates that men and women must be separated during public liturgical or ritual events. In fact, Deuteronomy 31:12 and Nehemiah 8:2–3 seem to suggest that men and women were not separated. But the Talmud (Tractate *Sukkah,* 51b–52a) does describe such a separation during one of the celebrations of the Sukkot festival, and certainly most of the post-talmudic data suggest that synagogues erected a section for women, separated by a nontransparent curtain or an iron or wood grill. Reform abolished that practice in the early nineteenth century, and eventually most American Conservative synagogues followed suit. Today the presence of such a *mehitzah* (literally, "barrier" or "separation") has become the main differentiating mark of the Orthodox synagogue. Pictured here is the women's section of a synagogue.

The role and status of the Jewish woman—like everything else in Jewish religious life—were determined by biblical and talmudic law. In areas of civil and marital law she was largely considered to be someone else's property, first her father's and later her husband's. For example, in Jewish law, when a couple marries, it is the man who "acquires" the woman; the groom speaks during the marriage service while the bride is silent. A woman cannot initiate a divorce. If she is abandoned by her husband and he refuses to divorce her, she remains an *agunah,* literally "anchored" to him and unable to marry another. In most legal proceedings, she, along with minors, deaf mutes, and the mentally impaired, is not considered competent to testify.

In the synagogue she was an outsider, relegated to the balcony or to the back or sides of the sanctuary. The liturgy was written by men, for men. A prayer for the congregation recited in traditional synagogues every Sabbath morning asks God to "bless this entire congregation . . . their wives, their sons and daughters." Every morning the Jewish male praised God "for not having made me a woman." The woman played no role in the public service of worship. Her place was in the marketplace, where she frequently ran the family business, or in the home, where she ruled the kitchen, the table, and the children's education.

Of course, side by side with these legal restrictions are a multitude of classical texts exalting the Jewish woman and emphasizing the crucial role she plays in the home and in her family. As Jewish feminism began to make its way, however, these texts came to be perceived as apologetics, especially in contrast with the woman's official status in Jewish law.

Though polygamy (sanctioned by biblical and talmudic law) was formally abolished in the tenth century of our era, it wasn't until the Enlightenment and the Emancipation in the nineteenth century that Jewish women began to express their frustration with their role in Jewish life. These first expressions of a feminist spirit can be found, predictably, not in legal documents but in the fiction and poetry of the age, written, it should be added, by both men and women.

THE POINT OF THE *YOD*

A classic expression of early profeminist sensibility is in the poem "*Kotzo Shel Yod*" ("The Point of the *Yod*") by the radical nineteenth-century social critic and opponent of rabbinic obscurantism, Yehuda Leib Gordon (1831–1892). The poem, written in 1876, describes the fate of a beautiful young Jewish woman, long abandoned by her husband and now ready to remarry. Her Jewish bill of divorce, sent from abroad by her husband, is invalidated by a rabbi because the husband's name is misspelled; it lacks a *yod*, the smallest of consonants in the Hebrew alphabet. In the meantime, the husband is lost at sea, the woman can no longer be divorced or remarry, and she is left an *agunah*. The poem is suffused with compassion for the fate of Jewish women combined with a vitriolic attack on the rabbinate and its anachronistic institutions. Its opening lines are: "Jewish woman, thy life who knows? . . . / Unnoticed thou dost enter the world, unnoticed depart from it./ Thy heartaches and thy joys, thy sorrows and thy desires spring up in thee and die within thee."

The advent of Reform in early-nineteenth-century Germany broke the stranglehold of Jewish law as a whole, including its dictates on the place of the Jewish woman. A conference of Reform rabbis meeting in Breslau in 1846 abolished the offensive benediction from the morning service; it granted women full equality in Jewish education and in public worship, including being counted in the *minyan*, and it accorded girls the right to celebrate their coming of age at thirteen. These breaks with traditional practice quickly entered American Reform practice as well. It wasn't until 1972, however, that the Reform movement ordained Sally Priesand as its first woman rabbi. Predictably, the Reconstructionist Rabbinical College, which Mordecai Kaplan founded in 1968, admitted women from the outset. Its first woman graduate, Rabbi Sandy Sasso, was ordained in 1974.

We can date the American Jewish feminist movement from roughly 1970, when Jewish periodicals began to manifest a powerful undercurrent of rebellion against the role American Jewish women had inherited. The year 1971 saw the creation of Ezrat Nashim, a national consciousness-raising women's group that began to lobby for Jewish feminist causes. In the spring of 1972 a group of Ezrat Nashim representatives attended the annual convention of the Rabbinical Assembly. Denied an official place on the convention program (though clearly encouraged by individuals within the leadership of the Assembly), the women demonstrated in the corridors, held their own prayer services, and lobbied individual rabbis on the full range of Jewish feminist issues. The revolution had now touched the Conservative Movement.

Women in Conservative Judaism

The Seminary vote to admit women to its Rabbinical School took place eleven years later, in 1983. In retrospect, however, that decision was the climax of a gradual process of development stretching back to the Movement's very beginnings.

From the outset, in most Conservative synagogues men and women were permitted to sit together during services of worship. By the mid-1950s some form of *bat mitzvah* ceremony had been accepted by most Conservative synagogues. A series of majority or legitimate minority decisions of the Committee on Jewish Law and Standards gradually extended full equality to women in synagogue rituals: having *aliyot* (1955), being counted in the minyan (1973), voting and holding office in the synagogue (1973), serving as witnesses in judicial proceedings, such as marriage, divorce, and/or conversion (1974), and even serving as rabbi or cantor (1974).

Of course, the vote on this last issue had no impact whatsoever on the Seminary, which was always more traditionalist on *halakhic* issues than the rest of the Movement, but the pattern as a whole clearly reflects the direction the Movement was taking. A 1987 survey conducted by Edya Arzt, Education Director of Women's League for Conservative Judaism, indicates that of 705 affiliated Women's League groups, close to 500 counted women toward the minyan and over 500 gave them *aliyot*. More important, a follow-up survey conducted two years later indicated that both figures had risen slightly.

Even at the Seminary, however, the process of rethinking the issue was under way. The faculty had never accepted the curricular strictures against women that were inherent in traditional practice.

For example, to this day, in almost all right-wing Orthodox schools women are not taught Talmud because of the talmudic injunction (*Mishnah Sota* 3:4) that liken teaching a woman Torah to teaching her frivolity, since (according to Maimonides' explanation of the passage) women are known to be light-headed!

As early as 1903 one of the most notable of American Jewish women, Henrietta Szold, later to become the founder of Hadassah, the international organization of Zionist women, was permitted to attend all Seminary classes, with the understanding that she would not be ordained. This policy became standard at the Seminary. In practice, most women students were enrolled in the Seminary's undergraduate school (or, later, in its Graduate School) rather than in its Rabbinical School, but the curriculum of the Graduate School did not differ in substance from that of the Rabbinical School, apart from those few courses that trained the rabbi for his professional role.

Even more notable, from a long-range educational perspective, were the religious policies practiced at Camp Ramah, the Movement's network of educational summer camps. From the time the first Ramah camp was founded in 1946, the responsibility for setting its educational and religious policy was vested in the faculty of the

■ MORDECAI KAPLAN used to say that he had four good reasons for initiating the *bat mitzvah* ritual in the United States—his four daughters.

Most of us today take the *bat mitzvah* for granted. Even some left-wing Orthodox synagogues are in the process of evolving some ceremony to celebrate a young Jewish woman's coming of age as an adult Jew, although these ceremonies would not include her being called to the Torah. In the context of American Judaism in 1922, however, Kaplan's decision to give his daughter an *aliyah,* in the sanctuary itself and at a Shabbat service, has to be viewed as wildly revolutionary. Judith Kaplan Eisenstein is pictured here reading from the Torah on the 70th anniversary of her *bat mitzvah.*

Teachers Institute, as the Seminary undergraduate program was then called. Somewhat astonishingly, however, in matters of religious observance this faculty exercised total autonomy, acting independently of the Committee on Jewish Law and Standards and frequently in opposition to Seminary practice itself.

At Ramah, mixed seating at compulsory worship services was the practice from the very beginning. Women were soon permitted to lead *Birkat HaMazon* at Ramah, to recite *Kiddush* and *Havdalah*, to lead the *Kabbalat Shabbat* portion of the Friday evening service (but not the *Ma'ariv* service, which is more ancient and carries more *halakhic* weight than *Kabbalat Shabbat*), and to chant the book of Lamentations at Tishah B'Av services. In 1974, women at Ramah were given the right to receive *aliyot* and read from the Torah. These public roles were still in dispute in many Conservative congregations, and of course, none of them was accepted at the Seminary itself until 1984. Yet all of these policies were introduced at Ramah without fanfare.

Finally, there was simply no question that Ramah's formal educational program—the classes in Hebrew, Bible, Talmud, theology, history, and literature—was addressed to men and women campers and staff alike, without the slightest hint of discrimination.

The net result of these policies was that the elite female youth of the Movement, those young women who had benefited from its most sophisticated educational program, had been raised to expect full access to Jewish religious life. It was only natural, then, in the spirit of the feminist revolution that was sweeping the country, for some of these women to press the Seminary for formal admission to its Rabbinical School.

The Ordination Issue

Admission to the Rabbinical School was a different matter than was participation in synagogue ritual. Ordination was a singularly complex issue. It had *halakhic* dimensions (rabbis usually serve as witnesses in judicial proceedings and frequently lead the congregation in prayer); ethical dimensions (did not justice and human dignity demand the full equalization of women's status and role in Jewish life?); and professional dimensions (would congregations engage women rabbis, and would these women drive men out of the field, as was perceived to have happened in education and social work?). It also raised theological questions (in what way and to what extent are Jewish legal precedents authoritative?). Above all, it had monumental symbolic significance; it crystallized the full range of identity issues that the Movement had been struggling with for a century. In the last analysis, was the Movement designed to preserve tradition or to seek an accommodation with modernity? It was, of course, designed to do both, but in this concrete case, how was the mix to be achieved?

Breaking with the Past

The ordination issue portended a major break with the past. The very fact that in none of Judaism's classical texts is there even a hint that this was an issue worthy of serious discussion, even to be explicitly forbidden, is itself an indication of the distance that separated the modern community from its predecessors. The feminist revolution spoke to primitive, deeply buried instincts. It threatened to overthrow the carefully constructed structures of Jewish communal life. In a word, it represented anarchy.

The issue could not be ignored; it had galvanized the entire movement. From 1972 on it was on the agenda of every United Synagogue, Women's League, and Rabbinical Assembly convention. The 1973 convention of the United Synagogue, for example, passed a resolution urging its member congregations to "take such actions as will insure equal opportunity for its women congregants to assume positions of leadership, authority and responsibility in all phases of congregational activity." The body "looks with favor upon the inclusion of women in ritual participation, including but not limited to participation in the minyan and *aliyot*." Finally, it "wishes to note that it looks with favor on the admission of qualified women to the Rabbinical School of The Jewish Theological Seminary of America."

However, on the issue of ordination, only the Seminary could act. In fact, for the first time in its history the Seminary was confronted with a complex religious issue that by its very nature could not be settled by any other body. As a school, the Seminary could easily avoid discussing the *kashrut* of cheeses or the use of electricity or driving on the Sabbath. Even the decisions of the Committee on Jewish Law and Standards regarding women's role in the synagogue were not binding on the Seminary synagogue—or, for that matter, on any congregation or rabbi; they simply delineated the range of permissible options. But now the issue was admission to an academic-professional training program. Who else could make that decision but the school itself?

At least in the early stages of the debate, undoubtedly many members of the faculty fervently prayed that the issue would simply go away. But it didn't. Instead, the calls for action grew stronger and louder. Ducking the problem might destroy the Movement, and the school could not afford to pay that price.

At its annual convention in May 1977 the Rabbinical Assembly passed a resolution petitioning the Chancellor of the Seminary "to establish an interdisciplinary commission to study all aspects of the role of women as spiritual leaders in the Conservative Movement." The makeup of the Commission was to "reflect the pluralism and diversity of the Conservative Movement." Its final report and recommendation was to be presented to the 1979 convention of the Rabbinical Assembly.

The Commission on the Ordination of Women

The formation of the Commission was announced five months later at the opening of the 1977–1978 academic year. Chaired by Chancellor Cohen, it was composed of fourteen men and women, including members of the Seminary faculty, rabbis, academicians from other schools, and representative laypersons from Conservative synagogues. In addition to meeting as a body in New York, the Commission held public meetings in six communities throughout the country, at which anyone affiliated with the Movement was invited to testify.

The Commission's final report, signed by eleven of its fourteen members, concluded by recommending that "the Seminary revise its admissions procedures to allow for applications from female candidates"; that "this revision of policy be accomplished as quickly as possible"; that the Seminary "set up appropriate apparatuses for the recruitment, orientation and eventually, career placement of female rabbinical students"; and that "the major wings of the movement immediately begin discussion of procedures to be followed to educate the community concerning issues raised in this report so as to ensure as smooth and as harmonious an adjustment to the new policy as possible."

Three members of the Commission—two rabbis and one member of the Seminary's Talmud Department—filed a minority dissenting opinion. It recommended that "appropriate roles be created for Jewish women short of ordination so that their commitment and talents may be a source of blessing and not of unnecessary controversy." Four considerations led this minority to their conclusion: certain *halakhic* problems relating to the issue remained unresolved; the decision threatened the unity of the Movement; given the Seminary's dominant position in the movement, its unprecedented intervention into *halakhic* decision making would effectively foreclose the options of those who disagreed with the decision; and finally, the decision threatened to alienate the more traditional members of the Movement.

FEMALE ORDINATION AND *HALAKHAH*

The Commission's report on women and their role in religious life was thorough and comprehensive. It dealt at length with the *halakhic* dimensions of the issue ("there is no direct *halakhic* objection to the acts of training and ordaining a woman to be a rabbi, preacher and teacher in Israel"); with its ethical dimensions (it is "morally wrong to maintain an educational structure that treats males and females equally up to the final stage, but distinguishes between them at that stage, without a firm and clearly identifiable *halakhic* reason for doing so"); and with what it called "other considerations" (e.g., a decision not to ordain women would mean "the rejection of a pool of talented, committed, and energetic women . . . who could play a major role in revitalizing Jewish tradition and values in the Conservative Movement").

The final report of the Commission was presented at the January 1979 convention of the Rabbinical Assembly in Los Angeles. The Assembly took note of the report but determined to take no further action prior to further study of it by the full membership and "the study, analysis and decision of the Seminary faculty on its [the report's] recommendation."

Two further steps were taken to stimulate public discussion of the issue. Members of the Seminary faculty were encouraged to write statements expressing their personal views. Eventually, eleven such papers were written and circulated. (Nine of these have been published, along with the majority and minority reports of the Commission, in a volume, *The Ordination of Women as Rabbis: Studies and Responsa*, edited by Seminary Vice Chancellor Simon Greenberg.)

Simultaneously, as another way of surveying the sense of the community at large, in the summer and fall of 1978 the Seminary commissioned the market research firm of Yankelovitch, Skelley, and White to conduct a survey of congregational opinion on ordination and a wide range of other issues pertaining to the beliefs and practices of lay Conservative Jews. A questionnaire was prepared, and the rabbis of fourteen congregations deemed to be representative of the Movement at large were invited to distribute it to their congregants. Three hundred completed questionnaires were returned (an acceptable return for a survey of this kind), the results were tabulated and cross-related, and the final report was submitted to the Chancellor at the end of 1978 and to the Seminary faculty in February 1979.

One of the people who gained access to the Yankelovitch data was Dr. Saul Shapiro, a prominent Conservative layman and professional computer analyst. Shapiro's study of the data convinced him that apart from whatever they had to say about the ordination issue, the truly alarming message was that the Conservative Movement was heading for a demographic crisis; young Conservative Jews were simply not affiliating with the Movement in the way that their parents had.

Independent of Shapiro's work, a similar conclusion had been reached by Dr. Charles Liebman. Now on the faculty of Bar Ilan University in Israel, but then (1978–1979) serving on the Seminary faculty, Liebman based his conclusions on his study of the 1970 National Jewish Population survey and the 1975 survey of Jews in the Boston metropolitan area.

Liebman and Shapiro met in January 1979 and presented their conclusions to Chancellor Cohen. Cohen's response was to commission them to undertake a second survey of the Movement and its religious attitudes. They designed a new questionnaire, which was mailed directly to almost 18,000 households, selected at random from the master list of Conservative congregants. Close to 5,000 were returned.

In May of 1979 a draft of the Liebman–Shapiro report was presented to the Chancellor and shared with the faculty. It confirmed the authors' fears regarding the demographic trends in the Movement at large. Their further conclusions, however, generated sharp and controversial debate. On the ordination issue, the authors concluded from the data that first, most Conservative Jews simply did not care one way or the other and second, that the most Jewishly educated and observant of Conservative laypeople opposed the ordination of women. Predictably, the Liebman–Shapiro data added fuel to what was an already frenzied and confrontational mood both at the Seminary and in the Movement at large.

Rarely had the Seminary community been more polarized. From the time the Commission on the Ordination of Women was formed in 1977, the issue had been on the agenda of just about every meeting of the Seminary faculty, but now a decision was imminent. Professors and students caucused, lobbied, and argued. Seminary classrooms, offices, and hallways echoed with the clash of the debate.

Prospective vote counts were tabulated, revised, and retabulated. "Undecideds" were avidly courted. Hovering in the background but very much present and involved were the women whose careers hung in the balance, many of whom had enrolled in the Seminary's Graduate School pending the faculty vote. The process was blatantly political; in the last analysis, numbers would tell, but what impelled the political infighting was nothing less than the ultimate issue—a community's religious commitments.

A Decision Is Made

As September arrived and the 1979–1980 academic year opened, the decision-making process came to a head. The Commission report—with both its majority and its minority recommendations—was public; the Yankelovitch and Liebman–Shapiro data were available. The date for the faculty vote was set for late December.

As the fateful date drew near and the size and makeup of the two blocs emerged, it became clear that those in favor of women's ordination held the majority, but just barely. A handful of votes—4 or 5 out of the roughly 40 to be cast—separated the two groups. At that point a subgroup of the majority bloc reached the conclusion that an issue of such significance should not be decided by such a small majority. The outcome would split the faculty and might destroy the school. No issue was that important. This subgroup approached Chancellor Cohen and proposed that the entire question be tabled for further study. Cohen himself had vigorously supported the policy change, but confronted with the vote count and the breakup of the majority bloc, he reluctantly agreed. The faculty meeting was held on December 19, 1979. The motion to table was made, seconded, and passed by a vote of 25–19.

For four years the issue lay dormant. In the background, however, forces were at work that would bring it to a head once again. As before, the catalyst was a convention of the Rabbinical Assembly, this time in Dallas in May 1983.

The Rabbinical Assembly is composed largely of Seminary-ordained rabbis. In accord with a long-standing agreement between the Seminary and the Assembly, any rabbi ordained by the Seminary is granted automatic membership in the Assembly. In addition, however, the Assembly admitted rabbis ordained at other schools. Unlike Seminary graduates, these candidates are screened by the Assembly's Membership Committee, and their membership has to be endorsed by a 75-percent vote of an Assembly convention.

It was inevitable that sooner or later a woman ordained at the Reform or Reconstructionist school would apply for membership in the Assembly. That woman was Rabbi Beverly Magidson, ordained at Hebrew Union College in 1979 and then serving as advisor to the

B'nai B'rith Hillel Foundation in St. Louis. The Membership Committee had screened Rabbi Magidson and determined that she met all of the qualifications for membership in the Assembly. But on the issue of recommending her for admission to the Assembly, the vote of the Committee was split. In the end, the Committee determined that its responsibility was simply to implement the Assembly's policy for admission, not to determine what that policy should be. Since the constitution of the Rabbinical Assembly stipulated that gender was irrelevant as a criterion for membership, the Committee referred the issue to the Dallas convention for a decision.

The convention debate was long and bitter. (Its transcript fills 33 pages in the 1983 *Proceedings of the Assembly.*) It encapsulated all of the theological, *halakhic*, ideological, and programmatic tensions that had characterized the Movement's religious message from the outset. In the vote that followed, Rabbi Magidson's admission missed the 75-percent requirement by 2 votes out of 278 cast. In a recount, it missed by 3 votes out of 285.

The Dallas vote galvanized the Seminary community once again. It was now clear that close to 75 percent of the Rabbinical Assembly favored the ordination of women. Further, the debate itself revealed that a number of the no votes had reflected the view that it was the Seminary and not the Assembly that should take the lead in accepting the principle of women rabbis. Finally, it was also patently clear that if the Seminary would not act, and act quickly, the Assembly would, probably at its next convention.

Three months later, at the beginning of the 1983–1984 academic year, Chancellor Cohen announced his determination to place the issue on the agenda of the faculty once again, at a meeting to be held at the end of October. Once again the school was ablaze with controversy. This time, however, the outcome was never in doubt. On the afternoon of October 24, 1983, the Seminary faculty voted, 32–8 (although five members of the opposition simply boycotted the meeting), to admit women for ordination beginning with the academic year 1984–1985. Nineteen women were admitted as part of that 1984 entering class (an unusually large number because of the backup of candidates who had put their training on hold pending the faculty decision), and one of their number, Rabbi Amy Eilberg of Philadelphia, was ordained in May 1985. (Rabbi Eilberg had completed most of the Rabbinical School course requirements as a student in the Graduate School.) Conservative Judaism had its first woman rabbi. In fact, it had three, for at its 1985 convention the Rabbinical Assembly accepted into its membership not only Rabbi Eilberg, but also Rabbi Magidson and Rabbi Jan Kaufman of Washington, D.C. (also ordained at HUC). Since 1984, women have constituted roughly one-third of each entering Rabbinical School class.

What had changed in the four years separating the two votes and in the 100 years since the founding of the Seminary? Everything. Both school and Movement had undergone a profound transformation, and while we may still be too close to the events to understand all of the subtleties of that change, some factors emerge as absolutely decisive. If any one of them had not been present, the decision might have gone the other way.

A New Chancellor

Gerson Cohen's personal involvement in the ordination issue was the primary factor.

Cohen became the chancellor of the Seminary because he fit the classical mold of Seminary leadership: He was a brilliant scholar. In this capacity, he was an apt successor to Schechter and Finkelstein, but in another respect he was very much not in the Finkelstein tradition. He was not, at least in the minds of most of the Seminary

■ AMY EILBERG of Philadelphia was the first woman ordained at the Seminary. She had completed most of her required Rabbinical School course work while formally enrolled in a master's program in the Seminary's Graduate School. After the 1983 decision to admit women, she needed but one more year to complete the remaining Rabbinical School courses. She was ordained on May 12, 1985.

community, associated with the traditionalist wing of the Movement. He was also a historian, the first such to head the Movement (Finkelstein was essentially a scholar of early talmudic texts), and that scholarly orientation was to prove significant.

■ GERSON COHEN (1924–1991) was a charismatic teacher, acerbic in manner and dramatic and challenging in the classroom and lecture hall. (This author recalls the striking first sentence of Cohen's lecture on the Ptolemaic dynasty in third-century-B.C.E. Egypt: "The Ptolemaic kings were interested in two things: sex and money.")

Cohen assumed the chancellorship of the Seminary in 1972, just as the Jewish feminist issue began to emerge. Educated at the College of the City of New York and ordained at the Seminary in 1948, Cohen obtained his doctorate in Semitic languages at Columbia University. He taught at the Seminary from 1953 to 1963 (and served as Seminary Librarian from 1950 to 1957) and then joined the Columbia faculty. In 1970 he returned to the Seminary as the Jacob H. Schiff Professor of Jewish History. When Cohen returned to the Seminary, he was acknowledged to be his generation's outstanding historian of ancient and medieval Judaism.

Cohen's address to the 1979 Rabbinical Assembly convention, introducing the final report of the Commission on the Ordination of Women, is an extraordinary document. He had heard from all quarters, he says, that he was in a "no-win situation," that whatever the recommendation of the Commission, the Movement would be split. He is grateful that the Assembly had insisted the issue merited careful study, that it was too momentous an issue to be railroaded through, and that by requesting the establishment of the Commission, the Assembly had reaffirmed the Seminary's role as "the fountainhead of Conservative Judaism." He is also clear that the issue could not be side stepped: "We can vote yes or no but we may not delay or equivocate."

Then, astonishingly, he confesses that when he originally broached the issue, he had hoped that the findings of the Commission would be negative. (On social and political issues Cohen was known to be, by instinct, conservative; he appreciated the indispensability of communal structures and social discipline. These instincts had likely been strengthened when, as a faculty member of Columbia University in the spring of 1968, he watched helplessly as the radical student movement disrupted the school's programs, vandalized its buildings, and violated its academic integrity.) Now, however, he has been persuaded to go against his instincts and become "a passionate advocate" of ordination, for a variety of reasons: *halakhic*-theological, moral, sociological, and institutional.

The bulk of his address is built around a study of three critical moments in the past when the Jewish community had to confront the choice of consolidation or creativity. The third of these was the tension between what he refers to as "the spirit of Baghdad and the spirit of Cordova."

"The world in the eighth century" he said, " was burning with sectarianism, with Karaism, and with new forms of Arabic assimilation. . . . The Jewish world was aflame, the Baghdad Yeshiva was suffering terribly and had lost authority." At this moment, the head of the Yeshiva, Rabbi Shmuel ben Ali, could only insist on the supremacy of his authority. He alone had legitimacy. He was the leader of the Jewish community, and he was prepared to assert his authority in a rigidly inflexible way. In these stress-filled times, there was to be no democratization, no yielding of authority, no sharing of power.

But generations later, quite another response was offered by a man who had no official standing. Moses Maimonides, originally of Cordova and later of Egypt, confronted these new challenges by compiling a code of Jewish law that would make Jews independent of any central institution or rabbinic authority. This code recognized the legitimacy of local custom and would thus enable the Jews to respond to their contemporary challenges with both legal structure and diversity. Maimonides composed his *Guide to the Perplexed* so that Jewish thought could also adapt to contemporary intellectual currents.

"If choose I must," Cohen continues,

> my choice would be the spirit of Cordova. My world, your world is aflame . . . with secularism . . . , with intermarriage . . . , with the decline of the Jewish birth rate . . . , with ignorance. To me, the spirit of Cordova is the response of a community that seeks creativity . . . , the opening of the gates of thought and practice . . . , the creation of new vehicles to unite Jewry in spirit and practice as a consequence of challenge.

This was a historian speaking, and suddenly the rhetoric of a chancellor sounded strikingly new. Here was a chancellor of the Seminary, Finkelstein's successor, responding to a call for guidance from the Movement at large. That was unprecedented. Even more, he was leading the Seminary into the thicket of a complex issue of religious practice. That was also unprecedented. Finally, and astonishingly, he was advocating a significant break with a centuries-old tradition. That was simply unheard of. The appeal to history had returned to impel the Movement into dangerously uncharted waters.

Back at the Seminary, with his address on record, Cohen was in an awkward position. As Chancellor of the entire school and President of the entire faculty, he would have to chair the decisive meeting. Yet his position was known, and he simply could not remain above the struggle. He was indeed in a "no-win situation," and he alienated a significant bloc of the faculty. The 1979 vote to table the issue was a personal defeat. The 1983 vote was a personal triumph.

וְשָׂעֵרְךָ צִמֵּחַ וְאַתְּ עֵרֹם
וְעֶרְיָה

וַיָּרֵעוּ אֹתָנוּ הַמִּצְרִים וַיְעַנּוּנוּ וַיִּתְּנוּ עָלֵינוּ עֲבֹדָה קָשָׁה

■ GERSON COHEN's appeal to the "spirit of Cordova" reflected his long-standing conviction as a historian of Judaism that Judaism is most vital and most creative when it is able to assimilate the best of the "outside" or non-Jewish culture into the fabric of Judaism. That was the essence of "The Blessing of Assimilation," his 1966 commencement address delivered to the Boston Hebrew Teachers College. Never was this thesis more illuminating than in the case of Spanish Jewry: An open society and a shared language, Arabic, enabled this community to create a grand synthesis of two great cultures. This illustration, a page from the thirteenth-century Prato Haggadah, is an excellent example of this assimilation process. The portrayal of grotesque animals, the initial word panels, the scenes in the margins, and the gothic decor reflect the style and technique of the great French and Spanish illustrators of the era. Their artistic genius is now mobilized to glorify a Jewish liturgical text.

The New Talmudists

Seminary chancellors have always wielded a great deal of power, but Gerson Cohen could never have accomplished this revolutionary change in Seminary policy without significant faculty support. The heart of the Seminary faculty was its talmudists, the largest single grouping within the faculty, the source of its scholarly eminence, and not incidentally, the most traditionalist group in matters of religious practice. Louis Finkelstein's control of the Seminary's religious life was accomplished through a carefully cultivated alliance with this group of men, particularly with Professor Saul Lieberman, commonly acknowledged to be the outstanding talmudic scholar of his generation (at least outside the Orthodox *yeshivah* world), and an uncompromising traditionalist.

Lieberman's scholarly agenda was founded on the assumption that Judaism's rabbinic tradition did not grow in a vacuum but was, rather, part and parcel of the broader culture of antiquity that permeated it throughout. His mastery of this culture enabled him to illuminate countless Jewish texts and institutions that had puzzled Jewish authorities for centuries.

■ LOUIS FINKELSTEIN (left) wooed Saul Lieberman (right) to the Seminary in 1940—he was then teaching and writing in Israel—and he soon became the luminary of the Seminary faculty, the rabbi of its synagogue, and its unchallenged *halakhic* authority.

Earthy, imperious, gracious, and generous to friends and disciples yet devastating to scholarly opponents and to students who fell short of his scholarly or religious expectations, Lieberman (1898–1983) exercised unparalleled influence at the Seminary as well as in the Jewish scholarly world at large. His authority rested in his encyclopedic knowledge not only of the entire range of rabbinic literature but of Greek and Roman literature as well.

Finkelstein's retirement in 1972 marked the decline of Lieberman's influence on the Seminary's religious life. (Lieberman eventually retired, in 1981, and died on a flight to Israel on the eve of Passover 1983, just months before the faculty vote on ordination.) Cohen's accession to the chancellorship, his support of women's ordination, and Lieberman's retirement and death had a liberating effect on the younger members of the Talmud Department. In contrast to their teachers (all European born and all educated in European or Israeli academies), these young men (and soon, women as well) were American born and Seminary educated. Many were products of the Conservative Movement, of synagogue schools, and of Camp Ramah. They were involved personally in the feminist revolution. They were by instinct much closer to the center and liberal wings of the Movement than their predecessors had been. Ironically, their training and subsequent appointment to the Seminary faculty were the result of Finkelstein's determination to create a new generation of American-born scholars of Judaica.

More important, some of them were inclined to view the *halakhic* process in a more flexible way than had their predecessors. A number of them welcomed Cohen's invitation to write personal statements on the ordination issue. Some of these were, in fact, *halakhic* responsa, or formal legal opinions, buttressed with citations of precedents from the entire range of Jewish legal literature. Predictably, the statements prepared by Lieberman's disciples adamantly opposed the ordination of women. But the responsa of some of the younger scholars supported it. For the first time on a complex religious–*halakhic* issue, the Seminary's Talmud Department was split.

The most influential of this latter group of responsa was written by Rabbi Joel Roth. Raised in a Conservative synagogue in Detroit and educated at the Seminary, Roth was then Associate Professor of Talmud. His opinion is a long (with its footnotes it fills 60 pages in *The Ordination of Women* volume) and intricately argued case for the *halakhic* legitimacy of women rabbis.

The core of Roth's argument centers on the issue of the Jewish woman's relation to "time-bound" commandments, such as thrice-daily prayer. According to the tradition, women are freed from observing all positive commandments that have to be performed at a specific time, ostensibly because a woman's time is not always her own. According to Jewish law, a Jew who is not personally obligated to perform a specific commandment may not fulfill that obligation for another Jew. In our day the rabbi is constantly asked to observe certain commandments (e.g., leading the congregation in prayer as a *shaliah tzibbur,* literally "the representative of the community") in place of other Jews who cannot themselves fulfill the obligation. But how can a woman serve in this role as a rabbi if she herself is not obligated to observe these commandments?

Roth's answer is that Jewish law provides for the possibility of a woman's obligating herself to perform all the positive commandments, effectively overriding the freedom given to her by the tradition. His recommendation is that women who wish to enter the rabbinate should privately and personally perform this act of self-obligation; should they subsequently renounce that obligation, they should cease functioning as rabbis.

Roth's argument hardly convinced the traditionalists among the faculty. It was bitterly attacked by some of his colleagues in the Talmud Department. It served, however, as a powerful weapon for other talmudists and for many of their colleagues in other disciplines. There was clearly a sense among many of these scholars that, in principle, women should be ordained, but there was also a yearning for authenticity—specifically, *halakhic* authenticity. Roth's argument provided that element of security. For many, it was decisive. Even though the 1983 faculty vote explicity rejected the Roth proviso regarding self-obligation as a condition of women's admission to the school, it was later reintroduced by Chancellor Cohen's fiat.

■ THE FACT that Joel Roth, a product of a Conservative synagogue in Detroit, of Camp Ramah, and of the Seminary's own Rabbinical and Graduate schools, should have emerged as a respected talmudic scholar and *halakhic* authority is testimony to the Movement at its most effective.

In earlier years, even some members of the Seminary faculty voiced their conviction that only a product of a traditional *yeshivah* education could possibly do first-rate Talmud scholarship. That claim has long been discredited. Each year the Seminary's Graduate School produces academicians in Talmud as well as in every other field of Jewish studies. In 1992 Roth completed a term as Chair of the Rabbinical Assembly's Committee on Jewish Law and Standards and embarked on a second term as Dean of the Rabbinical School. He is commonly consulted on *halakhic* issues by rabbis throughout the Movement.

A New Faculty

The ordination vote was not simply the result of a new Talmud faculty, however. Death and retirement had taken their toll on the Finkelstein faculty as a whole. Their replacements, too, tended to be younger, American born or educated, and more flexible and liberal in religious outlook; some were women, and some were married to women who were professionals in their own right.

The traditionalists argued that an issue such as this one, with *halakhic* implications, should not be submitted to the democratic process, whereby every member of the faculty—including, for example, Hebrew-language instructors—enjoyed the same right to vote as the talmudists. They proposed that the vote be restricted to the rabbis on the faculty (thereby excluding faculty women, among others) or that it be referred to the reigning *halakhic* authority (Professor Lieberman in his day) or to a panel of *halakhic* authorities. Above all, non-*halakhists* or, more fuzzily, nonobservant faculty, should not have a voice. There was, however, no way of determining which members of the faculty should have a vote and which should not. Moreover, in the final analysis, Cohen responded, the issue facing the school was primarily one of academic policy, not *halakhah*. Who determines a school's academic policy if not the faculty as a whole? The entire faculty was to have its say, he insisted.

A New Consensus

Taken together, these changes within the Seminary have led to a reworking of the relationship between the school and the Movement. Louis Finkelstein's agenda had centered on reestablishing the chain of Jewish scholarship in America and on transmitting the enduring religious message of Judaism to America at large. It had little room for cultivating the Movement. However, that agenda, thoroughly justifiable in its day, had been largely accomplished. Jewish studies was on the curricula of most American schools, and American Jewish scholars, many of them Seminary trained, were producing a rich body of literature of enduring merit. Judaism itself had become one of the three recognized mainstream religious communities in America. Will Herberg's *Protestant, Catholic, Jew* (1955), a landmark study of the sociology of American religion, concluded that these three religious communities constituted "the three faces of American religion, the three 'pools' or 'melting pots' in and through which the American people is emerging as a national entity after a century of mass immigration." Judaism had arrived in America. Finkelstein's work was done.

Cohen was now free to turn to the Movement, and he headed a faculty that was itself largely a product of that Movement and sensitive to its needs. The ordination issue helped crystallize this new concern. The impulse had originated from outside the school, among the women who had been educated in the Movement; it had found expression in conventions of the United Synagogue, the Rabbinical Assembly, and the Women's League for Conservative Judaism. The call for direction finally reached the Seminary. This time the Seminary listened and responded.

In the process, the Movement was realigned. The issue was too divisive to have led to total integrity and consensus, of course. But instead of the horizontal divisions that had characterized the Movement for the better part of a century—Seminary versus rabbis versus laypeople—this new alignment was structured vertically: Seminary faculty, rabbis, and laypeople united on both sides of the feminist issue, roughly in a 3:1 ratio.

The Union for Traditional Judaism

The ordination vote served to bring to a head a long-simmering disaffection with the new directions being espoused by both school and Movement. Much of the criticism was directed at Cohen's religious posture, at specific political or personnel decisions he had made and more generally at the waning of the influence of Saul Lieberman and his disciples on school policy and at the school's abandoning its role as the bastion of traditionalism in the Movement. Even before the ordination vote in October 1983, the minority consensus had crystallized into a new organization, originally called the Union for Traditional Conservative Judaism but changed in 1990 to simply the Union for Traditional Judaism. The Founders' Conference of the Union took place on May 28, 1984.

The most significant aspect of the Union's break is that it took place at all. The break is testimony to the greater ideological cohesion that Conservative Judaism acquired under Gerson Cohen and in the light of the ordination of women. Until then, the Movement's ideology was so vague that no one had to break with it; its pluralistic impulse left room for the widest possible range of beliefs and programs. Gerson Cohen's own proclivities and the ordination issue alienated the right wing of the Movement, and the split was inevitable.

At the outset, the Union insisted that its goal was not to create further divisions within the Jewish community. It sought, rather, to serve as a lobby within Conservative Judaism for a more traditionalist approach to issues of belief and practice. The Union believed that the Conservative Movement had abandoned its roots, most dramatically in the ruling on ordination. The Union's goal was to guide the Movement back to its founding ideology.

The Union's membership currently numbers about 8,000 families, including about 325 rabbis. It publishes a quarterly newsletter, *Hagahelet* ("The Ember"), and an annual, *Cornerstone*. It sponsors its own Panel of *Halakhic* Inquiry (parallel to the Movement's Committee on Jewish Law and Standards), which rules on questions submitted to it and whose responsa are published periodically in a volume entitled *Tomeikh kaHalakhah* ("In Support of Halakhah"). It conducts an informal placement service, which tries to match rabbis and congregations who share the concerns of the group. More recently (March 1990) it announced the formation of a new rabbinical seminary, the Institute of Traditional Judaism.

The Union's initial statement identified the organization as being "in the spirit of Solomon Schechter." This is an accurate capsule summary of the group's agenda. It was founded on the assumption that the Movement's classical ideology—that *halakhah* must change by evolution and not revolution, that *halakhic* change must be "neither arbitrary nor open-ended," that such change must be guided by the leading rabbinic authorities of the day—which is represented most prominently in Schechter's writings, remains sound but that the Movement has abandoned Schechter and its own roots, most dramatically in the ruling on ordination.

Hagahelet

'A publication of the Union for Traditional Judaism'

Volume 3 / Number 3

UTJ •261 East Lincoln Ave.• Mt. Vernon, NY 10552 •Summer 5750/1990

"Tov shem mishemen tov"
A Good Name ...
by Rabbi Ronald D. Price, Executive Vice-President

■ THE UNION for Traditional Judaism began as a lobby for a more traditionalist approach to *halakhic* issues within the Conservative Movement, but it has since separated itself more and more from the Movement's institutions. The Union's decision to drop the label Conservative from its name symbolizes its independence. To all intents and purposes, it is now an independent movement, situated between Conservative Judaism and Orthodoxy. It has even negotiated a merger with a group of left-wing Orthodox rabbis (The Fellowship of Traditional Orthodox Rabbis). Pictured here is *Hagahelet,* the Union for Traditional Judaism's quarterly newsletter.

From Biblical times through to the present, names and their connotations have been matters of real import. The name by which the Jewish nation is known today results from a change in the patriarch Jacob's status and his subsequent change of name to Israel. Names are expected to reflect the essence of that which they name.

Several months ago our members received a letter which explained the thinking behind the proposed change in the name of our Union. I enclosed with that letter copies of resolutions which, if passed by at least a two-thirds majority of those members present at our annual conference, would put that name change into effect.

On May 27, the first day of the conference, these resolutions were passed by an overwhelming majority.

The name of our organization will now be the Union for Traditional Judaism. I am very pleased with the mandate to make this change. It does reflect the essence of that which it names. I believe that the community will henceforth be able to judge us based on our own actions and our contributions, rather than first measuring us against any particular movement. The trans-denominational nature of the Union can now more easily flourish.

Our name is a reflection of our identity. The Union for Traditional Judaism is the organization which teaches traditional observant Judaism to a community which today, by and large, is secular in its lifestyle. Our goal is *keruv*, to bring Jews into the world of Jewish observance. Our desire is to create and

nurture traditional communities which will be characterized by a lifestyle based on the values and observances of the Jewish tradition while remaining open to the modern world. Regardless of organizational affiliations, any individual can benefit from the programs and teachings of the UTJ. We hope that our name now makes us accessible to a broader constituency.

While the decision to change our name has received very positive reaction among our members, we were concerned for those of our constituents who are also members of Conservative synagogues and organizations. It is important that they not feel abandoned by our decision to remove the word Conservative from our title. As we develop our truly trans-denominational program, it is more important than ever that our Traditional Conservative constituents receive our services and our *hizzuk*. If you are one who shares this concern, I ask that you

call or write to me directly to express it. I assure you that the Union continues to be prepared to assist you in maintaining and enhancing the traditional nature of your community and your lifestyle.

In *parashat beha'alotkhah* Aaron is given instructions on the lighting of the seven branched menorah in the Tabernacle. Rashi is puzzled at the special word used here for "lighting" (*beha'alotkhah*) which literally means "raising up". He explains that "he (Aaron) must kindle the light until the flame goes up by itself..." The Union for Traditional Judaism has this goal set before it. Each Jewish soul is a light that should burn brightly with passion and love for the Holy One Blessed Be He and for His Torah. We must try to kindle those lights "until the flame goes up by itself", and then we must kindle still another. We pray that our change in name will help us reach more souls that are waiting to be kindled.

Douglas Aronin, UTJ Vice President, presents proposal for name change at Conference '90

The name of Saul Lieberman is regularly invoked in Union publications (the name of its publication, "The Ember," is taken from a letter Lieberman addressed to the Union's founders, in which he referred to the group as the last surviving "ember" of the

Movement's classical traditionalism), but its regnant religious authority is Rabbi David Weiss-Halivni, currently Professor in the Department of Religion at Columbia University. A Holocaust survivor, Weiss–Halivni came to the Seminary as a young man, shortly after arriving in America. He was ordained and obtained his Doctorate of Hebrew Literature degree in Talmud (the highest degree then offered by the Seminary) under the tutelage of Saul Lieberman, and he soon joined the Seminary faculty. Very quickly Weiss–Halivni achieved international fame as a master of rabbinic literature and the most accomplished talmudist of his generation outside the Orthodox *yeshivah* world.

Most of Weiss–Halivni's writings are devoted to his scholarly concerns, but he has also written on contemporary issues. His approach is consistent with that of his teachers at the Seminary and with the Seminary's founding ideology: an open, critical, scholarly mind-set combined with a strong traditionalist bent in matters of religious practice. He clearly provides the Union with its stamp of scholarly authenticity.

The Union's ideological position emerges notably in an address given by Weiss–Halivni at the Seminary on the occasion of the first anniversary of Lieberman's death. Was Lieberman troubled, Weiss–Halivni asks, by the lack of synthesis between "his simple beliefs and scrupulous observance and his classical sophistication and sense of historical development?" Weiss–Halivni's answer: "Not at all! The truly great need no synthesis. . . . The truly great do not need to trim edges, as it were, to make genuine experiences fit with each other. They preserve them intact. And if their experiences appear contradictory, they build an emotional bridge spanning them allowing both the landscape and the water to be seen." Here is the Frankel-Schechter-Finkelstein tradition, with a vengeance!

Weiss–Halivni opposed the ordination decision. In the fall of 1986 he left the Seminary to accept an appointment at Columbia. It is not clear how decisive a role the ordination issue played in that decision, but it was certainly one factor among others.

At this writing, the future of the Union will depend largely on how it handles two critical challenges. First, will it remain a one-issue organization, devoted only to fighting the feminist issue again and again? By and large, it is the feeling of most Conservative Jews that the Movement has made its peace with the new feminism, that the tide cannot be reversed, and that those remaining rabbis and congregations that refuse to go along will eventually drop out.

The Union claims that it has put the feminist issue behind it. It has moved aggressively into promoting Sabbath and *kashrut* observance among the laity, a challenge that the rest of the Movement has only begun to take seriously. It is also possible that the Movement will hand the Union some other issue—it might have been patrilineal descent, but on this issue the Movement has reaffirmed the traditional position. Whatever happens in the future, the Union's survival may well depend on its ability to expand its agenda in a convincing way.

The second, and more important challenge, is whether Schechter's ideology is adequate and even viable for the Movement today. Most Conservative Jews would question whether it is. The perspective of this volume is that Schechter's ideology was seriously flawed; it was filled with unresolved tensions, it sidestepped the central theological issues, and it led to a message that the lay community could only find bewildering, for it offered no clear way of justifying why certain departures from traditional practice were legitimate and others were not. All of these problems persist in the Union's various ideological statements. But clearly, the Union would disagree with that assessment.

The presence of a loyal opposition within the confines of the Conservative Movement could serve as a source of increased vitality. It could sharpen the issues, present alternative options for many congregants and rabbis, and serve as a reminder of the Movement's roots. If Conservative Judaism takes its commitment to pluralism seriously, it should have room for a grouping of this kind. But this scenario assumes that the Union is serious about working within the Movement.

That intention is admittedly uncertain. Can you have your own Panel of Halakhic Inquiry and your own placement service (effectively sidestepping the Movement's Committee on Jewish Law and Standards and its Placement Committee) and still claim to be working within the Movement? Possibly. But the Union's two most recent decisions—to drop the word *Conservative* from its name and to establish its own rabbinical seminary—seem to remove any shade of ambiguity. It would seem that even though individual members of the Union, lay and rabbinic, have retained their formal affiliation with the United Synagogue and the Rabbinical Assembly, the Union itself has effectively forfeited its opportunity to influence the future course of Conservative Judaism.

A New Integrity

The ordination of women is a landmark in the history of Conservative Judaism. It lent the Movement the integrity it lacked for the better part of a century. In one stroke, it erased the inner tensions of the Movement's founding ideology. Seminary, rabbinate, and lay community together had effectively affirmed that whatever else Torah is, it is also a cultural document, that it has always been and will continue to be affected by historical considerations, and that it is the Jewish community in every generation that serves as the authority for the ongoing shape of Judaism in matters of belief and practice.

Of course, the decision itself did not proclaim all of these ideas in any explicit way. Yet a year after that first body of women rabbinical students began their Seminary studies, in the fall of 1985, a group of rabbis and academicians representing the Seminary and the University of Judaism met for the first time as the Commission on the Philosophy of Conservative Judaism. Close to three years later, in the spring of 1988, the fruit of the Commission's work, a pamphlet entitled *Emet Ve-Emunah: Statement of Principles of Conservative Judaism,* was unveiled at a Rabbinical Assembly meeting. The Movement had its first platform. What the ordination decision had only implicitly affirmed, *Emet Ve-Emunah* said clearly and forthrightly.

9 | A STATEMENT OF PRINCIPLES

" Given our changing world, finality and certainty are illusory at best, destructive at worst. Rather than claiming to have found a goal at the end of the road, the ideal Conservative Jew is a traveler walking purposefully towards 'God's holy mountain.' **"**

——*Emet Ve-Emunah*

A Virtue of Necessity

The decision of the Seminary founders to avoid producing an ideological platform made a virtue out of a necessity. What was necessary above all was to avoid splintering their anti-Reform coalition. In this, the founders were eminently successful. Within a decade of Schechter's death in 1915, the newly created Conservative Movement was on solid footing.

It took over a century for the Movement to produce its own ideological platform. As long as the Movement was flourishing, the nagging sense of inner vapidity and ideological confusion could be successfully repressed. Toward the end of the Finkelstein chancellorship, however, as the sense of a movement in crisis began to emerge, it became apparent that this strategy had become counterproductive.

The women's ordination issue brought the problem to a head. First, it was inherently divisive; it could not but bring the strains and tensions in the founding ideology to the surface. Further, the Yankelovitch and Liebman–Shapiro surveys of the beliefs and practices among the lay community highlighted the demographic crisis facing the Movement and the wide and growing gap that separated the Seminary's understanding of Conservative Judaism from that of its lay body. Finally, Orthodoxy and Reform had become explicitly ideological. The ideological issue had to be tackled again.

Early Attempts at Ideology

The Movement had made earlier attempts at defining its ideological stance. The creation of the United Synagogue in 1913 forced Solomon Schechter to compose a statement of objectives for this new body, and that statement achieved some authoritative standing as the Preamble to its Constitution. The statement deserves mention, not only for what it says but for also what it leaves unsaid. According to Schechter, the "purpose" of this new body would be:

> The advancement of the cause of Judaism in America and the maintenance of Jewish tradition in its historical continuity,
>
> To assert and establish loyalty to the Torah and its historical expositions,
>
> To further the observance of the Sabbath and the dietary laws,
>
> To preserve in the service the reference to Israel's past and the hopes for Israel's restoration,
>
> To maintain the traditional character of the liturgy, with Hebrew as the language of prayer,
>
> To foster Jewish religious life in the home as expressed in the traditional observances,
>
> To encourage the establishment of Jewish religious schools, in the curricula of which the study of the Hebrew language and literature shall be given a prominent place, both as the key to the true understanding of Judaism, and as a bond holding together the scattered communities of Israel throughout the world. It shall be the aim of the United Synagogue of America, while not endorsing the innovations introduced by any of its constituent bodies, to embrace all elements essentially loyal to traditional Judaism and in sympathy with the purpose outlined above.

The statement (given here in its entirety) is fascinating. The bulk of the statement is clearly directed against Reform. In fact, it would be difficult to find an Orthodox Jew who would disagree with any of its specifics. Who but a Reform Jew would not support the references to Israel's restoration, the traditional liturgy, Hebrew, Sabbath and dietary laws, and traditional home observances? True, the reference to Judaism's "historical expositions" might be construed as acknowledging the appeal to history that was integral to the school's founding ideology, but both the phrase itself and the way in which history was to be viewed are vague enough to blunt the force of the reference.

But note the absence of even the slightest reference to theology, to God, to revelation, or to why Torah is authoritative in the first place. And note also the last sentence. This was Schechter's oblique acknowledgment that this movement was going to come up with innovations that would be potentially divisive. He would not stop that process, and the new organization would never "endorse" them, but as long as these elements were "loyal to traditional Judaism," a phrase broad enough to drive a truck through, they would be welcome. But eventually both Mordecai Kaplan—who had joined the faculty just four years earlier and was beginning to propound those theories that would make him a center of controversy—and the traditionalists in the coalition eventually felt more and more alienated, and they broke away.

STRUGGLES WITH SELF-DEFINITION

As early as 1931 the Rabbinical Assembly passed a resolution urging the organization to "define [its] attitude toward the fundamental problems of Judaism"; a committee was appointed to do just that, but its work came to naught. The diversity of views within the committee itself, let alone within the Movement at large, precluded the possibility of agreement. In 1956 the Rabbinical Assembly made still another attempt to address the ideological problem when it created a Continuing Conference on Conservative Ideology, chaired by Rabbi Jacob Agus of Baltimore. The Movement needed a body of this kind because it "suffers from the absence of deep convictions and from the shallowness of formal allegiance." This Conference, like its predecessor, yielded neither platform nor program.

The Formation of the Commission

It is to be expected that the relationship between the Chancellor of the Seminary and the President of the Rabbinical Assembly will be strained. The two individuals represent different constituencies with different agendas. This tension was particularly strong during the years of the Finkelstein chancellorship. Finkelstein was concerned primarily with building the Seminary's academic reputation and preserving the traditionalist cast of the Movement. The Assembly, for its part, was becoming more and more independent. It was tackling the problems of the community in an innovative and creative way. It was publishing prayerbooks, and its Law Committee was trying to deal with contemporary issues, such as the new feminism. But the new prayerbooks were never accepted in the Seminary synagogue, and the Law Committee's responsa were generally derided by Seminary talmudists. The tension was blatant.

As Chancellor, Gerson Cohen tried to reverse that trend. Cohen did not have Finkelstein's stake in *halakhic* traditionalism, and he was much more concerned with the fate and direction of the Movement. Cohen's relationships with Rabbinical Assembly presidents were generally marked by a shared concern for the problems facing the congregational rabbi. It was in this context that Cohen and Rabbi Alexander Shapiro, President of the Assembly from 1984 to 1986, evolved the notion of forming a Joint Commission to write a Statement of Principles for Conservative Judaism.

As originally conceived, the Commission was to be made up of eight academicians from the Seminary (this writer being one of them) and its West Coast school, the University of Judaism, and eight congregational rabbis (hence, the Joint Commission). An attempt was made to include representatives of the various ideological perspectives within the Movement. It included, for example, Rabbi David Novak, a founder of the Union for Traditional Judaism and a member of its Panel for Halakhic Inquiry, as well as Rabbi Ludwig Nadelmann, prominently identified with Kaplan's Reconstructionist movement. (Nadelmann's sudden and untimely death in the course of the Commission's deliberations was a severe blow to its work.) To chair the Commission, Cohen and Shapiro selected Robert Gordis. That choice was inspired and decisive.

Gordis was one of the handful of the Movement's leaders who had successfully combined a career as an academician and a congregational rabbi. Although he was primarily a Bible scholar, he had written extensively on theological, philosophical, and social issues

■ TALL, IMPERIOUS, and authoritative, Robert Gordis (1909–1992) was known for his unique ability to compress more ideas and words in a one-hour lecture than most other humans could do in two (for which his students affectionately dubbed him "Rapid Robert"). He was a veteran of the Movement's ideological warfare and past president of the Rabbinical Assembly. Though he had campaigned vigorously for the ordination of women, he was as close to the ideological center of the Movement as one could be. At the time of the Commission's formation, Gordis, then in his 78th year and retired from both pulpit and classroom, was universally recognized as one of the Movement's genuine elder statesmen.

facing Judaism, all the while holding a pulpit in Rockaway Park, New York. Throughout the more than two years of the Commission's work, Gordis' chairmanship was exemplary. He achieved a perfect balance of authority and collegiality, cutting through discussions that seemed to be getting no place quickly yet respecting the views of even the most junior members of the group. His uncanny skill with words enabled him to suggest a formulation of a complex and potentially divisive issue in a way that would satisfy every point of view.

The Commission met for the first time on October 15, 1985. It would meet for ten additional two- to three-day sessions until November 10, 1987, when the document called *Emet Ve-Emunah: Statement of Principles of Conservative Judaism* was substantially completed. The text of the document was unveiled at a Rabbinical Assembly gathering in March 1988.

The first meeting of the Commission was devoted to a discussion of the general shape and tone of the document that the Commission hoped to produce. A list of topics to be covered was prepared, and each member of the Commission volunteered to be responsible for shepherding one or two of these topics through the process of drafting and rewriting. As a preliminary assignment, Gordis requested that each member of the Commission prepare a personal ideological statement, which was to be read and discussed by the Commission as a whole. This assignment was to prove invaluable; it enabled the participants to get to know each other and to sample the range of positions on all the issues facing the Commission before beginning the work of drafting the statement itself. (One of the precious memories of those early meetings was the sight of the members of the Commission, all Gordis' former students, tearing into Gordis' personal statement with as much gusto as they did into each other's.)

That first meeting also produced the Commission's first overt clash—over an issue that was symptomatic of the very conditions that had brought the group together. Some members voiced their disappointment that the lay community was not represented on the Commission. If the ultimate goal was to give the Movement an ideological identity and if the ultimate "consumer" of the Commission's work was to be Conservative congregants, should they not participate in the preparation of the document? In contrast, the defenders of the Commission's makeup were motivated by the fear that its deliberations promised to be stormy, and there was no guarantee that its work would be successful. Why should laypeople be exposed to still additional confusion? Wouldn't their presence inhibit the rabbis and academicians from exposing the full range of their disagreements? The issue was joined, and the Commission voted to restrict its membership to the original appointees. That decision was reversed at the next meeting, and six laypeople joined the Commission as full-fledged members.

Early on, the Commission decided that it would be impossible to submit whatever document emerged from its deliberations to a formal vote by any of the branches of the Movement. Who should vote? The United Synagogue? The Rabbinical Assembly? The Seminary faculty? And on what should they vote? The entire document as a whole? Each section? Paragraph? Sentence? Even possibly specific words? The spectacle of any such procedure was simply ludicrous. The Commission itself almost never resorted to a formal vote in determining the wording of even the most controversial passages. The Statement would have to stand on its own and be accepted or rejected to the extent that Conservative Jews would decide either to use it or ignore it.

Emet Ve-Emunah

The Commission's final document is 40 pages in length; a shorter or longer statement was ruled out, the former because it would be excessively vague, the latter because it would be too cumbersome. It is divided into three sections: "God in the World," on theological issues; "The Jewish People," on issues of communal concern; and "Living a Life of Torah," on issues of Jewish religious expression.

God in the World

The most remarkable aspect of this first section is that it is there at all. The five short statements on "God," "Revelation," "*Halakhah* (Jewish Law)," "The Problem of Evil," and "Eschatology: Our Vision of the Future" provide, for the first time in any authoritative Conservative document, a theological underpinning for the Movement's ideology.

The Commission's policy was to try to produce a consensual statement, to settle on a language that would satisfy all members of the group, but theological issues rarely lend themselves to clear and precise formulation. When it was impossible to achieve consensus, the statement would list a number of possible options and indicate that any or all of these positions are equally legitimate. To everyone's surprise, that second strategy was invoked far less frequently than was anticipated, but a disproportionately large number of those instances occur in this first section, particularly on the first three issues.

Regarding God, the statement articulates two different positions on God's nature: a traditionalist image of God as "a supreme, supernatural being" who "has the power to command and control the world through His will," and a more Kaplanian image of God as "not a being to whom we can point" but rather "a presence and a power that transcends us," a God who is "present when we look for meaning in the world, when we work for morality, for justice, and for future redemption." (p. 18)

Regarding revelation, the statement concedes that it can be understood either as a personal encounter between God and human

■ THEOLOGICAL CONSENSUS was never as important in Judaism as it was in Christianity. The essential authenticating act for the Christian is the belief that God became incarnate (i.e. flesh) in the person of Jesus of Nazareth and that Jesus' death and resurrection are the source of salvation for all human beings. The Christian who does not accept these ideas is simply not a Christian. That claim can be understood in many different ways, however. Therefore, the theological elaboration of this belief becomes absolutely indispensable to the very viability of Christian religion.

There is no Jewish parallel to this Christian authenticating belief. The Jew is a Jew by birth (or by conversion), and if there is any criterion for religious authenticity, it is much more a matter of behavior—of observance—than of belief. In this context, then, *Emet Ve-Emunah*'s openness to theological pluralism is an authentically Jewish position.

Very rarely in Jewish intellectual history has anyone even tried to specify what the Jew must believe in order to be an authentic Jew. Moses Maimonides (1135–1204), the premier Jewish philosopher of the Middle Ages, represents the major exception—his Thirteen Principles of Faith is the most famous of these attempts—but on this issue, Maimonides was a lonely voice. Not only his choice of principles but even the very notion that there exists such a list were roundly criticized.

beings that has "propositional content" (i.e., that God revealed actual thoughts and/or words to Israel); or as an "ineffable human encounter with God" where the words of the Torah were formulated by human beings, though with divine inspiration; or, again in the Kaplanian tradition, as Israel's "continuing discovery, through nature and history, of truths about God and the world." (p. 20)

Finally, regarding the *halakhic* process, the statement legitimizes two approaches to dealing with laws that appear to be immoral (such as the issue of the *agunah,* the woman who cannot get a bill of divorce from her husband) and laws that are not susceptible to the normative processes of legal change (i.e., by writing responsa that try to find a precedent or by finding extralegal factors that would justify modifying the law). "Some within the Conservative community are prepared to amend the existing law by means of a formal procedure of legislation." Others "are willing to make a change only when they find it justified by sources in the *halakhic* literature." (p. 24)

These divergent opinions in no way cancel out the substantial consensus that was reached on much of the material. The statement affirms "the critical importance of belief in God" and, much more controversially, states that "proponents of both views use metaphors to speak of God"; it insists that revelation is "the uncovering of an external source of truth emanating from God"; it affirms that *"Halakhah* is indispensable . . . because it is what the Jewish community understands God's will to be." Further, the last two sections of this portion of the document are concise summaries of classical Jewish thinking on the problem of evil and on the end of days.

THE END OF DAYS

The chapter of Jewish thought dealing with the events that will take place at the end of days—the coming of the Messiah, the last judgment, the return to Zion, the rebuilding of the Temple and the resurrection of the dead, and so on—poses manifold problems for most Jews. Traditional Jewish teachings on all of these topics vary widely; since no one really knows what will take place at the end, the imagination was given wide latitude.

Since the descriptions of these scenarios are invariably touched with fantasy and seem to strain our credulity, most rabbis simply avoid discussing this material. Is it to be taken literally? As metaphor or myth? As great poetry? The problem with avoiding these topics, however, is that they are to be found everywhere in Jewish literature—in the Bible, in rabbinic literature, and in the liturgy. Anyone familiar with these texts can only wonder how they are to be understood. The section of *Emet Ve-Emunah* that deals with these issues represents one attempt to convey their meaning in a way that coheres with a modern mind-set.

One more word on this section of the document is needed. What is most significant about *Emet Ve-Emunah* is that it provides the first consistent and coherent theological grounding for much of what the Movement has said and done for generations. We should not forget that although Conservative Judaism has always affirmed the binding nature of Jewish law, it had also just sanctioned a major departure from classical Jewish practice by voting to ordain women, and this decision was but the latest in a series of such departures: mixed seating in the synagogue, driving on the Sabbath, and the marriage of a *kohen* to a convert or to a divorcée, among others. We also know that the implicit ideology of the Movement viewed Torah, whatever its divine source, as a cultural document that has always responded to changing historical conditions and that can therefore be studied with all of the resources available for the study of any human creation.

The statement that Torah is a cultural document is a complex theological claim. It says something about God, about how God's will was transmitted to a human community, about what happened at Sinai, about the respective roles of God and a human community in formulating the content of revelation, and about what we mean when we say that we are commanded to observe the Sabbath. In order to address all of these issues, the Movement needed to define its theological position. With *Emet Ve-Emunah,* it finally articulated a theological basis for what it had stood for since its founding.

Consider the following three statements, one from each of the first three sections of *Emet Ve-Emunah:*

1. "Although proponents of both views [on the nature of God] use metaphors to speak of God . . ." (p. 19)
2. "We also reject fundamentalism and literalism, which do not admit a human component in revelation, thus excluding an independent role for human experience and reason in the process." (p. 20)
3. *"Halakhah* is . . . what the Jewish community understands God's will to be." (p. 21)

Taken together, these three statements articulate a theology that reads something like the following: No human being can say precisely and objectively what God is. That's what makes God God (i.e., totally other than anything within human experience). All of our characterizations of God, then, are metaphors, human approximations of a reality that remains beyond human understanding. As a result, any statement about God as revealer of Torah is also metaphorical. God could not really "speak" at Sinai because to attribute speech to God is another one of the classic Jewish metaphors. But if God did not speak at Sinai, then the words of Torah are human words—whatever God's role in revelation may be—and Torah as it has come down to us is legitimately a human document. It can be studied as any other human document, and its authority rests in the community, for in the last analysis, it is the human community, not God, that formulated the contents of that document. *Halakhah* is thus the community's understanding of God's will, not—note well—God's will but, rather, Israel's understanding of that will.

The implication of this position is that a modern community of Jews can introduce changes in *halakhah* to the extent that it wishes to do so. It does not have to change anything. But it must understand that if it remains bound to traditional practice, it does so because of where it *decides* to set its parameters, not because of where the parameters are intrinsically set; in addition, it has to acknowledge that other communities within the Jewish people may set their parameters elsewhere. That is also their right.

The above is admittedly a selective reading of *Emet Ve-Emunah's* theology. It is not the only possible reading, and it is certainly possible to read the text in a more traditionalist mode. This reading is also one attempt at making the implicit theology of Conservative Judaism explicit. It accounts for the way in which *halakhah* has developed within the Movement; it explains for exam-

ple, why the Movement has accepted feminism but rejected patrilineal descent, why it has maintained a host of Sabbath regulations but permitted driving to the synagogue.

The Jewish People

The Commission achieved substantial consensus on most of the six sections that make up this portion of the document: "God's Covenant: The Election of Israel," "The State of Israel and the Role of Religion," "Israel and the Diaspora," "Between Jew and Fellow Jew," "Relations with Other Faiths," and "Social Justice: Building a Better World." There are no "some of us believe X, others believe Y" formulations in this material. However, the debate on the relations of the American wing of the Movement to its Israeli confreres was long and bitter.

When the Commission was put together, an attempt was made to include representatives of every significant interest group in the Movement at large. In retrospect, it is striking that the one significant group that was not originally represented was the Israeli branch of the Movement. This omission was probably the result of logistical considerations; it was simply unrealistic for Israelis to travel to New York three or four times a year to participate in the Commission's deliberations. Still, it's not wildly speculative to suggest that on an unconscious level this omission was a reflection of the Movement's priorities. Our study of the Movement's founding

■ THE NOTION that all of our characterizations of God are metaphors is not original with *Emet Ve-Emunah.* It is also a cornerstone of Maimonides' theology. He devotes much of the first part of his monumental *Guide to the Perplexed* to disabusing his readers of the belief that the Torah's anthropomorphic descriptions of God (e.g., "The hand of God" in Exod. 9:3) are literally true. In his *Mishneh Torah* he enunciates the principle that all such expressions are "adapted to the mental capacity of the majority of mankind who have a clear perception of physical bodies only. The Torah speaks in the language of men. All these phrases are metaphorical. . . . But God's essence as it really is, the human mind does not understand and is incapable of grasping or investigating" (*Book of Knowledge,* 1:9). In other words, literal God-language is unacceptable because it demeans God. Whether Maimonides would have carried his position to as radical a conclusion as did the authors of *Emet Ve-Emunah* is another issue. Pictured here is Michelangelo's *The Creation of Man* from the Sistine Chapel.

ideology showed that Conservative Judaism never had an anti-Zionist streak—Zionism was one of the issues on which it broke with Reform—but its Zionist commitments were never very forcefully articulated, at least in any authoritative way.

Besides, the Conservative Movement was a Diaspora movement, created by and for a Diaspora Jewry. Its very existence assumed the legitimacy and viability of Jewish religious life in the Diaspora. It was thus inevitable that however sympathetic the Commission's feelings about Israel, any statement it produced in that regard would be balanced with an affirmation of loyalty to Diaspora Judaism.

The members of the Commission were largely in agreement on these issues. The conflict arose when early drafts of these statements were sent to the official bodies of the Movement in Israel.

The final version of the document deals with two issues: the place of religion in Israeli life and the relationship between Israeli and Diaspora Jewries. On the first, the Commission vigorously protests Orthodoxy's monopoly of Israeli religious life in matters of conversion, marriage, and divorce and insists that a Conservative reading of Judaism be granted legitimacy for those who want to associate with the Movement. Israel "is and ought to be a democratic state" that must express the will of the majority and protect the right of minorities. Since the State was founded for all Jews, it "must in its actions and laws provide for the pluralism of Jewish life." (pp. 34–35)

In this spirit, "The State should permit all rabbis, regardless of affiliation, to perform religious functions, including officiating at marriages, divorces and conversions." "We regard it as an overriding moral principle that neither the State nor its political subdivisions and agencies employ coercion in the area of religious belief and practice." The document insists that matters of personal status (e.g., marriage and divorce) should fall under secular, not Jewish, law and that the State "should provide civil options for marriage and divorce for those who so prefer, while empowering each religious community to handle its own ritual requirements." (p. 35)

On this issue the statement is powerful and unambiguous. It reflects over four decades of the Movement's frustration with the systematic delegitimization of all non-Orthodox religious communities at the hands of a small but militant Orthodox minority—a minority that controls the religious life of the State through sheer political coercion.

It was the second statement, the one dealing with Israel and the Diaspora, that kindled the ire of Israeli Conservative Jews. Rabbi Benjamin Segal, then Director of Camp Ramah in Israel, soon came to New York, joined the Commission, and argued in support of their position.

The debate revolved around the issue of the exclusive centrality of the State of Israel for the Jewish community around the world. The consensus of the Commission was to espouse a dual-center model. It argued that Jewish life had flourished and could continue to flourish both in Israel and in the Diaspora, that each center enjoyed different advantages and faced unique challenges, and that each could enrich the other.

What else could a group of American Jews say on this issue unless it was prepared to advocate that the entire Movement pack its bags and move to Israel, something it was clearly not prepared to do? At the same time, their position was not the kind that a community made up largely of former American Jews who had moved to Israel was prepared to endorse.

Rabbi Segal argued on two fronts. First, he proposed the inclusion of a separate statement entitled "Israel: People and Land," which would precede the "Israel and the Diaspora" section and would capture the sense in which *Eretz Yisrael* was the promised land since the beginning of our history as a people, designated by God as Israel's unique home, the focus of generations of Jewish loyalty, yearnings, and expectations. A straightforward statement of this kind, Rabbi Segal argued, was absolutely mandatory if only because this is what Jews have believed for centuries. No document claiming to express classical Judaism could possibly ignore it.

Second, on Israel–Diaspora relations, Segal argued that only Israel can serve as a center for Jewish life. Israel alone provides the Jew with the opportunity to live a life totally informed by Jewishness. Only in Israel is Jewish self-determination assured, is Hebrew the language of the community, is the Bible taught in all schools at all levels,

■ THE MOST pernicious effect of the polarization of the religious right in Israel is its impact on the large majority of Israelis who are either staunchly secularist or religious moderates. They view the ultra-Orthodox Jews as angry, confrontational, imperialistic, exclusivist, and aggressively political in achieving their aim, which is nothing less than imposing their reading of Judaism on Israeli society as a whole. The ultra-Orthodox Jews believe that if Jewish law forbids one to attend the cinema on the Sabbath, then no Israeli Jew, whatever his or her proclivities, should be permitted to attend the cinema! In effect, they use political clout and confrontational tactics to achieve what they have been unable to achieve by education and persuasion. The ultimate loser is Jewish religion itself. What sensitive and spiritually inclined Israeli would want to identify with a tradition of this kind? Pictured here is an ultra-Orthodox Jew in Jerusalem protesting the practice of Saturday film screenings, which the Orthodox believe desecrate the Sabbath.

is the calendar a Jewish calendar, are the Sabbath and festivals national holidays. More important, only in Israel does the Jew have to struggle with the issues raised by sovereignty and political power.

Ultimately, the Commission decided to retain the substance of the original Israel and Diaspora draft but to incorporate into it some of the language of Segal's two statements. In its final form the statement recalls that "throughout the ages, we have revered, honored, cherished, prayed for, dreamed of, and sought to settle in Jerusalem and the Land of Israel." (p. 37) It also lists Israel's unique opportunities for "an all-encompassing Jewish life."

Then, however, it adds, "Paradoxically, the very ease with which Jewish identity may be expressed in the Jewish state may give the false impression that religion is not needed in Israel for Jewish survival as it is in the Diaspora." (p. 39) In that spirit, the statement also acknowledges the unique problems of Diaspora Judaism, preeminently its failure to "resolve the problem of assimilation," but it also lists the manifold contributions of the Diaspora in the course of Jewish history, tracing the ways in which the two communities "interacted in a continual symbiotic process of mutual enrichment." (p. 39) The thrust of the statement is best captured in the sentence "Our religion has been land-centered but never land-bound; it has been a portable religion so that despite our long exile (*Galut*) from our spiritual homeland, we have been able to survive creatively and spiritually even in the *tefutzot* (Diaspora)." (p. 38)

It is not surprising, then, that *Emet Ve-Emunah* has not been translated into Hebrew. It has, in fact, been largely ignored by the Israeli movement.

Of the remaining four statements in this portion of the document, two merit special attention. "God's Covenant: The Election of Israel" affirms unapologetically the classical doctrine of the chosenness of the Jewish people, an integral part of traditional Jewish thinking until the modern period. Reform Judaism, and later Mordecai Kaplan, perceived this doctrine as conflicting with the universalism of the age. It also became too easily confused with doctrines of racial or national superiority. Although Kaplan's influence pervades much of *Emet Ve-Emunah*, on this issue he was repudiated.

To the surprise of some members of the Commission, the section on "Relations with Other Faiths" occasioned a good deal of debate within the group. The thrust of the draft statement affirmed that Judaism does not hold a monopoly on religious truth, that religious truth is relative, not absolute, that the most we can say is that Judaism is true for us, as other religious traditions are true for other religious communities.

This position was simply an inevitable implication of much of what had been propounded in the theological section of the statement. If all of our references to God are human metaphors, if revelation involves a substantive human component, if Jewish law is Israel's understanding of God's will (not God's will itself), then it would seem only natural to affirm that different communities may view God and God's will in ways different from those of the Jews. Although the explicit religious relativism of this position disturbed

some members of the Commission, the final version of the statement retains this thrust intact. It affirms that "God may well have seen fit to enter covenants with many nations." And again, "theological humility requires us to recognize that although we have but one God, God has more than one nation." (p. 43)

Living a Life of Torah

The five sections in this final portion—"On Women," "The Jewish Home", *"Tefillah* (Prayer)," *"Talmud Torah* (Jewish Study)," and "The Ideal Conservative Jew"—provided little reason for controversy, though some members of the Commission felt that to include a separate statement on the role of the Jewish woman was in itself demeaning: If women are truly the equal of men, they should not be singled out for separate treatment, however positive that treatment might be.

■ BY THE late 1950s, Abraham Joshua Heschel had emerged as American Jewry's premier spokesperson on a wide range of social and political issues. His theological writings, describing the religious experience as a fundamental *human,* as opposed to *Jewish* impulse, were widely read in Christian circles. He was therefore the natural choice of American Jewish organizations to negotiate with the leaders of the Catholic Church in Rome, before and during Vatican Council II, to eliminate or modify passages in the Catholic liturgy that demeaned Jews and called for their eventual conversion to Christianity. Heschel argued vigorously that no single religious community could claim an exclusive monopoly on religious truth.

■ THE SECTION in *Emet Ve-Emunah* on the Jewish home marks a startling but inevitable turnabout in the priorities of the Movement. Conservative Judaism had never explicitly said that it had given up on the Jewish home, but, in fact, it had focused its energies on the synagogue and the synagogue school. This statement constitutes a belated recognition that if the home does not provide a rich environment for the Jewish experience, there is little hope for transmitting identity from generation to generation.

There is still much in this portion that merits attention. The section on prayer, for example, is the longest single statement in the entire document. It is a sensitive and insightful delineation of the many purposes of Jewish prayer. The statement on study reaffirms the classical Conservative commitment to both traditional exegesis and "modern, historical methods."

Finally, "The Ideal Conservative Jew" is a recognition that the Movement originated as a distinctive reading of Judaism designed to cultivate a "wholeness in Jewish personalities," in which "modernity and tradition inform and reshape each other." In that spirit, the document concludes, the ideal Conservative Jew is a "willing" Jew, a "learning" Jew, and a "striving" Jew: a willing Jew because Jewish commitment involves a decision to "refract all aspects of life through the prism of one's Jewishness"; a learning Jew because one cannot be whole as a Jew without commitment to serious and ongoing study of the tradition; and a striving Jew because "what is needed is an openness to those observances one has yet to perform and the desire to grapple with those issues and texts one has yet to confront." (pp. 56–57)

Criticisms of *Emet Ve-Emunah*

Emet Ve-Emunah has been attacked on a variety of fronts: specific word choices, omissions (or inclusions), positions advocated, and the style of the document as a whole. Some examples of each are examined here.

Wording

The section on "The Problem of Evil" includes the following sentence: "Given the enormity of the horror represented by Auschwitz and Hiroshima, this dilemma [of reconciling faith in God with the existence of evil] has taken on a new, terrifying reality in our generation." (p. 25) Critics have protested this equating of Auschwitz and Hiroshima. It has been perceived as diminishing the impact of the Holocaust by universalizing it. Furthermore, since the destruction of Hiroshima was a legitimate act of war against an enemy aggressor, why does it pose a theological dilemma? Others have defended the pairing of these two atrocities. Interestingly, not once in the many internal debates over the wording of this section did any member of the Commission question this particular sentence.

Omissions and Inclusions

There is no statement on Jewish ritual behavior, such as the dietary laws, the wearing of *tallit* and *tefillin*, and Sabbath and festival observances. In fact, a draft statement on ritual was prepared by the late Rabbi Nadelmann and hotly debated. Rabbi Nadelmann was asked to rewrite his statement but he died in the interim, and the issue was shelved. When it was raised once again toward the end of the Commission's work, it was decided that much of what the Commission had to say on the issue was included in the sections on *halakhah*, prayer, and the Jewish home. In retrospect, that decision was probably a significant error in judgment. Conservative Jews have not been noted for their devotion to the rituals of Jewish life, and part of the reason is that the Movement has never been clear on just what these observances mean and why they should be taken seriously by Jews who no longer believe that we do them simply because "God says so."

As to inclusions, we referred earlier to the protests surrounding the separate section on Jewish women. The Commission anticipated this criticism but concluded that the issue was still controversial enough to merit separate treatment.

■ BY AND LARGE, in the course of the Movement's first century, Conservative Jews abandoned many traditional Jewish ritual forms, such as the dietary laws, the use of *tefillin* for daily prayer, and Sabbath and festival observances. These rituals were perceived as anachronistic and separatist, they did not seem to infuse a modern Jewish lifestyle with any significant spiritual dimension, and Conservative rabbis were not trained in educational strategies for convincing their congregants that ritual was an indispensable dimension of religious life. Recently this trend has begun to be reversed. A new Rabbinical School curriculum now addresses these issues, and the younger generation of Conservative rabbis have pursued them with their congregants much more vigorously than in the past.

Positions Advocated

Predictably, the Israel and Diaspora statement displeased the more ardent Zionists in the Movement, as did the section on relations with other faiths. Also, there was either too much or not enough Kaplan in the document, depending on the critic's position on Kaplan's ideology.

More to the point, on some issues the document is self-contradictory. For example, a statement on revelation reads, "We reject relativism, which denies any objective source of authoritative truth. We also reject fundamentalism and literalism, which do not admit a human component in revelation, thus excluding an independent role for human experience and reason in the process." (p. 20) It can justly be asked, Once we admit a human component into the shaping of revelation, how is it possible to exclude a modicum of relativism? As soon as the human factor enters into the equation, the wide range of human needs and perspectives will inevitably be introduced, and then relativism simply can't be avoided. Such is the fate of a document written by a committee.

The Style of the Document as a Whole

Criticisms about style are more serious. They reflect two different and—it must be noted—contradictory perspectives. The first criticizes the document for being too authoritarian or too dogmatic, for threatening to straitjacket the Movement, for eliminating potentially divisive positions. The second perspective criticizes the document for being too pluralistic, for resorting too often to "some of us believe X, others believe Y" in theological sections. "We wanted a guide for belief and practice," these critics complained. "What we got was a menu."

Of course, it is possible to respond that if the document is perceived as being both excessively dogmatic and excessively pluralistic it is probably just where it should be. However, that would trivialize the criticisms; they deserve more serious consideration.

The fear that any statement of principles would become an ideological straitjacket that would eventually splinter the Movement is precisely what prevented the writing of such a document in the first place. Of course the enterprise was risky; everyone was aware of that. But the leadership of the Movement—and it is fair to say, the overwhelming majority of thinking Conservative Jews—felt that the risks involved in continuing to duck the problem of self-definition were far greater. Time alone will tell which of the two parties was correct, but as of this writing, *Emet Ve-Emunah* has not split the Movement. (The Union for Traditional Judaism was created five years before the statement was published, and some of its founding members were active and articulate members of the Commission.)

The other criticism—that the statement is too open and pluralistic, that it provides too many options—is more serious. It reflects the human need for authority and for absolutes and the expectation that if religion does not provide them, where will they be found? How can we live without absolutes, especially in an age that is already far too relativistic?

This criticism goes to the heart of what Conservative Judaism has always been about. This movement may well have begun as a reaction against the excessive liberalizations of Reform Judaism, but it quickly found itself equally distant from the authoritarian character of Orthodox Judaism. Orthodoxy, in all of its guises, is founded on one theological premise: "We know what God expects of us in matters of belief and practice. We know this because God spoke at

Sinai, and we have an authoritative record of what God revealed in that encounter. True, the message is sometimes obscure, and sometimes it does not seem to relate to contemporary conditions, but the Torah contains all truth, implicitly if not explicitly, and a qualified scholar can unearth its message on every human issue. His verdict represents what God wants of us in this specific situation." With this theological premise in place, it is easy for any religion to claim to stand for absolutes. A religious tradition of this kind will inevitably speak in monolithic terms, for on all but the most peripheral of issues God doesn't deal with options. There is one truth, and we know, or can find out, what that truth is.

We have seen that the founders of Conservative Judaism rarely discussed theology, but from the very outset their approach to Torah made it impossible for them to view it as the explicit word of God. As the Movement developed independently of the Seminary, its distinctive style suggested that even if it were possible to ascertain what God wanted from our ancestors, those obligations had changed throughout history and would continue to change. How then could the Torah be viewed as providing absolute, eternal truths? Instead the Movement flaunted its pluralism, both in practice and, given the fluid state of theological formulations throughout Jewish history, in belief. And where there is pluralism, authority is blunted and absolutes are relativized.

This is in no way intended to dismiss the yearning for this kind of "old-time religion." Those yearnings are genuine and legitimate. However, the Commission could not possibly come up with a monolithic statement, even if it wanted to—and it didn't want to. Where possible, it tried to reach consensus. When it couldn't, it was fully prepared to present two, three, or even more possible positions, any of which the reader could appropriate as he or she saw fit.

That stance should be viewed as empowering the lay community. It appeals to its strength, maturity, and intellectual competence. It is an expression of confidence in the layperson's ability to think and weigh contrasting positions and to resolve which position best captures his or her feeling at that time.

There are many, including this writer, who value the document and think that it represents an impressive achievement. Others may differ, and time alone will tell who is right. But whatever the fate of this particular statement, Conservative Judaism has finally overcome a century-long inhibition about telling the world what, in the view of this group of Conservative Jews, this Movement stands for. That fact alone represents a radical turnabout from the past. If for no other reason, the document is a milestone.

EMET VE-EMUNAH

אמת ואמונה

STATEMENT OF PRINCIPLES
OF CONSERVATIVE JUDAISM

The Jewish Theological Seminary of America
The Rabbinical Assembly
United Synagogue of America
Women's League for Conservative Judaism
Federation of Jewish Men's Clubs

■ AS OF this writing, all 50,000 copies originally printed of *Emet Ve-Emunah*'s first printing have been distributed or sold, and a second printing is available. Publication costs were shared by the three major wings of the Movement. There has been no formal survey of how it has been used, but what is known is that it has been taught in adult education classes through lectures and sermons and studied in confirmation, Hebrew High School, Ramah, and U.S.Y. classes. To facilitate its use, two study guides have been published, one for adult education courses and one for use with adolescents.

THE ISRAEL EXPERIENCE

"We feel that large numbers of Israelis in all walks of life, young and old, male and female, if given the opportunity to discover the true meaning of Conservative Judaism, would wish to affiliate with the movement and thus find their place within Jewish tradition without resigning from the twentieth century. "

——Robert Gordis

■ GOD'S ORIGINAL promise to Abraham (Gen.12) included posterity, blessing, and land. Our tie to *Eretz Yisrael,* then, dates as far back as our historical consciousness. Despite our accommodation to Diaspora existence, the land remained the focus of our loyalties, our dreams, and our prayers. The dream of a return to the land was omnipresent in our liturgy. In the modern age, political Zionism mobilized these impulses and gave them a practical and programmatic focus. In our own day, in the wake of the Holocaust, which accentuated our vulnerability as a people, and with the State of Israel a vivid reality, that ancient nexus between a people and its land has received wide, public recognition throughout the world. Pictured here is the Western Wall, where Jews from all over the world come to pray.

The story of Conservative Judaism's involvement with the State of Israel is a drama in three acts. Act I (from the Seminary's founding to roughly 1960) was marked by an extended period of ambivalence on the part of the Seminary, counterbalanced by the active involvement of the rest of the Movement. Act II (dating roughly from the early 1970s to the late 1980s) was marked by a broad-based and aggressive engagement by all wings of the Movement, spurred by the determination that the Conservative approach to Judaism must have an impact on the religious life of Israel. In Act III (beginning in 1989–1990 and still in progress) the Seminary has been forced to redefine and refocus its Israeli-based activities, largely because of its strained financial resources. During this period an indigenous Israeli Conservative Movement, the Masorti movement (from the Hebrew *masoret*, or "tradition"), has begun to flower and to take the initiative in developing a wide range of activities in Israel and elsewhere. These most recent developments have had the effect of forcing both school and Movement to reconsider their respective missions.

Act I: Initial Ambivalence

The Seminary's initial ambivalence was well documented in the earlier chapters of this study. The school was founded in the Diaspora by and for Diaspora Jews. Its very existence assumed the ongoing legitimacy and vitality of Diaspora Judaism. That reality could not but blunt its commitment to the Zionist cause.

To speak of the Seminary's "ambivalence" on this issue is far too imprecise, however. In 1906 Solomon Schechter published a pamphlet, *Zionism: A Statement*, in which he unequivocally espoused the Zionist cause as "the great bulwark against assimilation." In his Preface to his *Seminary Addresses and Other Papers*, however, Schechter cautioned the reader that his personal allegiance to Zionism "cannot be predicated of the Institution over which I have the honor to preside, and which has never committed itself to the [Zionist] movement, leaving this to the individual inclination of the students and Faculty, composed of Zionists, anti-Zionists, and indifferentists."

In fact, the large majority of Schechter's faculty, and of the later Adler and Finkelstein faculties, were committed Zionists. Mordecai Kaplan, Louis Ginzberg, and Israel Friedlander of the Schechter faculty, for example, were outspoken Zionists. So were the vast majority of Rabbinical School students throughout these years. But neither the student body nor, for that matter, the faculty had much influence over official Seminary policy. That was in the hands of the Seminary president and its board, and they, to use Schechter's term, were largely "indifferentists" or even "anti-Zionists." Cyrus Adler, for example, was articulate in expressing his conviction that an allegiance to Zionism would compromise his American loyalties, and the Finkelstein years were characterized by much simmering faculty discontent with the Chancellor's highly restrained enthusiasm for the Zionist cause.

To this day the Conservative Movement flaunts the fact that it alone of the three major Jewish movements never harbored an outright anti-Zionist spirit. (In contrast, Reform's Pittsburgh Platform rejected any expectation of "a return to Palestine," and significant groups on Orthodoxy's right view Zionism as a rebellion against God, Who alone can bring about an end to the Exile.) It is important to remember, however, that the Movement's Zionist rhetoric was confined to the expectation that an independent Jewish state could serve as a haven for homeless Jews and would foster Jewish cultural creativity, not that it would signal the end of the Diaspora community. To use a different measure of commitment, until the 1980s the Movement never explicitly and aggressively pushed *aliyah* as a desideratum for Conservative Jews. Until the 1960s there was no coordinated Movement-wide program to foster the development of a Conservative approach to Judaism in the Holy Land. It is not surprising, then, that prior to the 1960s a Seminary rabbinical student who wanted to spend a year studying for academic credit in Israel had to petition the faculty for permission. To this day Seminary alumni recall the difficulty in obtaining this permission, and although it was usually granted, many simply decided to go on their own and forgo academic credit.

FINKELSTEIN AND ISRAEL

A fascinating chapter in Seminary lore recalls that the 1948 Rabbinical School graduating class petitioned Chancellor Finkelstein to add the singing of "*Hatikvah*," the Israeli national hymn, to its Commencement exercises. The Commencement took place about a month after the establishment of the State. Finkelstein's refusal prompted a student protest (the Israeli flag was draped over the Seminary buildings but was whisked away before the beginning of the ceremonies), but to no avail. In later years the singing of "*Hatikvah*" was justified by the presence of the Israeli consul. Today it is very much part of the program, as it is of just about every significant event in American Jewish life.

The Seminary leadership's ambivalence toward studying in Israel was the result of a number of factors, above all its prized academic integrity: It simply did not believe that Israel harbored scholarly resources in Judaica that could match what the student would gain by studying in New York. It should also be noted that throughout the Schechter, Adler, and Finkelstein eras the Seminary Board was composed largely of Reform Jews who reflected classical Reform's powerful antipathy to Zionism. As a result, the Seminary leadership, whatever its private inclinations, may have been inhibited from expressing its own views. The school's later about-face on Israel was the result of an entirely new set of realities after 1948, but Reform's own turnabout and the change in the complexion of the Seminary Board in the past several decades were also factors.

The Movement's Involvement

The Seminary was not the whole of Conservative Judaism. On the Zionist issue, as on so many other issues, the school and the Movement soon found themselves very much in conflict. Conservative rabbis and their congregations were much more in tune with the fervent Zionist instincts of the Jewish community at large. In fact, Samuel Halperin's *The Political World of American Zionism* (1961) notes that "The American Zionist movement derived its most unanimously enthusiastic and dedicated supporters from the ranks of Conservative Judaism."

It was the United Synagogue that took the lead in advocating the Zionist cause. Schechter's preamble to its 1913 Constitution voices as one of its purposes, "to preserve in the service the reference to Israel's past and hopes for Israel's restoration." From 1917 on, the annual reports of the United Synagogue feature some reference to the Zionist cause. That 1917 report includes a resolution to the effect that the body "joins with the Zionists throughout the world in voicing the claim to a legally recognized and internationally secured homeland for the Jewish people in Palestine." That resolution, however, was hotly debated by Cyrus Adler, then President of the body, who voiced passionate disagreement. "I strongly object to this resolution," Adler proclaimed, "which I think is against the constitution of the United Synagogue. . . . I shall not vote for it; I shall not be bound by it. This is a matter of principle and conscience which no vote can force upon a man." What seems to have troubled Adler was the reference to a "legally recognized and internationally secured homeland" (which he felt implied a conflict in loyalty with America) and the absence of any overt "religious" cast to the resolution.

From 1927 on (the first year for which we have published convention *Proceedings*), Zionism is also omnipresent on the agenda of Rabbinical Assembly conventions. To choose but a few examples, in 1927 two lectures on Jewish Law in Palestine were part of the convention program, Mordecai Kaplan's 1933 Presidential Message included an extended discussion of Zionism, three resolutions at the 1934 convention dealt with Palestine, and the 1939 *Proceedings* include a report from "The Convention Committee on Palestine."

Zionism was equally pervasive in the congregational field. Many Conservative synagogues observed Palestine Sabbath, others voted to join the Zionist Organization of America, billing members for ZOA dues and synagogue membership dues simultaneously, and still others created Permanent Palestine Committees. The Seminary may have been ambivalent, but the rabbis and congregations in the field were firmly committed to active engagement in a wide range of activities in the Holy Land.

Act II: Aggressive Engagement

The congregational movement and its rabbinate set the pace on the Zionist issue, but when the Seminary did respond, that response was aggressive and wholehearted.

It is difficult to put ourselves into the situation of the leadership of American Jewry during the first four decades of the twentieth century. From our perspective now, with the State of Israel a throbbing reality and clearly the single most powerful focus for the aspirations of Jews everywhere, it is hard to imagine how it was even possible for anyone to be so cautious about the Zionist cause.

But certainly until World War II, the hope that there would be an independent State on the Jewish homeland seemed a wildly improbable dream; in contrast, the needs of the Diaspora community were real and immediate. If the Jewish community were to have continuity, it seemed that it would have to be primarily in America; and even that continuity was in doubt, given the seductions of the modern age and the openness and individualism of the American setting. It is therefore not surprising that the primary energies of Conservative Judaism should have been devoted to ensuring some minimalist kind of survival on American soil. Finally, whenever we are tempted to indulge in second-guessing, we should remember that throughout this period the Seminary was never far from financial insolvency. It simply could not do everything it wanted to. We shall see that the problem of allotting already limited resources to Movement activities in the Holy Land is still very much with us.

All the ambivalence evaporated as the horrors of the Holocaust seeped into our awareness. As the postwar momentum of the Zionist cause inflamed the Jewish world, Israel simply could not be ignored by any movement that claimed to speak for classical Judaism. The post-Independence years saw a surge of *aliyah* on the part of American and, more generally, English-speaking Jews. Quite naturally, these families recreated on Israeli soil the religious institution most familiar to them from their native lands—the synagogue. The first Israeli Conservative synagogue was Jerusalem's Emet Ve-Emunah, which was originally founded as a Reform synagogue in 1936 by a group of German Jews but later transferred its allegiance to the Conservative Movement. The 1960s saw the founding of three congregations—in Haifa, Ashqelon, and Omer—populated by recent English-speaking immigrants and older immigrants from Europe. As of this writing, some 40 congregations are affiliated with the Israeli branch of the United Synagogue. The Israeli region of the Rabbinical Assembly numbers over 120 members, some serving as congregational rabbis, others as educators or academicians, still others in a variety of professional positions. Also, many Conservative rabbis have chosen to spend their retirement years in Israel.

■ ALTHOUGH THE Holocaust and the creation of the State of Israel are the two major events in recent Jewish history, the attempt to tie the two together raises a host of problems. On one hand, the need to find a safe haven for the survivors of the Holocaust certainly impelled the political process of creating the State and helped win international support. On a more theological level, however, to the extent that we believe, as does classical Judaism, that God acts in history, we may be tempted to see Israel as some form of divine compensation for our suffering. To many Holocaust survivors, that thought is simply obscene. In any event, the culture of the State from the outset was fired with the conviction that it alone represented our ultimate safeguard against another holocaust. That impulse, for example, has inspired much of Israel's foreign policy. *Yad Vashem* (from Isa. 56:5, literally, "a monument and a name"), established in Jerusalem in 1953 as a memorial museum and library for the 6 million Jews lost in the Holocaust, serves as a striking affirmation of that conviction. Pictured here is the Valley of the Destroyed Communities at *Yad Vashem.*

■ NEVE SCHECHTER, erected in 1962 on a tract of land near the Israel Museum in Jerusalem, served as the hub of the Seminary's Jerusalem Campus. It provided dormitory space, a dining hall, classrooms, a synagogue, and a library for Seminary rabbinical students spending a year of study in Israel. It also housed *Midreshet Yerushalayim* and the administrative offices for the Jerusalem Campus as a whole. In 1990 the Jerusalem Campus was dissolved, and the responsibility for educating Seminary students in Israel was vested in the *Bet Midrash*, which is now housed in Neve Schechter. The shift from a Seminary-sponsored Jerusalem Campus to an indigenous *Bet Midrash* symbolizes the recent shift in the Seminary's understanding of how it can best serve the Israeli community.

Still, it was not until 1962 that the Seminary acquired a tract of land in Jerusalem on which to erect a building—the first of three contemplated buildings but the only one ever completed. This building was to serve as a dormitory and academic center for Seminary students studying in Israel. Funded by contributions from Conservative congregations around the country—with the final $100,000 (of a total $500,000) provided by one of the Movement's preeminent congregations, Philadelphia's Har Zion—the new building, originally called The American Student Center and, later, Neve Schechter, became the hub of the Seminary's Jerusalem Campus. That campus later came to include the Schocken Institute for Jewish Research, which houses an extraordinarily rich collection of rare books and manuscripts in Judaica and Hebraica, and still later, *Midreshet Yerushalayim,* an intensive program in basic Jewish studies for young Americans seeking an academic and religious experience in Israel. It also included the Saul Lieberman Institute for Talmudic Research, a center for computer-based research into rabbinic texts, named after the dean of Seminary talmudists. In 1975 a new Rabbinical School curriculum instituted a year of study in Israel as a requirement for every Seminary rabbinical student.

There were other efforts in these years to establish the movement as a presence in Israel. Seminary Vice Chancellor Simon Greenberg, probably the faculty's most outspoken and fervent Zionist, personally raised funds to introduce Seminary scholars and scholarship into the curriculum of Oranim, the teacher-training school for the secular kibbutz movement located near Haifa. Many Oranim students eventually studied at the Seminary and formed the nucleus for an Israeli academic community identified with Conservative Judaism. Also Rabbi Morton Leifman, Seminary-trained Director of Neve Schechter, invited secular Israelis to live and study with rabbinical students in Neve Schechter.

These efforts, however, remained scattered and fragmentary. The Seminary's Jerusalem Campus remained just that, an Israeli outpost of an American institution. These various outgrowths of a Conservative approach to Jewish living and thinking lacked any integrating structure. More important, there was no distinctive body that would initiate and sponsor the kind of wide-ranging activity necessary to make a significant impact on Israeli life. Nor was there an adequate source of funding for the enterprise. It simply was not a Movement priority.

To this day, no Conservative rabbi has ever been sent by the Movement to Israel to create a synagogue; the initiative has invariably come either from the rabbi or from groups of congregants themselves. The *laissez-faire* attitude on the part of the Seminary toward the Israeli movement was in all likelihood a reflection of the school's strong American focus and its financial straits.

There was also an emerging recognition that if the Movement were to take root in Israeli society, the impulse for its growth would have to come from within Israel, not from America. In effect, Conservative Judaism in Israel would have to develop its own style, its institutional structure, and even an ideological and *halakhic* stance that would reflect its own indigenous setting. That this pattern of native Israeli growth might inevitably create tensions between the Israeli and American movements was only dimly perceived at the outset.

As with so many other areas, it was Gerson Cohen's chancellorship that provided the spark for change. In February 1979 Cohen responded to the initiatives of his associates in Israel and to the prodding of faculty members—especially Vice Chancellor Greenberg, who for years had been personally raising funds for the Movement's activities in Israel. Cohen announced the creation of the Masorti (literally, "Traditional") movement. For the first time, Israel would have its own indigenous Conservative Movement with its own executive director, board, and executive committee. The impulse that led to this restructuring was not simply a need for administrative integrity, financial security, and ideological coherence. It was also greatly motivated by the ever more strident animosity of Israel's religious establishment, firmly entrenched in the hands of the Orthodox chief rabbis and the members of a range of equally Orthodox political parties. These groups retained absolute

התנועה ליהדות
מסורתית בישראל

בית המדרש
ללימודי היהדות

*The Seminary of
Judaic Studies*

*The Movement of
Masorti Judaism
In Israel*

■ IN THE long run, of all of the Masorti movement's institutions in Israel, the most influential may come to be the *Bet Midrash L'limudei Hayahadut,* The Seminary of Judaic Studies, a school that creates Israeli rabbis and teachers in a Conservative mold to serve in Israel. The graduates of this school will be instrumental in evolving a reading of Conservative Judaism that will reflect the unique needs of Israeli Jewry. Pictured in this photograph is the first graduating class of the school at its ordination ceremony in 1988. Chancellor Ismar Schorsch stands behind the podium. To his right is Rabbi Lee Levine, Dean of the Seminary for Judaic Studies, and to his left, Rabbi Raphael Arzt, then Associate Dean.

authority over all Israeli religious life, and they were not about to yield any of that authority to movements (for Reform Judaism, too, had begun to invest heavily in Israel) that they viewed as patently heretical. The fight for recognition and legitimacy in Israel would require an integrated effort.

In its present form, apart from the associations of Conservative synagogues and rabbis, the Masorti movement encompasses the following:

1. Kibbutz Hanaton, a communal settlement located in the lower Galilee, with members from North and South America, Europe, and Israel

2. The *Bet Midrash L'limudei Hayahadut* (The Seminary of Judaic Studies), a school created to train Israelis to serve as rabbis and educators in Israeli settings

3. The TALI, or Religious Education Enrichment Program, an alternative stream (now numbering about fifteen schools ranging from kindergarten through high school) within the State's public school system, designed to add a more open and critical religious dimension to the secular Israeli educational experience. The Masorti movement supports these government schools by training teachers, writing curricula, and fostering the development of new schools. Even though the TALI program is ideologically and historically identified with Conservative Judaism, the schools' lay leaders prefer to distance themselves from a direct institutional affiliation in order to avoid conflict with the Israeli religious establishment.

4. Moshav Shorashim, a religious community based on Masorti principles, whose main industry is scientific, computer, and medical-testing equipment for export

5. Ramah Noam, a summer camping experience for Israelis

6. Noam Youth Movement, modeled on other Israeli youth movements, which stresses Conservative ideology and provides informal educational, social, and cultural programs for adolescents

7. The Center for the Study of the Galilee, a research center and educational field school devoted to furthering an understanding of the history, archeology, and traditions of the Galilee

8. Nahal Army Groups, groups of Masorti youth who enter the Israeli army as a unit to undergo basic training and to serve in the context of the army's settlement branch with the eventual hope of settling in Kibbutz Hanaton

9. Solelim, a social, cultural, and educational program for Masorti young men and women on Israeli university campuses

To round out the picture, the Masorti movement created MER-CAZ, a party within the structure of the World Zionist Organization. By the late 1980s, MERCAZ's position in the WZO was so strong that for the first time a MERCAZ member, Rabbi Joseph Wernick (ordained at the Seminary and a former president of the Masorti movement), was appointed head of the Organization Department of the Jewish Agency for Israel. The Movement is thus officially represented in the centers of decision making within the Zionist movement and can participate in the allocation of funds raised abroad for various religious and cultural endeavors in Israel, including, of course, its own.

■ THE TALI schools provide a format within the Israeli public school system for families who desire a religious educational experience for their children that is more pluralistic and more open to modern society and contemporary culture. They are thus an alternative both to the Israeli religious schools, which remain staunchly Orthodox, and to the regular public schools, which remain staunchly secular. Though institutionally independent of the Masorti movement, they are funded by the Seminary of Judaic Studies and also by the Israeli Ministry of Education and Culture. Their ultimate goal is to educate an Israeli lay population that will identify with a Conservative reading of Judaism. Pictured here is a parent and child holiday workshop at a TALI program.

The Seminary remained responsible for funding the schools and programs centered at its Jerusalem Campus. To fund the Masorti program, Cohen created an independent Foundation for Masorti Judaism in Israel, which was to have its own executive vice president, officers, and board (although the Chancellor of the Seminary would serve as Chairman of the Board). According to an initial three-year agreement, it was to conduct its own fund-raising among Conservative congregations, parallel to and independent of but coordinated with, the Seminary-sponsored joint campaign for funds to serve the American movement.

The achievements of the Masorti movement have been impressive, especially given the fact that this concerted effort is still young (founded in 1979) and that it has had minimal funding. The future of the enterprise rests on the success with which it deals with three hard realities: (1) the hostility of the Israeli religious establishment from without, (2) the chronic financial insecurity of the American movement from within, (3) and the inevitable conflict of interest within the Movement between a Diaspora- and an Israeli-centered perspective on Judaism.

Act III:
Persistent Hostility

It was only natural in the years preceding the establishment of the State of Israel that the religious needs of its Jewish population would be administered by the indigenous Orthodox rabbinate. What other kind of rabbis were there in that period? Besides, although the large part of the population was confirmed secularists—very few of the early Zionists were religious Jews—the Israeli religious community was entirely traditionalist. By informal agreement, those areas of Jewish life that were marked off as religious were entrusted to the Orthodox rabbinate and its interpretation of Jewish law: areas such as the supervision of *kashrut* in restaurants, religious life in the synagogues and *yeshivot* (or more generally, all institutions of religious education), and especially matters of personal status, such as marriage, divorce, conversion, and the laws governing inheritance.

That informal agreement became formalized in 1948 under the aegis of David Ben-Gurion, Israel's first prime minister. Ben-Gurion's primary concern was to unify the population of Israel and win broad political support for his government. For this political support, he was willing to pay a price, and the price exacted by the religious parties was the formal confirmation of what came to be called the "status quo" on matters of religious policy, that is, as in pre-1948 practice, whereby the Orthodox establishment controlled Israeli religious life. The net results of this decision were, first, the religious life of the community was entwined with its political system, and second, the non-Orthodox communities and their rabbis,

```
                        Foreign Office,
                              November 2nd, 1917

Dear Lord Rothschild,

        I have much pleasure in conveying to you, on
behalf of His Majesty's Government, the following
declaration of sympathy with Jewish Zionist aspirations
which has been submitted to, and approved by, the Cabine

        His Majesty's Government view with favour the
establishment in Palestine of a national home for the
Jewish people  and will use their best endeavours to
facilitate the achievement of this object, it being
clearly understood that nothing shall be done which
may prejudice the civil and religious rights of
existing non-Jewish communities in Palestine, or the
rights and political status enjoyed by Jews in any
other country"

        I should be grateful if you would bring this
declaration to the knowledge of the Zionist Federation.
```

■ THE BALFOUR Declaration, dated November 2, 1917, was a landmark in the history of the Zionist cause. Named after Arthur James Balfour, then Great Britain's Foreign Secretary, the declaration proclaimed the British government's basic sympathy with the notion of establishing a national home for the Jewish people in Israel. It may well have been motivated by moral and religious considerations, but it was also designed to help rally political support from Jews for the Allied cause against Germany. The last portion of the document is of particular interest, since it addresses areas of tension caused by the creation of the State of Israel that persist to this day: tension between Jewish and non-Jewish communities in Israel and the problem of dual loyalties among the Jewish populations of other countries.

who were never able to muster the clout of their Orthodox rivals, had no official standing. To this day, Israeli Conservative and Reform rabbis have no legal status in the Israeli system. They cannot officiate at marriages or divorces, their conversions are not accepted, and their supervision of *kashrut* is not recognized.

More recently, the issue of Orthodoxy's political clout has come to a head on the question of the Law of Return, more commonly known as the who-is-a-Jew issue. The Law of Return, as adopted in 1948, grants automatic Israeli citizenship to every Jew. For the purposes of the law, a Jew was defined as one who is born of a Jewish mother—the traditional *halakhic* definition—or one who has converted to Judaism. As part of a general policy of harassment of the non-Orthodox communities and capitalizing on the increasingly divided Israeli political scene, the religious parties decided to press for an amendment to this law as the price for their political support. The proposed amendment would add the words "according to *halakhah*" to the requirement for conversion. As a result, only a Jew converted "according to *halakhah*" would be granted automatic Israeli citizenship. The perception was that this amendment would add legal weight to the Orthodox parties' control of Israeli religious life, further delegitimatizing all non-Orthodox expressions of Judaism, for the assumption behind the amendment was that all non-Orthodox conversions were *ipso facto* non-*halakhic*.

As of this writing the proposed amendment remains in limbo, largely because of the collective outcry of Israeli secularists (who were appalled at the grab for power by the religious right) and by the Diaspora communities (largely made up of Conservative and Reform Jews, who saw themselves disenfranchised and who threatened to divert a portion of their financial investments in Israel to their own Movements' activities). The amendment put the Masorti movement in a bind. Conservative conversions are very much "according to *halakhah*," certainly in contradistinction to Reform conversions, which do not require immersion in a *mikveh*. In the eyes of the Orthodox, however, the Conservative conversions are not acceptable.

■ THE TENSIONS between Israel's secular and religious communities predate the establishment of the State. They are, in fact, inherent in the original Zionist impulse, which was predominantly secular at the outset but later won the support of some religious groups in the European community and later in the *Yishuv* (settlement in Palestine). These groups were given the right to control those areas of Jewish life that had a clearly religious component, notably matters of personal status (marriage, divorce, conversion, and inheritance), the supervision of *kashrut* and synagogue life, and religious education. Since this religious community was almost exclusively traditionalist, it was the Orthodox approach to these matters that became enshrined as normative. This was the "status quo" that David Ben-Gurion, here pictured reading Israel's Declaration of Independence on May 14, 1948, pledged to retain in exchange for the political support of the religious communities in forming Israel's first government.

The issue, then, had become not the authority of *halakhah* itself but, rather, one of conflicting interpretations of *halakhah*. More precisely, the issue was the authority of the particular rabbi and the theology standing behind a specific interpretation of *halakhah*. In short, the Masorti movement claimed that the issue was not who is a Jew but rather who is a rabbi. In fact, the issue was politics, an instance of a political party trying to achieve by coercion what it had failed to achieve by education or persuasion. By any but the most Orthodox reading, the religious establishment has abysmally failed to have any impact on the large majority of Israelis, who remain adamantly secularist. The American experience of a significant *Ba'al Teshuvah* movement, that is, a return to Jewish observance on the part of young Jewish adults, is in no way as widespread in Israel as it is in America. At the same time, the Orthodox establishment has systematically curtailed the availability of other readings of Judaism. The Israeli is thus left with two polarized options—traditionalism on the right and secularism on the left.

This picture is only slightly oversimplified. There are traditionalist groups on the left of the Orthodox spectrum who have tried to present a more attractive, accommodating face to their Judaism, who are open to dialogue with Reform and Masorti Jews, and who have tried to develop educational strategies that might reach out to the secular community. These groups, however, have remained relatively peripheral, and their efforts have been dwarfed by the impact of the religious right.

More pertinent to our concerns, for a number of reasons the Masorti movement has hardly had the kind of public impact that would attract a multitude of adherents because of Conservative Judaism's inherent ideological ambiguity, the subtle (in contrast to Orthodox and Reform) quality of its religious message, the lack of adequate funding for movement projects, and finally, the fact that it is branded in the Israeli mentality as an import from America. Furthermore, although the polarization between Israeli traditionalists and secularists would seem to leave fertile ground for a middle-of-the-road stance, the Masorti movement has not been successful in establishing an identity separate from that of Reform. This confusion is critical because Masorti Judaism is perceived as espousing Reform's radical position on *halakhic* issues, and this perception effectively denies it its legitimate centrist position.

Given the politicization of religion on the Israeli scene, the only effective way to combat the power of the religious right is to increase the political clout of the other religious groupings. However, the total membership of the 40 Masorti congregations numbers only 12,000 out of a total population of about 5 million. That number will surely grow as the TALI and Noam programs, the Masorti congregations, and the *Bet Midrash* continue to flourish, but to strengthen the existing congregations, create new ones, attract new rabbis and educators, and expand the congregational population would require a heavy subvention of funds. And even more funds would be needed to mount the kind of public education campaign needed to make an impact on Israeli life, which is already congested with multiple ideological, political, and religious voices all clamoring for adherents.

Limited Resources

The second hard reality the Masorti movement must confront is the limited financial resources available to the Movement as a whole.

The Seminary's budget allocation for its Jerusalem Campus in fiscal 1989 was close to $1.2 million out of $18 million. For the same period, the Foundation for Masorti Judaism in Israel set its own independent fund-raising goal at $2 million. As a result, about 18 percent of all funds to be raised to support the Movement's activities were allocated to its projects in Israel. Although the Foundation's campaign was to be conducted separately from the Seminary's, the Foundation's money was to be raised largely from the same population that the Seminary turns to for more than 60 percent of its own annual budget. In effect, it could be argued that the two campaigns were competing for the same dollar. (The response to that charge is that American Jews view their contributions to Israel as separate from those they make to American institutions. Even more, the presence of an Israeli dimension to Conservative Judaism might well attract more contributions to the American sector.) One other figure rounds out this picture. For the same fiscal year of 1989, the Seminary's operating deficit was roughly $2.6 million.

What these figures posed most sharply was the issue of priorities. Barring an unexpected increase in revenues, the leadership of the Movement would have to determine what its primary mission should be over the next decade.

The case for concentrating on its American constituency is easily made: The revitalization of American religious Jewry is the cause that brought the Movement into being in the first place. The school is already operating at a deficit. Its endowment is pitifully small. The expansion of its Rabbinic Training Institutes (a highly successful continuing education program for members of the Rabbinical Assembly), the development of a School of Education to train teachers and principals for congregational and Solomon Schechter schools, the purchase of a retreat center for family education programs—all of these and numerous other suggestions for the enrichment and expansion of its educational mission in the United States have been on the Seminary's planning board for years but have not been implemented because there was no funding. In fact, if anything, the Seminary has been cutting programs in order to erase its deficit.

At the same time, a case can be made for the importance of the Movement's mission in Israel. Israel remains the most significant focus for Jewish energy worldwide. No movement that claims to address the contemporary Jewish scene can ignore Israel. In fact, many would say that an imaginative outreach program in Israel could attract funding for the Movement's activities in America as well. "Success sells," these people say; "dreams sell." And Israel provides rich opportunities for successful programming and dreaming.

In February 1990 the hard budgetary realities impelled Chancellor Ismar Schorsch and the Seminary Board to announce a number of decisions that seriously affected Seminary activities in

Israel. The two fund-raising campaigns were merged; the Seminary would now run one central maintenance and capital campaign for the Movement as a whole; $900,000 of the funds raised would be allotted by the Seminary to the Masorti movement. The Rabbinical School year-in-Israel program was integrated into the Israeli *Bet Midrash*, now to be housed at Neve Schechter but without dormitories or food services. *Midreshet Yerushalayim* was closed. The future of the Lieberman Institute would depend on the availability of non-Seminary funding. The total budgetary allocation for Seminary activities in Israel was cut by half, from $1.2 million to just under $600,000. Finally, some of the capital funds to be raised would be used to acquire a new site in Jerusalem that would house an academic center and headquarters for all Conservative/Masorti activities in Israel. Effectively, these decisions meant that apart from the Schocken Institute, which remains under direct Seminary auspices, the Seminary's Jerusalem Campus was to be absorbed by the Masorti movement. With the coming of age of the Masorti movement, an independent Jerusalem Campus had become superfluous.

In early 1992 the Seminary's financial difficulties dictated an even more stringent curtailing of Seminary support in Israel. For the foreseeable future, the school would support only the *Bet Midrash*. The Masorti movement would have to go it alone, raising funds from American Jews and Israeli government sources in whatever way it could, inevitably competing for these funds with the Seminary itself.

This budgetary issue conceals a much more central ideological tension that Conservative Judaism must now confront.

Diaspora Versus Israel

In a sense, we have returned to the initial ambivalence, but with a difference. For the first half of this century there was no problem claiming, as the Movement's founders insisted, that Conservative Judaism was created by Diaspora Jews for Diaspora Jews. At that time, the Diaspora Jew was the only kind of Jew there was. But can that claim be made with equal conviction at the end of the twentieth century, with world Jewry soon to celebrate the fiftieth anniversary of the creation of an independent State of Israel? Clearly not. The issue now is this: Since the State of Israel is a reality, where lies the heart of the Jewish world?

The leadership of the Israeli movement does not speak in one voice on this issue. The issue is rather one of emphasis, but it, too, is divided between those who view Israel as the center *par excellence* for world Jewry and those who foresee an ongoing, supportive, and even creative role for Diaspora communities. What they do agree upon is that Israel provides a unique setting for living Judaism to the full. Only in Israel do Jews have sovereignty. Only there are we masters of our own fate. Only there are we totally free to create the kind of

■ TO JEWS who are born and educated in America, it is tempting to view the Jewish world as composed exclusively of two large centers of Jewish life, one in Israel and one in North America.

What gets lost in that picture are the viable concentrations of Jews throughout the world, in South America, Europe, the Orient, South Africa, Australia, New Zealand, and elsewhere. Each of these communities faces challenges and needs that are frequently very different from those in Israel and North America. To the extent that the leaders of world Jewry are located in the two major centers, their scope of vision may well become parochial. The Masorti movement can take credit for focusing on the needs of some of these other Jewish communities and mobilizing the resources to serve them. Pictured here is the synagogue in St. Petersburg, Russia.

Jewish environment we wish to have. All of Jewish life will inevitably be centered in Israel. For a movement that claims to stand for the ongoing validity of the Jewish religion, Israel alone provides an arena for the broadest possible engagement of that religious tradition with all of life, including a system of government, political and fiscal affairs, a military and penal system, and cultural life. To the extent that the Conservative Movement refuses to acknowledge that fundamental new reality, it will have forfeited a precious opportunity to validate the impulse that brought it into being in the first place.

The spokespersons for the Israeli movement contend that the Seminary has become excessively parochial in its outlook, too much wedded to the North American scene. Conservative Judaism may well have developed in North America, but in fact the Movement is not wedded to any one space. It is, rather, a reading of Judaism in a modern idiom. That reading is universal and demands universal application. There are substantial centers of Jewish population in Europe and South America. In fact, they say, it is the Masorti movement that has maintained and expanded programs originally created by the Seminary for training rabbis and educators from Eastern Europe and South America. It has also established Masorti day schools in various communities in Eastern Europe. Israel has shown that it can provide a worldwide perspective for the expression of Jewish concerns.

We saw, previously, that the men and women who wrote *Emet Ve-Emunah* were forced to confront this series of claims by their Israeli colleagues and in essence rejected them. *Emet Ve-Emunah* espouses a dual-centered view of Jewish life, as opposed to the more Israel-centered view of the Masorti movement. *Emet Ve-Emunah* carefully balances the claims of both Israel and Diaspora Jewries; it insists that both centers can claim legitimacy, that each has its distinctive strengths and vulnerabilities, and that the Jewish world needs both. Not surprisingly, the Masorti movement has ignored *Emet Ve-Emunah*. It has been identified as the work of the North American Conservative Movement, and it has not been translated into Hebrew.

The issue can be put another way. *Emet Ve-Emunah* clearly reflects the reality of Conservative Judaism today in America. The overwhelming majority of American Conservative Jews seem to be here to stay. Although *aliyah* is now officially part of Masorti rhetoric (and is acknowledged as a "value, goal and *mitzvah*" in *Emet Ve-Emunah*), it has never attracted more than a trickle of Conservative congregants. Masorti protestations to the contrary notwithstanding, Conservative Jews seem to be totally comfortable with the dual-center model articulated by *Emet Ve-Emunah*. They will support Israel in countless ways, but they will also build a Jewish life for themselves and their children in America.

In contrast, some members of the Masorti leadership hoped that *Emet Ve-Emunah* would serve as an advocacy statement. They felt that it should articulate not the reality of where Conservative Judaism is today but, rather, what it should seek to become, what it should embody at its best. In their minds, Israel should become the exclusive center of Jewish life worldwide, and the Conservative Movement should support and encourage that achievement.

This tension between an Israel-centered and a bipolar model is fundamental, but there are other tensions as well, reflecting the different experiences of the two communities.

The Masorti movement, while prepared to ally itself with Israeli Reform in combating the Israeli religious establishment, is more sensitive to being grouped with Reform than is its American counterpart. This precarious tightrope act has led the Masorti leadership to espouse a more traditionalist *halakhic* posture than does the American Movement. Initially the Israeli *Bet Midrash* did not admit women to programs for rabbinic ordination; it does now.

In general, the Masorti movement turns to its own Law Committee for guidance on *halakhic* issues, effectively sidetracking the American Law Committee. An agreement was negotiated whereby the Israeli Law Committee would deal exclusively with Israel-related issues and would accept the rulings of the American committee (in which Masorti rabbis could participate) on more general issues. In practice, however, that distinction does not seem to have worked, and the tension remains unresolved. For example, the question regarding drafting Jewish women into the Israeli army is a distinctive Israeli issue. But what about the ritual observance of the fast of Tishah B'Av (which commemorates the destruction of Jerusalem and the Temple)? The Israeli Law Committee has ruled on both of these issues, on the latter to the displeasure of the committee members' American colleagues.

On the other hand, in a step that has striking symbolic importance, a woman, Rabbi Gila Dror, in 1991 was appointed rabbi of the Masorti congregation in Be'er Sheva. Rabbi Dror was educated in the Israeli *Bet Midrash* but ordained (after an additional year of study) in New York. The Masorti movement now has its first female congregational rabbi.

The fact remains that for the foreseeable future the issue of the Movement's role in Israel will be a source of tension. The American wing of the Movement desperately needs nurturing. It is also true that the Masorti movement enjoys substantial emotional support from the rabbinic and lay leadership of the American movement, and from the leadership of the Seminary. Israel is far too important for any movement to ignore, and the needs of the Masorti movement are clearly genuine. To abandon it at this point would be a symbolic statement of enormous power. It would be viewed as the Movement's abandonment of Israel itself. Finally, it is obvious that for the forseeable future, the Masorti movement will not be able to support itself.

■ BY AND LARGE, North American Jews are not prepared to do the one thing that would benefit Israel most of all: make *aliyah*. Yet they usually support Israel's interests—emotionally, monetarily, and politically. Sometimes this stance may conflict with their civic loyalties as Americans. More recently, as on the issue of Israel's policy regarding Palestinians and the West Bank, it may also conflict with their understanding of authentic Jewish values. In these situations, the tension underlying this complex relationship rises to the surface. In their relationship with Israel, then, American Jews walk a tightrope. Pictured here is a Los Angeles celebration, Solidarity Day with Israel.

Institutions do not like to make hard-and-fast either/or choices. The ultimate impact of the budget reductions and of the institutional reorganization is not yet clear, but the likelihood is that the leadership of the Conservative Movement will try to hold on to as much of the best of both programs as possible. It cannot, however, do everything it would like to do as well as it would like to do it. In the last analysis, the question is, Where is Conservative Judaism's heart and soul? What, above all, does it want to achieve? Wherein lies its *raison d'être*?

How the Movement chooses to confront this and a number of other areas of conflict will determine much about the course of the Movement as it enters its second century.

11 | RETROSPECT AND PROSPECT

"It is time to reassert with courage and conviction in word and by deed the wisdom of Conservative Judaism. Though but one movement in modern Judaism, we have the power to convey the greatest religious good to the largest number of Jews. It is to that historic challenge that I summon you today; the welfare of all Israel hangs in the balance. **"**

——Ismar Schorsch

In Retrospect

Before we try to anticipate the course of Conservative Judaism in the decades to come, we should briefly survey the accomplishments of the Movement during the last hundred years.

Remember that during the first decade of the Movement's history there were Jewish leaders who insisted that Judaism could never make it in America, that America's open society, its individualism, its pragmatic temper, and its scientific and technological spirit spelled the doom of any form of meaningful religious commitment. In short, Judaism could never compete with secular America for the spiritual, intellectual, and cultural energy of its young people. The Seminary's founders never shared that pessimism. They believed that America would be good for the Jewish people, and that Judaism had the resources to handle the challenges of modernity and its new American setting. That confidence is what impelled them to launch the Seminary and the Movement in the first place. In retrospect, it is largely because of that stunning act of faith that there is an American religious Jewry today. Not for a moment should we take that fact for granted.

Nor should we take for granted the fact that there is a Conservative Movement. For all of its ambivalence, the Seminary, together with its students, its alumni, and the laypeople it won to its cause, created a major Jewish religious movement on American soil. The simple fact that hundreds of congregations and hundreds of thousands of American Jews have chosen to identify with that Movement says something about the inherent attraction of Conservative Judaism's message.

■ IN ADDITION to its Rabbinical School, the Seminary now includes a Graduate School, which offers M.A. and Ph.D. degrees, as well as a D.H.L. (Doctor of Hebrew Letters, a second-level doctorate), in every field of Jewish studies (including a Dual M.A./M.S. Degree Program in Social Work with Columbia University's School of Social Work) and trains students for academic positions in colleges and universities around the world; the Albert A. List College of Jewish Studies, founded originally in 1909 as the Seminary's Teachers Institute, an undergraduate school that offers a joint degree program with Columbia's School of General Studies and a double degree program with Barnard College; the Cantors Institute/Seminary College of Jewish Music, founded in 1952, which trains men, and now women as well, for positions as congregational cantors and as specialists in Jewish music; and a supplementary high school division, the Prozdor, founded in 1951. Also housed at the Seminary is the Melton Research Center, which produces educational texts and trains teachers who work in Jewish supplementary schools.

There is still more. The Seminary, almost single-handedly, can be credited with creating a new link in the 2,000-year-old chain of Jewish scholarship; it laid the groundwork for the Jewish scholarly enterprise in America, populating colleges and universities with its first generation of professors of Judaica and stimulating an outpouring of scholarly work in all areas of Jewish culture. Never forget that as recently as the 1960s, only a handful of universities offered college-level courses in Judaica; today such courses are numerous. The membership of the Association for Jewish Studies, a grouping of academicians in Judaica, numbers over 1,000, and its annual December convention in Boston attracts close to 400 scholars and students. If the century-old dream of the European emancipators—that Jewish studies would become an accepted academic discipline—has been realized, it has been so as a direct result of the Seminary's scholarly achievements.

As we noted earlier, if Will Herberg was correct when he claimed in 1955 that Judaism had taken its place as one of the three mainline American religious traditions, then some of the credit for that accomplishment is Louis Finkelstein's. It is nothing short of miraculous that as far back as 1938 a small academy devoted solely

■ THE SEMINARY created the Jewish Museum, housed since 1947 in the former Warburg Mansion on Manhattan's Fifth Avenue. The museum collects, maintains, and exhibits over 14,000 ritual and art objects and antiquities. The museum also houses the National Jewish Archives of Broadcasting, established in 1979, which preserves and exhibits television and radio programs, over 2800 thus far, relating to Jewish history, culture, and religion. Its educational department provides adults and children with programs created to teach Jewish culture.

to Jewish studies should have hosted major conferences where academicians in the humanities and sciences and theologians and clergy of all denominations could sit together to discuss their interlocking concerns. That every week a radio program sponsored by the Seminary should reach into millions of American homes, that "middle America" should hear that Judaism has something important and interesting to say about the range of issues faced by modern-day Americans was also, in retrospect, a significant accomplishment.

The Ramah experience—the creation of a setting where Judaism can be lived 24 hours a day in a natural environment within a community of like-minded Jews—is a major achievement. Ramah has served as an educational model that has been widely copied by other branches of the community. It can also be credited with giving birth to the *havurah* movement; the early leaders of that movement were all Ramah alumni and picked up the notion of a *havurah*-type worship service from Ramah. It is arguably the twentieth century's most creative contribution to Jewish education.

In addition, the Rabbinical Assembly can take credit for creating the model of the American rabbinate as a profession. Its retirement plan and its placement service, designed to protect both the

■ IN 1947 the Seminary created the University of Judaism in Los Angeles, an academic center that also serves as the hub for a network of Conservative institutions and programs on America's West Coast. In addition to academic programs in Judaica, the UJ, as it is called, devotes a good deal of effort to training in the arts and to adult education.

rabbi and the congregation from unseemly competition, have become the norm for all the movements. Much of this work was accomplished under the aegis of the late Rabbi Wolfe Kelman, Executive Vice President of the Assembly from 1951 to 1988, who is credited with having done more to define the rights and responsibilities of the modern American congregational rabbi than any other single Jewish leader. Rabbi Kelman was commonly regarded as the rabbi to the Conservative rabbinate.

The United Synagogue, for its part, can take credit for serving as the face of Conservative Judaism in the public arena. Its network of regional branches, each with its own leadership, board, and commissions, provides the broad communal framework for the work of individual synagogues. The United Synagogue spearheads the Movement's involvement in social action. It also created the World Council of Synagogues, which extends membership to congregations around the world—in Europe, South America, and especially in Israel. The United Synagogue's Department of Jewish Education oversees the work of congregation-based supplementary schools and of the Solomon Schechter Day School movement, which now numbers over sixty schools.

■ BECAUSE RAMAH can create a total environment for its campers, it is in many ways an ideal religious community. That it can be so is its unique strength as an educational resource. For two months, campers are surrounded by a world that is totally Jewish: They worship daily, hear Hebrew spoken, keep the dietary laws, create ritual objects, observe the Sabbath, study Torah, and are constantly reminded that Judaism has something to say about their interpersonal relationships, even about how they play basketball. Memories of a Ramah experience have fueled the religious commitment of generations of young Jews throughout their lives.

THE WOMEN'S LEAGUE AND MEN'S CLUB

With a current membership of about 150,000, the Women's League for Conservative Judaism, founded in 1918 by Mathilde Schechter, Solomon Schechter's widow, provides educational, religious, and cultural programming designed specifically for adult women members of Conservative synagogues. Its Torah Fund program is a voluntary fund-raising effort that makes a significant (currently over $2 million) annual contribution to the Seminary's campaign for funds. The Women's League can also take credit for urging the Movement to recognize the significance of the feminist revolution in American life.

The Federation of Jewish Men's Clubs, founded in 1928, provides a parallel organization for the adult males in the Movement. Among recent programs, it has sponsored a Hebrew Literacy campaign to teach adults to read and understand the prayerbook in the original Hebrew, and The Art of Jewish Living, a series that instructs the lay population in bringing Sabbath and festival rituals into the home.

Finally, although we have been somewhat critical of the Conservative Jew's self-identification as "not Orthodox and not Reform," the reality is that Conservative Judaism alone of the three major movements devoted itself from the outset to walking the fine line between an uncritical acceptance of the Jewish past simply because it is the past and a radical rejection of that past as almost by definition anachronistic. Instead, this Movement tried, in an old phrase, "to grant the past a vote but not a veto." The Conservative Movement tried to retain as much of the traditional Jewish belief and practice as could be defended and to make the changes that had to be made in as conscientious and deliberate a way as possible. Shabbat remains Shabbat, but if you must drive in order to worship in the synagogue with a community of Jews, then drive, and try to observe the rest of the day as prescribed by the tradition. In retrospect, that goal was probably impossible to achieve; whatever you do, you are bound to offend both the right—which accuses you of betraying the tradition and compromising your standards—and the left—which accuses you of lacking courage.

Consider the range of issues surrounding feminism, for example. Orthodoxy remains unmovable. Whatever ferment the issue has stimulated is confined to a narrow range of possibilities and remains on the periphery of the community; the pressure on the national bodies to reject any change is overwhelming. At the other end of the spectrum, Reconstructionism acted quickly and easily. American Reform acted somewhat less quickly and easily, but the inherent dynamic of Reform encouraged a break of this kind; what had to change was not profound Jewish commitments but, rather, social attitudes.

In contrast, Conservative Judaism stewed over these issues for decades and did so in the public arena. The tension at convention after convention of both the United Synagogue and the Rabbinical Assembly was palpable. But why shouldn't there have been tension? Two equally powerful impulses were in open conflict. The issue marked a major departure from 2,000 years of tradition, and yet a profound social revolution was taking place before our very eyes. It could not be resolved by a mere stroke of a pen, and yet it had to be dealt with. The tension, then, was thoroughly appropriate for the situation. Any other reaction would have trivialized both the issue and the tradition.

The Conservative Movement also struggled overtly with the tension between unity and diversity. The notion that only in the modern age did the Jewish community become seriously splintered into competing, rivalrous factions is a romantic fiction. Students of Jewish history know that there was rarely an era when the community was essentially unified. We know of the conflict between priests and prophets in the biblical age, between Sadducees and Pharisees in the last two centuries B.C.E., and between the Schools of Hillel and Shammai a century later. We also know of the conflict between the Karaites and Rabbanites in tenth-century Babylonia, Maimonideans and anti-Maimonideans in the thirteenth century, rationalists and mystics throughout the Middle Ages, Hasidim and Mitnagdim in eighteenth-century Eastern Europe, and Zionists and anti-Zionists in the nineteenth and early twentieth centuries.

We were never free from internal tension, nor should we be, for we are far too vital a people. Conflict is a sign of caring, and there have always been seriously committed Jews who cared deeply enough about the fate of Jews and Judaism to fight about it. In this modern era, with its glorification of a sharply honed individualism, the disagreement, diversity, and tension are even more inevitable. The trick is not to avoid conflict but to ensure that our conflict is "for the sake of heaven." To put that criterion another way, we should make sure that our disagreements are designed to promote our commitment to God, Torah, and the Jewish people.

This criterion is difficult to apply, for our process of self-justification far too easily gets in the way. The fact remains, however, that there is an anarchic quality in Reform's fidelity to individual autonomy, while Orthodoxy's espousal of a literalist theology of revelation tends to discourage dissent. In contrast, both Conservative Judaism's theology and its institutional structure work to legitimatize cautiously defined pluralistic positions both in belief and in practice.

The long-standing implicit theology of the Movement, made explicit in *Emet Ve-Emunah*, insists that we view Torah as the work of the community as much as the work of God. With that claim in place, the Movement is saying that no human being knows precisely what God commands of us. Consequently, there can be multiple readings of God's will, and it is the responsibility of the caring community to establish the parameters for legitimate and illegitimate interpretations of that will.

Emet Ve-Emunah is but one instance of this community's attempt to establish ideological parameters. If we look at the work of the Movement's Law Committee, we can see the struggle to establish broad parameters for practice and observance. Within those parameters, the rules of the Committee acknowledge the legitimacy of certain minority positions and the right of the individual rabbi to be the final arbiter within his or her congregation. The spectrum of options within Conservative congregations is thus another testimony to the vitality and concern of the Movement. This process represents a deliberate and distinctive attempt to confront directly the tension between unity and diversity.

Our study ends, then, on a relatively optimistic note. The Movement's accomplishments are genuine and of monumental importance to the future of Judaism. The movement also seems to have weathered the crisis of the Seventies. For the first time in its history it has brought its theology, ideology, and *halakhic* posture into line. Its three wings—Seminary, Rabbinical Assembly, and United Synagogue— are working together in a way that was inconceivable decades ago. Its moderate traditionalism, now grounded in an explicit theological and ideological structure, seems to have found its niche in American Jewish life. The future would seem to be bright.

But much remains to be done. The previous chapter revealed the unresolved tension between an Israel-centered perspective and an Israel-Diaspora-centered perspective. That struggle is but one of a number of areas of tension that have to be addressed. The Movement's future will be determined by the way it chooses to deal with these issues. Not surprisingly, all of them are rooted in the past and in the way the Movement has evolved to this date.

A Great School or the Fountainhead of a Movement

Formal and informal surveys throughout Conservative congregations reveal that not more than 15 percent of affiliated Jews maintain a kosher home, attend the synagogue with regularity, or study in a formal adult education program. We have simply not produced an observant community, a praying community, or a studying community. That statistic is a devastating commentary on the Movement as a whole.

This issue was addressed for the first time in a sustained manner under Chancellor Gerson Cohen. Cohen understood well what had been only dimly perceived beforehand. First, the Seminary's role as the academic center for Jewish studies had been diluted by the spread of Judaica departments throughout the American academic world. Second, he perceived that the school desperately needed a constituency, and not only for financial support. Without a committed congregational base, the school would have no students, no place for its rabbis to serve, and no audience for its message. Most of all, Cohen understood that the Seminary stood for a commitment to the continuity and, indeed, the validity of a religious reading of Judaism in the modern age and in democratic America. Where else could that reading be concretized and tested if not in a congregational setting?

Cohen was the first chancellor to appoint an administrator to initiate outreach programs to the congregational movement. Cohen invited representatives of the lay community to participate in the writing of *Emet Ve-Emunah*. He also broached two new programs that were later launched by his successor, Ismar Schorsch: the Lehrhaus, an adult education program directed to Jews in the New York metropolitan region, and the Rabbinic Training Institutes, a series of five-day continuing education programs designed to help congregational rabbis work on their personal, theological, and religious agendas and evolve strategies to communicate these issues to their congregants.

Schorsch has extended Cohen's initiatives. He created the Leadership Council for Conservative Judaism, a group of the professional and elected heads of all wings of the Movement. This council meets periodically to discuss Movement-wide issues. More important, it is on call for any issue that demands concerted action. The

■ ISMAR SCHORSCH (1935–   ),
Chancellor of the Seminary since
1986, was ordained at the
Seminary in 1962 and received
his Ph.D. in Jewish History at
Columbia University in 1969. He
served as Chaplain in the United
States Army from 1962 to 1964,
taught at Columbia University
and at the Seminary, and also
served as Dean of the
Seminary's Graduate School and
as Seminary Provost before
assuming the chancellorship. His
scholarly field is modern Jewish
history, particularly German
Jewish history in the post-
emancipation period.

who-is-a-Jew crisis in Israel was the first issue of this kind. The leadership was polled, and the Movement's protest was out significantly before the rest of the Jewish world responded.

Despite these advances, there is still a problem, because there remains an inherent tension between Western-style graduate education and religious education.

Since antiquity the rabbi has been primarily a scholar but also the religious leader of the community, the primary Jewish religious role model. Until modern times, the two roles coincided: The scholarly role was the same as the religious role because the study of Torah was imbued with religious meaning. Since Torah was the explicit word of God, the study of Torah was an act of worship, a way of coming into touch with God's will for Israel. But modernity secularized Jewish scholarship, splitting the nexus between secular scholarship and religious meaning. The Seminary was instrumental in responding to that change.

The Seminary remains wedded to the scientific approach to the study of Judaism. Nor should it be otherwise. Its intellectual integrity is at stake on this issue! Not a single member of the Seminary faculty longs to return to the premodern, uncritical style of *yeshivah* study. However, if the study of Torah is to be approached in the same manner one approaches any other human discipline, that study becomes secularized. How, then, is it to be endowed with religious significance? And how is that significance to be communicated to a congregation of modern Jews?

The Seminary model of the rabbi was academic and scholarly, not religious or pastoral. It trained the rabbi to be the outsider, looking at the tradition from an objective point of view. But the rabbi's role demanded that he or she be on the inside, functioning from within a living religious tradition. It was the congregational rabbis who had to confront those eternal human issues, day after day, in the privacy of their office, by a hospital bed, and in a house of mourning. How were the rabbis to answer questions such as Why should I pray? Does God hear my prayers? What will happen to me after I die? Why did God take my son? Why do I have to suffer so much? What's supposed to happen to me on Yom Kippur? At moments such as these, much of the rabbis' training seemed irrelevant. They had been taught to analyze a biblical, talmudic, or liturgical text, break it up into its component parts, trace the history and provenance of each part, and compare it with other similar ancient texts. Rarely did their classes focus on the ultimate message of the text, on what it had to say to modern Jews, on how it addressed a persistent, existential human issue. And if the rabbis did not have the resources to cope with these issues, how could they expect their congregants to do so?

In the last analysis, after all of the psychological and sociological explanations for religious affiliation are exhausted, people turn to religion for one preeminent reason: to find meaning in their life experience. A religious tradition that does not have the resources to deal with the search for meaning in our lives will not long survive. Judaism has those resources, but the issue was how to extract and use them in a fully modern—that is, a critical and secular—setting.

With the creation of a separate Graduate School, the distinction between the religious role and the scholarly role could more easily be defined. The training of scholars could be assigned to the Graduate School, and the Rabbinical School could concentrate on its goal of creating a religious role model. That task took almost a century to accomplish. For much of its early history, the Seminary was still wedded to the older model without quite coming to terms with

■ THE PROBLEM of persistent, undeserved suffering that almost every human being experiences directly or indirectly is the single most powerful challenge to religion. In the course of its long history, Judaism has devised many responses to this challenge, none more powerful than that of the book of Job. Job is the paradigm of the man who suffers terribly, who tries desperately to make sense of his suffering and to reconcile his pain with his commitment to a just and omnipotent God. Every rabbinical student must be exposed to this book; however, it must be taught not simply as an ancient text but also as an existential document, deeply relevant to the human situation in every age. Pictured here is a drawing of Job by William Blake.

the fact that it was dysfunctional, that in fact rabbinic education at the Seminary was subverting of the rabbi's very role.

Again, it was Gerson Cohen who first asked the hard questions about rabbinic education at the Seminary, and again, it was left to Ismar Schorsch to implement the answers. A new curriculum for rabbinic education was introduced in the academic year 1989–1990. This curriculum aims at training students from their first semester to work on their theological, *halakhic,* and more broadly, personal religious agenda. They are asked to begin to think and speak as religious role models from the very outset. As of this writing, the new curriculum is just beginning to be tested. It has met with some resistance, largely because it represents a significant change, not only in the model of the rabbi but also in the culture of the school. Seminary professors are being asked to think and teach in ways for which they were not trained, ways that undermine everything they have been accustomed to do in the classroom and in their research and for which in the past they have not been rewarded by promotions and tenure.

Even if the effectiveness of the new curriculum is acknowledged, it will take a generation for these new approaches to enter into congregational life and transform the culture of the Movement. It will take a generation of rabbis preaching and teaching about God, prayer, revelation, the afterlife, and ritual observance rather than politics, anti-Semitism, and psychology, as their predecessors largely did, before a religiously committed Conservative Jewry may emerge. Whatever the fate of the new curriculum, if the Seminary is to serve as the fountainhead of a religious movement in modern-day America, it will have to cultivate answers to a whole series of questions that, for most of its history, it has systematically ignored. It will also have to train men and women to answer these questions.

The Issue of Authority

When you walked into a typical Conservative synagogue a generation ago and took a seat in the sanctuary, you felt that the sanctuary was designed to put you in a passive role. You were seated in a long pew; the people to your left and to your right made it awkward for you to get up and move. You sat in front of and below an elevated stage, on which the prime actors in the drama of the service—rabbi, cantor, president—sat or stood facing you. They were free to move about; you were not. They told you what to do: sit or stand, turn to page 152, read aloud or silently, in Hebrew or in English, in unison or responsively. The very structure of the service was such that you felt almost coerced to do exactly what they told you to do. (Just try to remain standing when the congregation is told to sit!)

THE DESIGN of a synagogue is not simply an architectural matter. It is also very much a spiritual challenge, for to a significant extent the design of the sanctuary will dictate how the congregation feels while worshiping within its walls. The design of the typical suburban Conservative synagogue dictated an essentially theatrical model of worship. Worship took place above and in front of the congregation, on a stagelike bimah. The congregant felt like an observer rather than a participant. It also gave a powerful message about the authority structure of the synagogue. The rabbi stood above the congregant and literally "spoke down" to the congregation, which was arrayed in rows before the rabbi. More recently, sanctuaries have been designed in the round, with the leaders of the service standing within and surrounded by the community. The message here is strikingly different. Pictured here is congregation Mishkan Tefilah in Chestnut Hill, Massachusetts.

One of the high points of the service was the rabbi's sermon. It was addressed "down" to you, from above. You sat and listened passively. You may have disagreed with what was being said, but the format deprived you of the opportunity to question or challenge. You also knew that on matters of ritual practice within the synagogue, the rabbi exerted final authority. There might have been a ritual committee that worked with the rabbi on these issues, but the rabbi was the religious authority for synagogue practice.

What I have described here, in only a slightly exaggerated way, was the classic authority structure in most Conservative synagogues. The rabbi served as the authority figure, and everything in the culture of the synagogue was designed to support and reinforce that role. In fact, however, the congregation retained (and still retains) a good deal of authority. It has the power to hire its rabbi and to decide whether or not to renew his or her contract. That authority represents the ultimate source of congregational power! Further, the rabbi's role as religious authority never extended beyond the doors of the synagogue. In their personal life and in their home, congregants retained the right to do what they wished with their Judaism, in defiance of what they knew full well their rabbi would have liked them to do.

The Conservative service of worship represented the most striking illustration of this authoritarian model. This model was operative throughout the Movement. The rabbi learned it at the

Seminary, for it reigned in the Seminary classroom as well. The faculty was composed of scholarly giants. There was never any question about the structure of authority in the Seminary classroom, about who had the power and who didn't. The instructors' authority was vested in their mastery of their discipline. The students learned their lesson well. They proceeded to create synagogues that would perpetuate the structure, except now they were the authorities and their congregants were on the receiving end of the message.

Even beyond this, the fact that the Seminary was the founding institution of the Movement, that from the very beginning the school was led by a small group of very strong presidents/chancellors (only two from 1915 to 1972), each of whom remained in power for decades, almost guaranteed the authoritarian style of the Movement. The power structure of the Movement enthroned the Seminary at the top of the pyramid, with the Rabbinical Assembly below the school, and the United Synagogue well below everyone else; the lay movement had little say in shaping Movement policy. Religious authority was ultimately vested in the scholar-traditionalist, that is, the Seminary faculty.

That authoritarian power structure was deliberately designed to distinguish Conservative Judaism from Reform and to protect the Movement's religious authenticity. Reform was perceived, at least in Seminary circles, to be sadly deficient both in genuine scholarship and in religious traditionalism. The congregational base of Reform, the Union of American Hebrew Congregations, held the ultimate authority to shape the course of that movement. Recall that it was the Union that created its school, the Hebrew Union College. The Seminary was never going to follow that pattern!

But this authoritarian model works only when both parties, the leader and the follower, are prepared to buy into it. The first generations of Conservative congregants were perfectly prepared to do so. They were largely unlettered Jews, certainly in comparison with their rabbis, and most of them never got beyond high school in their secular education. What authority could they have in Jewish matters compared with their rabbi? The very title "rabbi" was endowed with a mystique inherited from generations of Jewish experience. The Conservative rabbis were happy to draw on that mystique but soon realized that this status carried a trade-off. They were destined to be set apart; they could never enjoy the intimate friendship of their congregants. If they wanted to share the deeply personal burdens of their work, they could turn only to their family or to other rabbis. That was the price they had to pay for being "the Rabbi."

Since the 1980s, this authoritarian model has begun to crumble. First, the complexion of the lay movement has changed. Our laypeople are no longer unlettered. In their lives outside the synagogue they are powerful authority figures in their own right. They are the professionals, the academicians, the leaders of industry. Many control million-dollar budgets and supervise large staffs. They are gradually beginning to assert their authority in the synagogue as well.

Now the rabbi must learn to relate to congregants in a very different way. The rabbi must teach congregants to become as mature about their Jewish decisions as they are about the other decisions in their personal lives, decisions such as choosing medical care or a lawyer, writing a will or making investments. The rabbi must set forth expectations, primarily the expectation that the congregants will become responsible Jews. The rabbi must also be ready to share his or her authority in determining the religious style of the synagogue.

The empowerment model thus demands a very different kind of rabbi. This rabbi's authority does not lie in having final and definitive answers to questions congregants rarely ask. Instead, the rabbi becomes the authority in two processes—the process of wresting new meanings from a rich and ancient tradition, now in a very different cultural setting from the one in which it was originally formulated, and the process of urging the congregation to undertake its own struggle with that tradition. These processes demand patience, they demand respect for the integrity and independence of the congregant, they demand the ability to live with and indeed welcome divergencies of opinion on important issues and to work on achieving a consensus on these issues, and they demand the rabbi's readiness to expose his or her own struggles, achievements, and vulnerabilities.

This process of changing to an empowerment model is already obvious in many congregations. The most notable evidence is the change in the implicit message of the worship service. Many synagogues now sponsor alternative, *havurah*-style services that take place in the library or a classroom. The service is broadly egalitarian and democratic; chairs are arranged in a circle; the stage is dispensed with and, with it, any one single authority figure who "leads" the service; members of the group are responsible for chanting the service, reading the Torah, and leading a study session, which now takes the place of the traditional sermon. In fact, the traditional sermon is rapidly giving way to a discussion format, even in non-*havurah* services and even in congregations that still meet in traditional sanctuaries. The discussion format conveys a very different message from that of the traditional sermon. The authority is now being shared; the rabbi listens as well as talks; the congregant can disagree and challenge, immediately and on the spot. The sanctuary is transformed into an arena where rabbi and congregation participate together in a shared inquiry into the meaning and relevance of an ancient text for the life experience of modern American Jews.

There is still some resistance to this new paradigm, both from rabbis and from congregants. Some rabbis are uncomfortable with sharing their personal struggles with their congregants; but the new rabbinical school curriculum is designed to prepare the rabbi for this new role. Some congregants are resistant because of an apprehension that this new model might mean major changes in their home or lifestyle or in the investment in their children's Jewish education. If we are serious about a radical restructuring of Conservative congregational life, however, there simply is no alternative. The classical, authoritarian model failed to create a committed laity. It will no longer be abided by the best of our congregants. In short, empowerment represents the only hope for creating a lay community of serious, committed Jews. Without such a community, what future does the Movement have?

EMPOWERING THE CONGREGATION

In recent years, the culture of the Movement has accelerated the process of rethinking authority issues. Review the theological and ideological positions articulated in *Emet Ve-Emunah*. They clearly undermine the very possibility of the Movement's espousal of a strong authoritarian line. Recall that the document rejects the notion of Torah as the explicit word of God. In its place, it suggests that Torah represents Israel's understanding of God's will for the community. We can thus no longer speak of Torah as embodying eternal, absolute, and monolithic truth. That alone spells the death of any form of religious authoritarianism. Authority is now vested in the concerned community, in Schechter's Catholic Israel as the body responsible for determining what we are to believe and how we are to behave as Jews. This community does not include every Jew, or even every synagogue member, but it certainly should include more than the rabbis. In fact, the position can be viewed as providing a mandate for empowering as many members of our congregations as we can to be part of Catholic Israel.

We have claimed that Conservative Judaism is inherently a complex movement, and certainly this new approach to authority issues will make it more so. But the reality is that life is messy, that the issues are complex and subtle, that final and definitive answers on most important issues are difficult to come by, that extended periods of indecision are inevitable, that serious, clear-thinking, and committed people can disagree on many issues. That, of course, is an adult way of confronting life, and what this Movement must demand above all is that its membership be as adult in their Jewish decisions as they are elsewhere in their life.

Centers of Energy

The Movement, then, is rife with complexities and will likely become even more complex as it moves into its second century. But this complexity reveals an uncommon vitality that can be clearly perceived in the Movement's manifold centers of energy.

You can see it, for example, in the din of a lunch hour in the Seminary's dining room, when hundreds of students from around

the world crowd around tables to talk, both seriously and frivolously, about everything from that morning's lecture on the nature of God, to their next date, to the fortunes of a favorite basketball team, to Israel-Arab relations.

You can see it among the youngsters in any Ramah camp, learning to live as Jews on the ball field, around the lake, at arts and crafts, at a cookout, or on a Friday evening when 600 campers and staff, all dressed in impeccable white, sing *"Lecha Dodi"* as the sun sinks below the horizon.

You can see it in the passion of a Rabbinical Assembly convention debate, where motions, amendments, points of order, roll-call votes, speakers for and speakers against, open ballots and closed ballots give focus to a community's struggle with nothing less than its ultimate commitments.

You can see it on the faces of the 40 women who come to the Seminary for six hours every Monday to study in the Women's League Institute classes, struggling with a complex theological issue, a biblical text, a chapter in ancient Jewish history, or a short story by Agnon.

You can see it in the Seminary's Rare Book Room, where scholars from around the world pore over fragments of Genizah manuscripts, trying to decipher some obscure reference that may open a new chapter in medieval Jewish history.

You can see it in the faces of 30 couples from a congregation in Tulsa, Oklahoma, on a congregational retreat, scattered throughout an elaborate resort setting, quietly and seriously writing personal theological statements on how they understand God.

You can see it at a U.S.Y. convention, where over 1,000 adolescents take over a hotel for five days of study, worship, and discussion and fill its ballroom with the passion of Israeli singing and dancing.

You can see it around the table in a diner in Macon, Georgia, where four young couples discuss with a visiting Seminary professor just how they are to answer their children's questions about God's responsibility for the Holocaust.

You can see it in a synagogue's board room, where a group of men and women struggle to define the unique character of their congregation, the kind of service of worship they should create, the kind of a rabbi they want to hire, who should be teaching their children, how they should apportion funds that never really seem to be sufficient for what they want to do.

A rabbinic fantasy has Moses miraculously transported in time to Rabbi Akiba's *yeshivah*. To Moses' stunned dismay, he discovers that he cannot understand a word of Rabbi Akiba's teaching. When Akiba is pressed by a student as to the authority for his position, Akiba responds, "We know this law from Sinai as transmitted to us by Moses." Moses hears and is pleased.

Whenever I contemplate this statement, I wonder what Zechariah Frankel or Solomon Schechter would say if they, too, were miraculously transported to any one of the settings listed above. They, too, I sense, would be initially dismayed. Is this what they had labored to create? But if they stayed long enough, and if one of the students would press the instructor as to the authority for what was taking place, the instructor, too, might well respond, "We are simply continuing a process initiated centuries ago by Rabbi Akiba, continued in the Middle Ages by scholars such as Maimonides, and carried forward in much more recent times by two great modern Jews, Zechariah Frankel and Solomon Schechter."

And then Frankel and Schechter, too, would hear and be pleased.

End Notes and Suggestions for Further Study

The listing that follows makes no claim to be either complete or exhaustive. It records those sources I have found to be most useful in my own study of the issues. It also includes footnotes to the citations that appear in the text. Finally, it is designed to help the reader who would like to pursue more intensive study of the material in each chapter. Where possible, I have limited myself to book-length volumes, some of which, unfortunately, are out of print. "Pb" indicates availability of a paperback edition at the time of writing.

Chapter 1

On many of the personalities, institutions, and ideological currents discussed throughout this book, consult the *Encyclopedia Judaica* (16 vols., Keter, 1962) for the conclusions of the best of contemporary Jewish scholarship.

A valuable source book on both the Seminary and the Conservative Movement is *Conservative Judaism in America: A Biographical Dictionary and Sourcebook* by Pamela S. Nadell (Greenwood Press, 1988). This volume includes three summary essays on the history of the Seminary, the Rabbinical Assembly, and the United Synagogue, a generous collection of biographical essays on the Movement's leaders, and a comprehensive bibliography.

On Judaism's encounter with modernity, we are blessed with, first, Salo Baron's masterful overview, "The Modern Era" in *Great Ages and Ideas of the Jewish People*, edited by Leo. W. Schwarz (Random House, Modern Library, 1956), and second, a rich anthology of primary sources, *The Jew in the Modern World: A Documentary History*, edited by Paul R. Mendes-Flohr and Jehuda Reinharz (Oxford University Press, 1980 pb).

On the demography of American Jewry, see the pamphlet "Highlights of the CJF 1990 National Population Survey," published in 1991 by the Council of Jewish Federations.

The questions and replies debated by the assembly of French notables are found in *Modern Jewish History: A Source Reader,* edited by Robert Chazan and Marc Lee Raphael (Schocken, 1974 pb), pp. 14–31, and in Mendes-Flohr and Reinharz, pp. 116–121.

Mendelssohn's *Jerusalem* is available in two fine English translations, *Jerusalem and Other Jewish Writings,* translated and edited by Alfred Jospe (Schocken, 1969), and *Jerusalem or On Religious Power and Judaism,* translated by Allan Arkush (Brandeis University Press, 1983 pb). The latter is enriched by an Introduction and Commentary by Alexander Altmann, a distinguished scholar in the field of Jewish philosophy. Citations in this chapter are from the Jospe translation, pp. 104, 106–107.

On the Science of Judaism school, see Mendes-Flohr and Reinharz, Part V. On German Reform and, more generally, on the emerging patterns of religious adjustment in the nineteenth century and beyond, see especially Michael Meyer's *Responses to Modernity: A History of the Reform Movement in Judaism* (Oxford University Press, 1988 pb); also Mendes-Flohr and Reinharz, Part IV. Geiger's letter to Zunz is in *Abraham Geiger and Liberal Judaism: The Challenge of the Nineteenth Century,* edited by Max Wiener (Hebrew Union College Press, 1981 pb), pp. 113–115. W. Gunther Plaut's *The Rise of Reform Judaism: A Sourcebook of Its European Origins* (World Union for Progressive Judaism, 1963) is rich in original documents dealing with the emergence of Reform in Germany.

Chapter 2

The story of the 1845 Frankfurt Conference is traced in W. Gunther Plaut's *The Rise of Reform Judaism: A Sourcebook of Its European Origins* (World Union for Progressive Judaism, 1963), pp. 80–90. Frankel's address is on pp. 85–87, his letter of resignation is on pp. 87–89, and Abraham Adler's response is on pp. 163–165. There is unfortunately little by Frankel himself available in English, but apart from the material in Plaut, Frankel's essay "On Changes in Judaism" is in *The Jew in the Modern World: A Documentary History,* edited by Paul R. Mendes-Flohr and Jehuda Reinharz (Oxford University Press, 1980 pb), pp. 173–176, and more completely in the anthology *Tradition and Change: The Development of Conservative Judaism,* edited by Mordecai Waxman (Burning Bush Press, 1958). This latter volume, long out of print, includes many of the most significant statements on the ideology of Conservative Judaism from its founding to 1956. *Darkei HaMishnah* is not available in English, but see Ismar Schorsch's "Zacharias Frankel and the European Origins of Conservative Judaism" (*Judaism,* Summer 1991, pp. 344–354) for a summary of the impact of that work and of Frankel's thought in general, by the current Chancellor of the Seminary.

Holdheim's proposal to shift the service of worship from Saturday to Sunday is discussed in Plaut, pp. 190–195. Elias Bickerman's reflections on the significance of the Septuagint is in *From Ezra to the Last of the Maccabees* (Schocken, 1962 pb), pp. 75ff.

Samson Raphael Hirsch's "Religion Allied to Progress" is anthologized in Mendes-Flohr and Reinharz, pp. 177–181. The questions he addressed to Frankel are in Volume 2 of W. Gunther Plaut's *The Growth of Reform Judaism* (World Union for Progressive Judaism, 1965), p. 45. An excellent summary of Hirsch's thought is his *Nineteen Letters of Ben Uziel* (Feldheim, 1960 pb). For a book-length biography of Hirsch, see Noah H. Rosenbloom's *Tradition in An Age of Reform: The Religious Philosophy of Samson Raphael Hirsch* (Jewish Publication Society, 1976).

A superb one-volume history of American Jewry is Abraham J. Karp's *Haven and Home: A History of the Jews in America* (Schocken, 1985 pb). For documentary material, see Mendes-Flohr and Reinharz, Part IX. The early history of American Reform and the tensions between the various wings in the Reform coalition pre–Pittsburgh Platform are discussed in Michael Meyer's *Responses to Modernity: A History of the Reform Movement in Judaism* (Oxford University Press, 1988 pb) and in Moshe Davis' *The Emergence of Conservative Judaism: The Historical School in 19th-Century America* (Jewish Publication Society, 1963), especially Part II. This latter volume, long out of print, is a detailed history of the emergence of Conservative Judaism in America and its earliest years. On the Pittsburgh Conference and Platform, see *The Changing World of Reform Judaism: The Pittsburgh Platform in Retrospect*, edited by Walter Jacob (Pittsburgh: Rodef Shalom Congregation, 1985 pb). This volume includes the transcript of the Proceedings of the Conference. Kohler's opening address can be found on pp. 92–102; the Platform itself, on pp. 107–109.

On the early history of the conservative reaction to the Platform and the founding of the Seminary, see Robert E. Fierstien's fascinating *Different Spirit: The Jewish Theological Seminary of America, 1886–1902* (Jewish Theological Seminary of America, 1990 pb). The characterization of Isaac Mayer Wise is on p. 19, and the story of the *trefah* banquet is on pp. 20–23. See also Herbert Parzen's *Architects of Conservative Judaism* (Jonathan David, 1964), Chapters 1–3.

On the Kohut–Kohler controversy, see Fierstien, pp. 37–39, and Davis, pp. 222–225. Kohut's 1885 statement is included in *Tradition and Change*, pp. 65–74.

On Morais, see Fierstien, pp. 28–32, and Davis, pp. 354–356. On Kohut, see Davis, pp. 344–347. The final portion of Davis' volume contains biographies of the Seminary's founders along with documents relating to the founding of the Seminary. *Tradition and Change* includes "Can We Change the Ritual?" by Sabato Morais, a paper that captures his distinctive position on the issue.

Chapter 3

On the demographics of modern Jewish history, see the Appendix in *The Jew in the Modern World: A Documentary History*, edited by Paul R. Mendes-Flohr and Jehuda Reinharz (Oxford University Press, 1980 pb). Part V of this volume includes source material relating to the Science of Judaism school.

The founding of the Seminary is described in Moshe Davis' *The Emergence of Conservative Judaism: The Historical School in 19th-Century America* (Jewish Publication Society, 1963), pp. 231–241, and in Robert E. Fierstien's *Different Spirit: The Jewish Theological Seminary of America 1886–1902* (Jewish Theological Seminary of America, 1990 pb), pp. 41–70. Wise's reaction is in Fierstien pp. 49–50; Eisenstein's, on p. 51; Kohut's defense, on p. 50. The Certificate of Incorporation of The Jewish Theological Seminary Association can be found in Davis, pp. 386–387, and is discussed in Fierstien, pp. 52–55. The 1902 Agreement of Merger between the Seminary Association and the Seminary is in Davis, pp. 393–395. The early Seminary curriculum is described in Fierstien, Chapter 4.

The story of the founding of the Orthodox Union is narrated in Davis, pp. 314–320, and more briefly, in Fierstien, pp. 109–110. The new Seminary's problems in the 1887–1902 period, both fiscal and otherwise, are discussed in Fierstien, pp. 115–131.

On the circumstances surrounding Schechter's assuming the Seminary's presidency, see Davis, pp. 322–326, and Chapter 7 of Norman Bentwich's *Solomon Schechter: A Biography* (Jewish Publication Society, 1948). Schechter's 1893 letter to Kohut is cited by Bentwich on p. 167. Chapter 6 of that volume is an account of Schechter's discovery of the Cairo Genizah. His inaugural address, "The Charter of the Seminary," is in Schechter's *Seminary Addresses and Other Papers* (Burning Bush Press, 1959), pp. 9–34; the citations in this chapter are on pp. 15, 20–21, and 23–25. On the early history of the United Synagogue, see Herbert Rosenblum's *Conservative Judaism: A Contemporary History* (United Synagogue of America, 1983 pb).

Adler's involvement with the Seminary is described throughout his autobiography, *I Have Considered the Days* (Jewish Publication Society, 1941), and in the generous compendium, *Cyrus Adler: Selected Letters*, 2 vols., edited by Ira Robinson, Preface by Louis Finkelstein, and Introduction by Naomi W. Cohen (Jewish Publication Society and Jewish Theological Seminary of America, 1985).

Chapter 4

Most of the citations from Schechter's writings in this chapter are taken from his *Seminary Addresses and Other Papers* (Burning Bush Press, 1959 pb) and from *The Wisdom of Solomon Schechter*, edited by Bernard Mandelbaum (Burning Bush Press, 1963).

Schechter on America is in *Addresses,* p. 85; on Lincoln, p. 168; on modernity, p. 15; on the Science of Judaism approach, in Mandelbaum, p. 119; on Catholic Israel, in his paper "Historical Judaism" which is included in *Tradition and Change: The Development of Conservative Judaism,* edited by Mordecai Waxman (Burning Bush Press, 1958), pp. 94–95; on Zionism, in *Addresses,* pp. 91 and 100; that his own Zionist allegiance cannot be predicated for the Seminary, in his Preface to *Addresses,* p. xxiii; on Hebrew, pp. 110–111; on *halakhah* as binding, pp. xix–xx and 179–180. Schechter's *Some Aspects of Rabbinic Theology* (now titled *Aspects of Rabbinic Theology*), a masterpiece of popular scholarship, is now in print again (Jewish Lights, 1993).

Adler and Finkelstein on the binding quality of Jewish law are in their "Standpoint of the Seminary" and "The Things that Unite Us—An Address," in *Tradition and Change,* pp. 182–183 and 316–317, respectively. Frankel's discussion of *halakhic* development is in his "On Changes in Judaism," pp. 47–50 (*passim*), and Finkelstein's is on pp. 319–320 of the same volume.

On the code of Hammurabi and, more generally, on Ancient Near Eastern influences on the Bible, see Nahum Sarna's *Exploring Exodus: The Heritage of Biblical Israel* (Schocken, 1986). Sarna's discussion of the *lex talionis* is on pp. 182–189. Hammurabi's code itself can be found in *Ancient Near Eastern Texts Relating to the Old Testament,* edited by James B. Pritchard (Princeton University Press, 1955, 1968). The material on the *lex talionis* (paragraphs 196–197 and 200) is on p. 175 of this volume.

Chapter 5

On the denominational affiliation of American Jews today, see "Highlights of the CJF 1990 National Population Survey" (Council of Jewish Federations, 1991). Data regarding denominational affiliation are discussed on pp. 32–34 and in Tables 22–25; on synagogue affiliation, p. 37 and Table 29. The Jewish Identity Constructs used by the survey are introduced on pp. 3–6. Also illuminating, though reflecting the demographics of an earlier era, is Jack Wertheimer's "Recent Trends in American Judaism" in *American Jewish Year Book 1989* (American Jewish Committee and Jewish Publication Society), p. 77–82.

An intimate portrait of life at the Seminary during the Schechter-Adler eras is in *Keeper of the Law: Louis Ginzberg* (Jewish Publication Society, 1966), Eli Ginzberg's loving biography of his father, who served on the Seminary faculty from 1903 to his death in 1953. See also the extended discussion in Herbert Parzen's *Architects of Conservative Judaism* (Jonathan David, 1964), Chapter 5.

Cyrus Adler's autobiography, *I Have Considered the Days* (Jewish Publication Society, 1941) illuminates the wide-ranging career of this central figure in American Jewish history. Much of the

March 1989 issue of the periodical *American Jewish History* (78:3) is devoted to evaluating various aspects of that career. Of particular interest to us is Ira Robinson's "Cyrus Adler and the Jewish Theological Seminary of America: Image and Reality" (pp. 363–381). Robinson discusses the issues surrounding Adler's appointment as President and his relationships with the Seminary faculty.

A Bibliography of the Writings of Louis Finkelstein from 1921 through 1974 was published by the Seminary in 1977. For an example of Finkelstein's scholarly methodology at work, see his *Pharisees: The Sociological Background of Their Faith* (2 vols., Jewish Publication Society, 1938; revised edition, 1963).

Mordecai Kaplan's personal account of his religious odyssey is sketched in his "The Way I Have Come" in *Mordecai Kaplan: An Evaluation,* edited by Ira Eisenstein and Eugene Kohn (Jewish Reconstructionist Foundation, 1952). An excellent anthology of his writings is *Dynamic Judaism: The Essential Writings of Mordecai Kaplan,* edited and with Introductions by Emanuel S. Goldsmith and Mel Scult (Schocken and Reconstructionist Press, 1985 pb). But the most accessible point of entry into Kaplan's thought on just about any issue in Judaism remains his *Questions Jews Ask: Reconstructionist Answers* (Reconstructionist Press, 1956 pb), a collection of brief answers to questions that were submitted to Kaplan and originally appeared in the periodical he founded, *The Reconstructionist.*

Kaplan's "A Program for the Reconstruction of Judaism" appeared in *The Menorah Journal* VI:4 (August 1920). For a history of Reconstructionism see Richard Libowitz's *Mordecai Kaplan and the Development of Reconstructionism* (E. Mellen Press, 1984).

The American Judaism of Mordecai M. Kaplan, edited by Emanuel S. Goldsmith, Mel Scult, and Robert M. Seltzer (New York University Press, 1990) is a superb, wide-ranging anthology of studies on various aspects of Kaplan's thought. It includes a complete bibliography of Kaplan's writings.

The Ginzberg-Marx-Lieberman condemnation of Kaplan's prayerbook was published in 1945 in the Hebrew periodical *Hadoar* (*Tishre* 5706, No. 39).

The most accessible introduction to Heschel's thought is Fritz Rothschild's Introduction to *Between God and Man: An Interpretation of Judaism from the Writings of Abraham J. Heschel* (Free Press, 1959 pb). This volume also contains a bibliography of Heschel's writings and a selective bibliography of writings on Heschel, which in a later printing was updated to 1975. See also the book-length *Genesis of Faith: The Depth Theology of Abraham Joshua Heschel* by John C. Merkle (Macmillan, 1985).

Heschel's *The Sabbath: Its Meaning for Modern Man* (Farrar, Straus and Giroux, 1951 pb) remains his most popular and revealing work. His *God in Search of Man: A Philosophy of Judaism* (Jewish Publication Society, 1956 pb) is the most comprehensive statement of his personal theology. Heschel's political and social concerns are discussed in the anthology *The Insecurity of Freedom: Essays on Human Existence* (Schocken, 1972 pb).

Chapter 6

The Fall 1956 issue of *Conservative Judaism* (11:1) includes all the documentation relating to the issue of mixed seating at Congregation Adath Israel in Cincinnati.

Jack Wertheimer's "Conservative Synagogue" in *The American Synagogue: A Sanctuary Transformed*, edited by Jack Wertheimer (New York: Cambridge University Press, 1987) is a masterful overview of the history of the Conservative synagogue. This volume includes parallel articles on the history of the Reform and Orthodox synagogue as well as thematic studies related to American synagogue life.

The 1927, 1929, and 1930–1932 *Proceedings of the Rabbinical Assembly* record the early history of the Committee on Jewish Law. The resolutions of the 1948 Convention appear in its *Proceedings,* pp. 171–172 and 175–176. Morris Adler's 1949 Report is on pp. 46–57 of those *Proceedings,* his interpretation of the new Committee's mandate is on p. 47, and its "field of activity" is described on pp. 56–57.

The Committee's responsa on Sabbath observance are included in *Tradition and Change: The Development of Conservative Judaism,* edited by Mordecai Waxman (Burning Bush Press, 1958), Part III. A number of responsa are included in Part Two of *Conservative Judaism and Jewish Law,* edited by Seymour Siegel with Elliot Gertel (Rabbinical Assembly, 1977). Part One of this volume has a number of articles on approaches to legal development in Judaism by scholars generally associated with Conservative Judaism, including Louis Ginzberg, Louis Finkelstein, Mordecai Kaplan, Abraham Joshua Heschel, and the British rabbi–theologian Louis Jacobs. See also selected responsa in anthologies published by individual members of the Law Committee, such as Rabbi Isaac Klein in his *Responsa and Halakhic Studies* (Ktav, 1975). Klein's *Guide to Jewish Religious Practice* was published by the Seminary in its *Moreshet* Series (Ktav, 1979).

The Committee has also begun to publish its own *Proceedings.* The material from 1980 to 1985 appeared in 1988, and publication of the 1985–1990 material is in process. Extraordinarily valuable for any student of the Movement is David Golinkin's comprehensive *Index of Conservative Responsa and Practical Halakhic Studies: 1917–1990* (Rabbinical Assembly, 1992 pb).

On the process of *halakhic* decision making in Conservative Judaism, see also the excellent overview in Elliot N. Dorff's *Conservative Judaism: Our Ancestors to Our Descendents* (Youth Commission, United Synagogue of America, 1977 pb), Chapter 3. More concise but extremely accessible is David Golinkin's pamphlet, "Halakha for Our Time: A Conservative Approach to Jewish Law" (United Synagogue of America, 1991 pb).

Consistently illuminating are the articles by the late Robert Gordis anthologized in *Understanding Conservative Judaism,* edited by Max Gelb (Rabbinical Assembly, 1978). A number of these articles deal with both theoretical and practical issues related to Gordis' approach to Jewish law.

Finally, two more technical, book-length studies of Jewish law by scholars who are products of and strongly identified with the Movement as well as long-time members of the Law Committee: Joel Roth's *Halakhic Process: A Systemic Analysis* (Jewish Theological Seminary, 1986) and *A Living Tree: The Roots and Growth of Jewish Law* by Elliot N. Dorff and Arthur Rosett (Jewish Theological Seminary/ SUNY Press, 1988 pb). Rabbi Roth chaired the Law Committee from 1984 to 1992.

Current statistics on the rate of intermarriage in the American Jewish community are recorded in "Highlights of the CJF 1990 National Population Survey" (Council of Jewish Federations, 1991), p. 14, Chart 14.

Chapter 7

Schechter's use of *conservative/Conservative, orthodox/Orthodox,* and *traditional* as synonyms can be seen in his *Seminary Addresses and Other Papers* (Burning Bush Press, 1959), pp. xx and xxii, and in his "Work of Heaven" in *Tradition and Change: The Development of Conservative Judaism,* edited by Mordecai Waxman (Burning Bush Press, 1958), p. 165.

On Hirsch, see For Further Study, Chapter 2, in this volume. An excellent and up-to-date survey of the state of contemporary American Orthodoxy is Samuel C. Heilman and Steven M. Cohen's *Cosmopolitans and Parochials: Modern Orthodox Jews in America* (University of Chicago Press, 1989 pb).

Perhaps the most sophisticated presentation of an essentially traditionalist Jewish theology, however much it would be rejected by the right wing of contemporary Orthodoxy, is David Hartman's *Living Covenant: The Innovative Spirit in Traditional Judaism* (Free Press, 1985). Equally valuable as a statement of the ideology of what has come to be called centrist Orthodoxy is Norman Lamm's *Torah Umadda: The Encounter of Religious Learning and Worldly Knowledge in the Jewish Tradition* (Jason Aronson, 1990). Rabbi Lamm is the President of Yeshiva University, the academic center of that Movement.

A useful, point-by-point comparison of Reform's Pittsburgh, Columbus, and Centennial Platforms is published as a Supplement to Eugene B. Borowitz's *Reform Judaism Today* (Behrman House, 1983 pb). On the three Reform Platforms, see also the relevant pages in Michael Meyer's *Responses to Modernity: A History of the Reform Movement in Judaism* (Oxford University Press, 1988 pb). Borowitz's *Liberal Judaism* (Union of American Hebrew Congregations, 1990) is a thorough and systematic presentation of the ideology of contemporary Reform.

Marshall Sklare's 1972 evaluation of the state of Conservative Judaism is in Chapter 9 of the New, Augmented Edition of his *Conservative Judaism: An American Religious Movement* (Schocken, 1972 pb). Citations in this chapter are from pp. 261, 270, 277, and 281–282.

Chapter 8

For a study of women's ordination in the Christian churches, see *The Churches Speak On: Woman's Ordination*, edited by J. Gordon Melton (Gale Research Inc., 1991).

The literature on Jewish feminism is growing rapidly. Among the material I have found most helpful are the following: Anne Lapidus Lerner's " 'Who Hast Not Made Me a Man': The Movement for Equal Rights for Women in American Judaism" in *American Jewish Year Book 1977* (The American Jewish Committee and Jewish Publication Society), an excellent survey of the feminist struggle in each of the American Jewish religious movements; *On Being a Jewish Feminist: A Reader,* edited with an Introduction by Susannah Heschel (Schocken, 1983 pb); from a more traditionalist standpoint, Blu Greenberg's *On Women and Judaism: A View from the Tradition* (Jewish Publication Society, 1981 pb); and one of the earliest books in the field, Elizabeth Koltun's anthology *The Jewish Woman: New Perspectives* (Schocken, 1976 pb). Finally, a new and comprehensive anthology on the history, *halakhah,* and contemporary realities of Jewish feminism is *Daughters of the King: Women and the Synagogue,* edited by Susan Grossman and Rivka Haut (Jewish Publication Society, 1992). Rabbi Grossman was ordained at the Seminary and Ms. Haut is an Orthodox activist.

The translation of the opening verse of Gordon's *"Kotzo Shel Yod"* is taken from Shalom Spiegel's *Hebrew Reborn* (Meridian Books and Jewish Publication Society, 1962 pb), p. 182. Mordecai Kaplan's claim that he had "four good reasons" for initiating the *bat mitzvah* ritual is related in Mel Scult's "Mordecai M. Kaplan: His Life" in *Dynamic Judaism: The Essential Writings of Mordecai Kaplan,* edited by Emanuel S. Goldsmith and Mel Scult (Schocken and Reconstructionist Press, 1985 pb), p. 9.

A challenging statement on the range of issues associated with Jewish feminism from a radical theological perspective is Judith Plaskow's *Standing Again at Sinai: Judaism from a Feminist Perspective* (Harper and Row, 1990 pb).

On the history, aims, and achievements of Camp Ramah, see *The Ramah Experience: Community and Commitment,* edited by Sylvia C. Ettenberg and Geraldine Rosenfield (Jewish Theological Seminary in cooperation with the National Ramah Commission, 1989 pb). This volume is the transcript of a conference convened in 1986 to celebrate Ramah's 40th birthday.

Edya Arzt's survey of women's participation in Conservative synagogue ritual was published as "Our Rights to Rites" in *Women's League Outlook* (59:1, Fall 1988), pp. 17–18, updated in the Fall 1990 issue.

The Ordination of Women as Rabbis: Studies and Reponsa, edited by Simon Greenberg (Jewish Theological Seminary, 1988 pb), contains Gerson Cohen's address to the 1979 Rabbinical Assembly convention, the majority and minority reports of the Commission, and nine of the papers prepared by Seminary faculty, pro and con.

Neither the Yankelovitch, Skelley and White nor the Liebman-Shapiro reports are available in print. Consult the relevant annual *Proceedings of the Rabbinical Assembly*.

The pros and cons of women as rabbis is the subject of an entire issue of *Judaism* (33:1, Winter 1984). Volume 1 of The Union for Traditional (Conservative) Judaism's *Tomeikh kaHalakhah*, edited by Rabbi Wayne R. Allen, was published in 1986, and Volume 1, Number 1, of *Cornerstone*, edited by Rabbi Leonard L. Levy, in 1988.

David Weiss-Halivni's eulogy on the occasion of Professor Lieberman's first *yahrzeit* was published in *Conservative Judaism* (38:3, Spring 1986), pp. 5–9. For a taste of Saul Lieberman's scholarship, see his *Hellenism and Jewish Palestine* (Jewish Theological Seminary, 1950); for a taste of Weiss-Halivni's, see his *Midrash, Mishnah and Gemara* (Harvard University Press, 1986) and his *Peshat and Derash* (Oxford University Press, 1991). Chapter 4 of the latter deals with Weiss-Halivni's understanding of the theological underpinnings of *halakhic* development.

Chapter 9

On Conservative Judaism's ideological struggle, see Sidney H. Schwarz's "Conservative Judaism's 'Ideology' Problem" in *American Jewish History* (74:2, December 1984), an entire issue devoted to a reexamination of Marshall Sklare's *Conservative Judaism: An American Religious Movement* (Schocken, 1972 pb), Chapter 7 of which is devoted to "The Question of Ideology." Schwarz's discussion of the 1931 and 1956 efforts (among others) to clarify the Movement's ideology are on pp. 145 and 152, respectively. See also Chapter 4 of Elliot N. Dorff's *Conservative Judaism: Our Ancestors to Our Descendents* (Youth Commission, United Synagogue of America, 1977 pb) and Mordecai Waxman's Introduction to *Tradition and Change: The Development of Conservative Judaism*, edited by Waxman (Burning Bush Press, 1958).

The Preamble to the 1913 United Synagogue Constitution can be found in Appendix IV in Dorff and on p. 173 in *Tradition and Change*.

Louis Finkelstein's personal version of the Movement's ideology is his "Things That Unite Us" and "Tradition in the Making"; Mordecai Kaplan's is "Unity and Diversity in the Conservative Movement" and "Toward the Formulation of Guiding Principles for the Conservative Movement." All four, together with a wide range of other material bearing on these issues, are in *Tradition and Change*.

Simon Greenberg's "The Conservative Movement in Judaism: An Introduction," and Robert Gordis' "Conservative Judaism: A Modern Approach" were published as pamphlets (United Synagogue of America, 1955 and 1956, respectively). Mordecai Kaplan's critique of the ideological confusion in the early years of the Movement is in Chapters 10 and 13 of his *Judaism as a Civilization* (Reconstructionist Press, Enlarged Edition, 1957 pb).

Robert Gordis' lifetime struggle to define the unique ideological perspective of Conservative Judaism is reflected in the anthology of his collected papers, *Understanding Conservative Judaism* (Rabbinical Assembly, 1978). Two further volumes, both published by The Rabbinical Assembly, reflect the diversity of ideological opinions within the Movement: *God in the Teachings of Conservative Judaism*, edited by Seymour Siegel and Elliot Gertel (1985), and *Conservative Judaism and Jewish Law*, edited by Seymour Siegel with Elliot Gertel (1977).

Emet Ve-Emunah itself and *Willing, Learning and Striving*, the two Study Guides for youths and adults, were all published by The Jewish Theological Seminary, The Rabbinical Assembly, and the United Synagogue.

Chapter 10

We are blessed with an extraordinarily rich anthology of statements on the full range of Zionist issues in Arthur Hertzberg's *The Zionist Idea: A Historical Analysis and Reader* (Meridian and Jewish Publication Society, 1960 pb). Hertzberg's extended and masterful Introduction is a model of clarity and thoroughness, and the selections are generous and all-encompassing.

Schechter's "Zionism: A Statement" is in the Hertzberg volume (as is a paper by Kaplan) and also in his *Seminary Addresses and Other Papers* (Burning Bush Press, 1959); see also pp. xxiii–xxiv in the Preface on the personal nature of the statement. Adler's ambivalence is discussed in David Dalin's "Cyrus Adler, Non-Zionism, and the Zionist Movement: A Study in Contradictions," *AJS Review*, (10:1, Spring 1985). Louis Finkelstein's personal views on Palestine in "The Things That Bind Us" are on p. 322 in *Tradition and Change: The Development of Conservative Judaism*, edited by Mordecai Waxman (Burning Bush Press, 1958). His exchange with Milton Steinberg is recorded in Simon Noveck's *Milton Steinberg: Portrait of a Rabbi* (Ktav, 1978), pp. 133–134.

The Movement's enthusiastic rallying around the Zionist cause is elaborated in Samuel Halperin's *Political World of American Zionism* (Wayne State University Press, 1961), pp. 101–107; citations in this chapter are from pp. 101 and 102; Cyrus Adler's ambivalence is discussed on p. 118, Finkelstein's, on p. 245.

The *Annual Report of the United Synagogue of America* from 1913 on makes fascinating reading, particularly pp. 66–73 and p. 79 of the 1917 *Report* on the first resolution on Zionism, Adler's dissent, Friedlander's defense, and the reformulated resolution; Louis Ginzberg's forthright statement on pp. 20–21 of the 1918 *Report* and the resolution to establish a "committee on Palestine" on p. 46; pp. 44–45 in the 1919 *Report*, which describe the committee's work; pp. 29–35 of the 1927 *Report* which describe the Movement's fund-raising efforts on behalf of Palestine. See also the relevant material in the annual *Proceedings of the Rabbinical Assembly*.

Finally, the entire range of issues and positions (including that of the Masorti movement leadership) surrounding the Movement's involvement with Israel today are explored in *Deepening the Commitment: Zionism and the Conservative/Masorti Movement* (Jewish Theological Seminary, 1990), edited by John Ruskay and David Szonyi. This volume contains the proceedings of the September 1988 Movement-wide conference on "Zionism and Zionist Thought Within the Conservative/Masorti Movement: Deepening Our Commitments."

Chapter 11

An expanded version of some of the material in this chapter is in my "Inside or Outside? Emancipation and the Dilemmas of Conservative Judaism," *Judaism* (38:4, Fall 198), in "The Changing Paradigm of the Conservative Rabbi" in *Conservative Judaism* (43:2, Winter 1990–1991), and in "On the Religious Education of Conservative Rabbis" in *Caring for the Commonweal: Education for Religious and Public Life,* edited by Parker J. Palmer, Barbara G. Wheeler, and James W. Fowler (Mercer University Press, 1990). For a different perspective on these issues, see Abraham J. Karp's "The Future of Conservative Judaism" in the 1987 *Proceedings of the Rabbinical Assembly.*

Volume 26:3 (Summer 1977) of *Judaism* is devoted to an extended series of articles on "Conservative Judaism on Its Ninetieth Birthday." Included are reflections by Louis Finkelstein, Gerson Cohen, and Wolfe Kelman, among others, as well as more critical pieces representing "The View from the Right" and "The View from the Left."

Chancellor Ismar Schorsch's personal perspective on the Conservative Movement and its future is in a collection of his Seminary addresses, *Thoughts from 3080* (Jewish Theological Seminary, 5748 pb).

The Seminary at 100: Reflections on The Jewish Theological Seminary and the Conservative Movement, edited by Nina Beth Cardin and David Wolf Silverman (Rabbinical Assembly and Jewish Theological Seminary, 1987 pb), is a compendium of articles on the state of both school and Movement on the occasion of its centenary.

INDEX

Italicized page numbers indicate an illustration

The editor and publisher gratefully acknowledge the cooperation of the following sources of photographs for this book:

Acme Newspictures, Inc. p. 111; Alinari-Art Reference Bureau, p. 159; Bill Aron Photography, p. 89, 91, 102, 103, 116, 164, 166, 186, 188; Atlantic Photo, p. 87; American Jewish Archives, p. 26; Beth Hatefutsoth, p. 59; The Bettman Archive, p. 8, 52; Courtesy of the Leo Baeck Institute, New York, p. 16, 18, 21, 132; Bibliotheque Nationale, p. 11, 53, 97; Joyce Culver/Jewish Theological Seminary, p. 68, 137, 143; Murray Garber Photography/Jewish Theological Seminary, Joseph and Miriam Ratner Center for the Study of Conservative Judaism, p. 71; Grant M. Haist from National Audobon Society, p. 77; Hebrew Union College-Jewish Institute of Religion, p. 25; Japan National Tourist Organization, p. 75; The Jewish Museum, p. 6, 28, 39, 41, 50, 192; Jewish Theological Seminary, Joseph and Miriam Ratner Center for the Study of Conservative Judaism, p. 30, 37, 44, 66, 84; Arnold Katz Photography, p. 69; Suzanne Kaufman/Courtesy of the Library of the Jewish Theological Seminary of America, p. 140; Library of Congress, p. 9; Lou Malkin, p. 78; Masorti Movement, p. 179; Pierpont Morgan Library, p. 200; John Popper/Jewish Theological Seminary, Joseph and Miriam Ratner Center for the Study of Conservative Judaism, p. 138, 141; Reconstructionist Rabbinical College, p. 81; Ramah, p. 130; Reuters/Bettman, p. 161; Georgia and Steven Solotoff, p. 175; Herbert S. Sonnenfeld/Yeshivah University Photo Library, p. 114; Virginia Stern/Jewish Theological Seminary, Joseph and Miriam Ratner Center for the Study of Conservative Judaism, p. 35; Time, Copyright 1951 Time Inc. Reprinted by permission, p. 72; United Synagogue, p. 195; University of Judaism, p. 193; Wide World Photos, p. 109; Alan Zale/New York Times Pictures, 129; Zionist Archives and Library, 57, 181